"Joan Englander's *Joy in the Evening of Our Lives* is so much more than a guide for healing companions to the elderly. Beautifully written, and filled with creative inspiration, *Joy in the Evening* is a revitalising experience for readers of all ages. It is a key that enables us to open our heart to others, to ourselves, and to our lives."

> — Peggy La Cerra, Ph.D., Author of
> *The Origin of Minds: Evolution,*
> *Uniqueness and the New Science of the Self*

"An astonishing work. Joan Englander's ministry has blended her own deep courage and spirituality with the needs of the elders she serves. A must-read for all who work with elders, from Hospice to clergy."

> — The Reverend Gwynne K. Schultz

"We are on the brink of another revolution, a crisis of conscience. We are making incredible technological advances but we have a disease of the soul. We need to get back in touch with our humanity, we need to reach out to one another. We need to care. This book will help if we have the courage to heed its message."

> — Sylvia Hansen, Administrator,
> Consultant, former Director of Nurses

"Joan Englander is a sensitive, compassionate woman who has a unique understanding of the consciousness of aging. She is a pioneer in her field and makes a significant contribution for all of us."

> — Gloria Kaye, Ph.D., Psychotherapist,
> former residential home owner

*"**Joy in the Evening of Our Lives** has challenged my thinking about the coming changes of my own aging years. I want all my caretakers—especially my children—to read this book and understand its heart. It has given me hope that my life will continue to have many rays of joy. I wholeheartedly recommend this book to women across America caring for elders or who are concerned about the quality of life in their own later years."*

— Georgina Morin, teacher

"Joan Englander's integrity in approaching every aspect of her work with an open heart, a loving spirit and a creative mind is an inspiration for all of us who seek the sacred in every human experience. If caregivers everywhere took the wisdom of this book to heart, we might greatly lessen our cultural resistance and fear of old age or infirmity."

— Laurie Hope, MFT, Author of
*Creative Aging: The SAGE Guide
to Group Facilitation*

"This is a book that is needed, and will be on the cutting edge of a new paradigm for life enrichment for confined elders."

— Barbara Neighbors Deal, Ph.D.
Psychologist, nursing home music therapist

"Health care professionals who are attuned to the importance of holistic healing may, like myself, stop and assess how they interact with their patients. This book is the missing link in the healing process. The veil has been lifted and God's essence, love, has been captured by Joan Englander."

— Carole Cutler, R.N.
former Director of Nurses

"Finally someone comes who has time to love me, an old woman. Because of the unspeakable joy Joan brings, I will never feel quite so lonely again. I had forgotten such joy existed. At night before I sleep, I listen to Joan's comforting voice on the prayer tape she made me. Every night she is my Healing Companion. To Joan I am a treasure, she has my good at heart, and I can talk to her about God. When I am with my other caregivers, I have many needs and wants. When I am with Joan, I have none. Joan loves me and that's the only thing that counts. Now that I have Joan, the world seems lit up, and the light is shining."

— Rosemary Bleignier, age 90
Former interior decorator and
ecumenical minister

"Who tries to help our thoughts, to help the inside of our hearts to rejoice in God, if not for Joan? She brings such beautiful thoughts to all these people in the nursing home who do nothing every day. You never know whose heart she will touch. I see the spirit of God behind her work completely."

—Joseph W. Tousignant, age 98
Former brother of the Sacred Heart
Community in Canada and Maine

Joy in the Evening of Our Lives

Nurturing the Elderly Soul

By Joan Englander

HEALING RIVER PRESS
OJAI, CALIFORNIA

Healing River Press, Publisher
P.O. Box 385 • Ojai, CA 93024 • (805) 646-7700
www.joanenglander.com • email: healing@joanenglander.com

Publisher's Cataloging-In-Publication Data
(Prepared by The Donohue Group, Inc.)

Englander, Joan.
  Joy in the evening of our lives : nurturing the elderly soul / by Joan Englander. -- 1st ed.

    p. ; cm.

  Includes bibliographical references.
  ISBN: 978-0-9794681-0-0

1. Older people--Care. 2. Frail elderly--Care. 3. Spiritual healing. 4. Older people--Religious life. 5. Caregivers. 6. Music therapy for older people. I. Title.

HQ1061 .E54 2008
305.26   2007927423

PRINTER: McNaughton & Gunn, Inc. Saline, Mi.
COVER DESIGN AND TYPESETTING: Olga Singer
COVER ARTWORK: Elisse Pogofsky-Harris
COVER PHOTOGRAPHY: Eric Nivelle
BACK COVER PHOTOGRAPHY: Rosalinda Monroy

This book is dedicated to:

Mother Teresa of Calcutta,
who inspired me to do, and to write,
something beautiful for God;

Sri Sathya Sai Baba,
who taught me to forget myself and serve others;

Rabbi Shlomo Carlebach,
whose pathway to joy gives me strength
and has touched many older lives;

My mother,
who always encouraged and had faith in me;

Sonia Braverman, honored elder,
whose support blessed this book,
which may not have been written without her.

Contents

Copyright Permissions

Acknowledgments

This book could not have been published without the dedicated help of my two loving friends, Georgina and Ed Morin. They spent countless hours editing, repairing the computer, printing, and, most important of all, lending encouragement when exhaustion set in. Because of them, Joy is now a blessing to others. My friend and graphic designer, Olga Singer, also selflessly gave of herself with her artistic sensitivity and her belief in the book's message for the future of holistic eldercare. Chandra saved the project during the last deadlines by editing and proofing with care and dedication.

My deepest gratitude also goes to Barbara Gaughen Muller, who lived the vision with me and whose heart and generosity gave me the courage to go on; literary agent Michael Larson, and author, Gloria Arenson, who gave me the beautiful titles for the book; Dr. Phillip Taylor, whose medical interventions enabled me to complete the manuscript; Patricia Treece, who prayed for years that this book would be born and whose belief kept the fire burning through many trials; Laura Golden Bellotti whose editorial guidance crafted the shape of the book; editors Cynthia Anderson, Letitia Grimes, John Raymond; Father John Powell, Don Sloggy, Rabbi Arthur Gross-Schaffer, and Linda Sabbath, whose wisdom gave depth to the book's message; Marilyn Grosboll, for her work on self-esteem; and Linda Phillips, Chris Drucker, Judy and Craig Paulino, Linda Caldwell, Dorothy Johnson, Dr. Peter Milhado, Laurie Hope, Mazie and Michael Stange, Sylvia Hansen, Therese Gagnon, Paula Sandefur, Beverly Broadbent Beall, Barbara Deal, Tricia Branum, Bob Birk, Laura Paine, Rev. Gwynne Schultz, Carole Cowgill, Peggy La Cerra, and Sucinno for their support and encouragement.

Introduction

A Journey of Hope

When an elder is physically challenged or emotionally alone as he or she journeys toward death, what does our society offer? The time has come for a new vision in eldercare—and this book reflects that vision, at the core of which is the Healing Companion. This book is about touching lives, about the aspiration of the human spirit, about seeking wholeness. It is an odyssey that speaks about triumph over obstacles—a journey of hope.

As an adjunct to traditional caregiving, Healing Companions® services were created to support elders. This service honors the inner life of elders through intimate dialogue, music, movement, storytelling, art, dreams, poetry, and prayer. Doctors, nurses, aides, ministers, and family members often do not have the time or training to relate holistically to an elder's needs. Healing Companions are trained to listen to an elder's innermost longings, to offer spiritual and emotional support—and most important, to share love.

Healing Companions provide visits to elders, some of whom are quite ill and some of whom are relatively well, in nursing homes, assisted living facilities, or at home with their families. Their visits engage elders on an emotional and spiritual level that is rarely reached through mainstream eldercare activities. A Healing Companion offers the opportunity to strengthen and encourage an elder's resolve to be thankful instead of lamenting, to seek beauty and joy instead of grief and despair, to experience peace and a deep sense of well-being in the midst of physical pain and anxiety about what the future holds.

So often we view old age as a disease, a time when physical and mental functioning declines, leaving a worthless shell and not a real person. While some cultures revere elders, ours often perceives them as unwanted children. We think if we feed, clothe, and entertain our elders, that is enough.

What we miss is the inner person, the beautiful soul. We forget that within each worn-out body is a spirit that yearns for recognition and acceptance before death finally removes all opportunity for expression. By relegating the role of elder to that of a helpless child or, worse, a nonentity, we lose their rich heritage, which should be treasured by all of us. As an elder's soul cries out to be recognized, the Healing Companion concept addresses that need by valuing the uniqueness of every human person.

Joy in the Evening of Our Lives points the way to a new kind of eldercare, one that honors the whole self and cares for the inner person. A Healing Companion is in touch with his or her own spiritual nature, and is able to connect with an elder's inner self. The intention of Healing Companions is to create a sacred space for inner wellness to awaken and for unexpressed emotions to be safely shared.

Although healing implies physical cure, the purpose of healing is not simply to affect bodily change; it is to celebrate inner wellness in spite of bodily ailments. At a time in life when elders have less to do and spend more time in an interior world, Healing Companions are prepared to travel with them on this soulful journey. Companions and elders share joy, hope, and compassion.

This book reveals the inspiring effect Healing Companions can have on elders. Elders who were deemed by family and health care providers as unable to think with clarity, to reflect, concentrate, or remember, come alive with Healing Companions and are able to share profound thoughts with little difficulty. Some, through prayer, are released from pain; some, near death, sing and make joyful movements in their beds; some find joy in the midst of grief.

Many books honor the process of dying, but few focus on the need for living more profoundly during the last cycle of life. This book helps family members and caregivers to become Healing Companions by showing them how to guide elders through the last stages of life's journey. In the process, elders tap into their inner resources, enliven their daily existence, and give meaning and purpose to the precious time they have left.

The experiences recorded throughout this book offer a unique view of elders rarely seen by families and health care providers. The stories reveal the fascinating, funny, complex, and spiritually alive human beings who live inside the elderly bodies we tend to dismiss.

Pioneers in our culture are engaged in helping to shift our consciousness from simply treating the physical self to honoring the whole person. Medical doctors Bernie Siegel, Deepak Chopra, Larry Dossey, and Jeff Kane; psychologist Thomas Moore; and journalist Bill Moyers have undertaken research into the body/mind connection. And Rabbi Zalman Schachter-Shalomi's approach to "age-ing and sage-ing" is helping pave the way for a new perspective on elders.

A new wave of eldercare is on the horizon. As we lovingly guide our elders toward inner growth and healing, we help them embrace their lives as a blossoming flower in which to complete and round out with joy the circle of years they have lived. This book will inspire us to undertake our own Healing Companion journey, not only with the elders in our care but also in the care of our own selves.

Guidelines for using this book

Anyone who is drawn to becoming a Healing Companion can become one. The guidance at the end of each chapter offers many ways to prepare and to encourage emotional and spiritual growth, in both Healing Companions and elders.

Various art forms are included. The act of creation, through any art medium, can be thrilling. Just remember that the creative process is more important than the end result. Allow your elders to experiment with what feels comfortable to them. Creative expression and other suggested self-help techniques are only avenues; the real purpose is to encourage the unfolding of meaningful communication and connection with your elders.

Note:

With the exception of prominent health care professionals, public figures, and noted authors, all other names and places are changed to protect patients' and clients' privacy.

When writing about the late Rabbi Shlomo Carlebach, it is customary to say "Rabbi Shlomo Carlebach of blessed memory" after each mention of his name. This is done to indicate his memory will be a blessing to us. In honor of Rabbi Carlebach, I do this now. To save space, I have deleted the phrase from the body of the text. The reader will find Shlomo's first name often used in place of his full name. This reflects Shlomo's desire to have everyone in the world call him by his first name.

The Jewish stories in the book reflect my heritage and have become the core from which my work has deepened. They have been beneficial in the lives of elders. I have also included spiritual teachings from other cultures. These teachings have broadened the foundation of my work. Any one who becomes a Healing Companion will use stories, traditions, and teachings of their own.

Where biblical references and discussions about God are found, inclusive language has not been adapted. To honor the elders represented in this book, I have kept the language the way they express it. God is referred to as "he."

And there comes the evening over the lonely meadows deserted by herds, through trackless paths, carrying cool draughts of peace in her golden pitcher from the western ocean of rest.

Rabindranath Tagore, *Gitanjali*

*Let us take whatever God gives
and give whatever He takes
with a smile. That is holiness.*

Mc Teresa mc

(From a letter written by Mother Teresa of Calcutta)

Not too long
from now
the people in this book
could be
you and me.

PART ONE

Embracing the Inner Person

ONE

Don't Talk—Sing!

Give your life away . . .
You should have the feeling
that this birth and this life have
been given to you not merely
for the sake of eating and
sleeping, but rather to serve
others until your last breath,
until your death.
—Sathya Sai Baba

ROSETTA CLASPS MY hand in a vise, yanking me toward her. Bracing myself against the arm of her wheelchair, I look into pleading almond eyes and gaze into what is usually a cherubic face, now turned sour.

"Honey, please help me," she whines. "What am I going to do? The nurses refuse to get me a glass of water—please honey, get me a glass of water."

"Here's your water, Rosetta." Reaching for the paper cup wedged into the railing along the wall of the corridor in the nursing home, I hold the cup in front of her.

"Honey, why don't you get me some water?"

Every day her litany is the same.

"What do you think I'm doing? The cup is right here in

front of you." I resist shoving it at her; I try to stay calm and offer it gently.

"Isn't this the water you wanted?"

"Yes, honey. But why are the nurses so mean? I'm cold but nobody gets me a sweater."

"Your sweater is right here behind your back. I'll wrap it around your shoulders, okay?"

"Thank you, honey. At lunch they took away my plate before I finished eating. Now I'm hungry. Why do they do this, honey? Oh, please pray for me."

Rosetta's voice trails on. Not only the staff but even the other residents avoid her. Momentarily, I want to escape also—but a scene from the past flashes before me, urging me to stay.

Nurturing through Song

Years ago at Mother Teresa's orphanage in Bangalore, in southern India, I gazed into the face of a black-haired youth staring at the ceiling. Sitting on his mattress, I held a bowl of rice, put the rice into his mouth, and watched him swallow. The sight of his scrawny body, twisted into a deformed shape, grieved me. As the food went into his mouth, his eyes remained vacant; he barely moved.

Before I realized it, I began humming a spontaneous melody. Where had it come from? I listened as the melody became a soothing lullaby. Soon simple words flowed: "You and I are sharing love / You and I are giving love / This is our joy, this is our gift / This is our happiness."

The song seemed to enter the boy, as his face, a wooden mask moments before, now broke into a smile with crinkles of delight dancing around his eyes—a few brief moments of sunshine. The boy was suddenly alive to the act of hearing, eating, receiving.

The memory of this scene softens my response to Rosetta. As her Healing Companion, instead of trying to get through to her with words, I begin singing whatever comes into my mind: "Rosetta, do you want to know why people are tired of you?" A simple melody line flows easily into the singing words.

Her eyes widen in astonishment. Last week she told me how lonely she was, asked why no one wanted to be her friend.

Startled perhaps by my sudden singing and the directness of the question, Rosetta's mouth pulls down at the corners. Before she has a chance to whine, I quickly grab her, give her a big hug, bury my face in her thick, black braid, then stand back and watch the "please pity me" look turn into smiling brown eyes. I go right on singing: "You could have so much love in your life / But you exhaust everyone / Why not look for the good and the light / Why not see the healing sun?"

Rosetta listens intently; she doesn't stir in her chair.

"When you give instead of take and demand / A change will come into your heart / The love you seek will be close at hand / Your life will have a brand-new start."

Stunned, Rosetta just stares at me. She doesn't expect this type of response. Again I hug her and then continue: "You ask for help both day and night / But you don't need to beg and groan / You forget you've got an inner light / And that you'll never, never be alone."

The song stops.

"Oh honey, I'm so thirsty, I'm so hungry, I'm . . ."

To curb my impatience, I start singing again: "Rosetta, Rosetta, I'm, I'm, I'm . . . People get impatient with you often times / But God loves you no matter what you do."

"Yes, honey, but I need my custard, get it for me, will you?"

I keep singing. "I need my custard, yes, I do! Does it ever occur to you / There's more than just *you*—who lives in this great, wide world?"

Pausing, I let this musical sentence sink in. Rosetta is about to whine again, but I quickly sing with gusto the first melody that comes into my head: "Never mind, Rosetta, I still love you!"

Repeating the phrase, I hug her. Rosetta's teary-eyed face looks up at me with a broad smile.

Mother Teresa said that there is a greater poverty in America than in India—a hunger not for food but for love, a hunger born out of intense loneliness, abandonment, hopelessness. Here in America, Rosetta cries; the sick, old, and dying long to be held, listened to, loved.

"You love me?" Rosetta's begging for love breaks through my reverie.

"Yes, I do."

"I love you too, honey. God bless you. Now will you please pray for me?"

I begin to sing Rosetta's name, talk to God in melody, ask for joy to live in Rosetta's heart. I used to think joy was not possible amid great suffering. But when I first met Mother Teresa, I received an inkling of such joy. As she held my hand, her intimate smile of love and radiant joy seemed to look directly into my heart.

Healing Companions do not have to go to India or meet Mother Teresa to give joy and comfort to others. We may be inspired by someone whose life is lived with great love, whose spirit is elevated, whose acts of selflessness go beyond the ordinary. We may find this caliber of person in a teacher, minister, or friend who imparts to us a desire to mirror qualities of patience, loving kindness, unselfishness. Through such persons we are strengthened, inspired, and enabled to give light and joy to a broken world.

Today, when the pain I see threatens to overwhelm me, often a song of comfort, power, and peace bathes everything in light—refreshing, restoring, reviving the capacity for joy. Any caregiver can find this joy. It may be through music or any art form. An inner stream of guidance and love may arise through a song, painting, poem or dance. Right now, my song touches Rosetta, whose eyes are wide with wonderment as she holds out her arms to embrace me.

"Thank you, honey, Mary, Mother of Jesus; your name is Mary."

I laugh. "No, Rosetta, that's not my name!"

Placing her hand on the gold cross she wears around her neck, she replies: "Yes, it is, honey; you are Mary, like Jesus' Mother . . . I'm gonna call you Mary from now on."

Tears and smiles. Rosetta leans back in her wheelchair, her head lolls to one side, sudden sleep covers her like a gentle cloud. And her complaining comes to an end.

An Intimate Song Opens the Heart

Though a year has passed since this incident, whenever I see Rosetta she looks at me in a special way, as if we share a secret no one else knows. She continues calling me Mary, a symbolic gesture that reminds her of our first time together, when prayer and song touched her soul.

That initial song created a gateway to intimacy. Soon after, Rosetta told me about her life. The nursing home staff avoided listening to her and guaranteed I would burn out if I "got involved." Instead, I was moved by Rosetta's story:

"I remember when my mother used to go outside, walk up the hill and light a candle on the rock," she tells me. "She used to pray there. Sometimes she carried me in her arms to that place. Then she would walk back to the house, carrying the candle.

"My grandpa was killed by bandits. Before he died he said to Grandma, 'Hurry, get away, they might do something bad.' She and my uncle went quickly to the river; they swam across. Grandpa stayed behind . . . and was killed. When Grandma came back, she found him with the half-dead dog circling around his body to protect him from being eaten by coyotes."

How did this hidden story come to light? That first personal song created just for Rosetta called her to let go of loneliness and self-inflicted isolation. Music became a bridge beckoning her to cross over into an experience of love, healing, and renewal.

Not only was Rosetta renewed, so was I. Through song, I was no longer the "professional" dealing with Rosetta the "patient." By singing the truth, I risked losing my safe, separate, "professional" identity; instead, we met heart to heart. Out of this musical meeting came trust.

And from trust, came tears. We can inspire elders to reveal their inner stories when we are unafraid to move them to tears—and to be moved to tears ourselves. And what better way to do this than through song?

An exquisite example of healing through song occurred in an Israeli jail housing women prisoners. Rabbi Shlomo Carlebach was unafraid to move these prisoners to tears with his songs and stories, to touch them in the depths of the human spirit. He told about two of the women; one had blown up an Israeli airliner, the other a movie theater.

In the jail, Shlomo approached one of the Arab women and told her that he could feel her feelings, knew what was hurting her, and that he was her brother. She softened and reached out her hand.

Shlomo sang into the hearts of the women, reached into the souls of their prison guards, touched the core of their conflicts—with ecstatic melodies. Long-time enemies, hardened through a lifetime of bitterness, anger, and despair, suddenly opened their hearts, and hatred began to heal. Prisoners and guards began to dance and hug one another.[1]

For a few moments, enemies did not exist. Singing touched the worst of the human condition; it broke down barriers, as it did with Rosetta—whose enemy turned out to be herself. Momentarily, Rosetta, too, changed. Did it occur to her, maybe for the first time, that "I don't need to live in this prison any more, I want to get out?"

On a daily basis, Rosetta was often as cranky as ever. But success is measured in moments rather than in days or years. A musical outpouring of love became one of the ways to heal Rosetta's loneliness; a few moments of musical triumph gave her a dynamic challenge, a glimmer of hope. And it became a bond between us.

One night after our initial singing experience, Rosetta clutched my arm, pulling at it with both of her hands.

"Rosetta, what's wrong?" Irritated, I tried to extract myself.

"My family never comes to see me. Honey, please don't leave me, I'm so alone." Big tears fell on her ruddy checks.

Ashamed of my momentary resistance, I offered her both of my hands. "I'll stay as long as I can, Rosetta. Don't cry, I'm here with you, I love you."

"But *they* don't love me. Why don't they come, honey? They've forgotten me." This time her tears were not on the level of whining; they sprang from deep wounds. The staff told me Rosetta's daughter had been here an hour ago, but that Rosetta is always complaining and doesn't remember her daughter's visit.

Although Rosetta's behavior is illogical, it doesn't eliminate the truth: she is suffering from feelings of abandonment. What does it matter whether she had a visitor an hour ago? What matters is that her heart longs for love, and she needs that love to heal on a deeper level.

Soon after this incident, I ask Rosetta to sing for me. At first, she seems puzzled, uninterested. But then, suddenly, her eyes sparkle with joy. With a flair for drama I didn't know she had, she flings out her arms, and sings her song—a plea pouring from her heart:

"Ven, que necesito verte (Come, I need to see you)

Ven, mi corazón te llama (Come, my heart is calling you)"

This song became our bond. No matter how unreasonable, agitated, or tired she became, whenever I asked Rosetta to sing, her smile lit up her world, and her song revealed the energy of a young girl.

Melting the Anguish with a Wordless Song

"You son of a bitch, get out of my way," Vera fairly hisses at Dorothy whose wheelchair blocks her path. Vera pushes her wheelchair forward, lunges at Dorothy, swings her arm, and barely misses her.

Vera's anguish is this—after living in a nursing home for ten years, she wants out. Anger underlies feelings of depression. Yesterday she rolled her wheelchair out of the building, down the driveway, and onto the sidewalk. When the nurses found her, she sobbed as she resisted being brought back to her room.

Turning to Vera, I begin singing a haunting Jewish melody

called a *nigun*, a song without words. Singing melodies without words can sometimes be more powerful than songs that have lyrics. Such wordless melodies can open and soften the heart so that a feeling of love awakens a joy more powerful than sorrow.

The *nigun* becomes infectious. In the recreation room, the women uninhibitedly sing even though they have never heard the melody before. This would surprise anyone who is convinced elders only want to sing tunes from the good old days.

Beckoning Vera to join the other residents who sing with me, I practically sing her over to the table where the five women are sitting. Securing the wheel brake on her chair, I place my chair next to hers. Dorothy wheels herself around to sit across from us. Knowing that singing a *nigun* can melt the meanest heart, I wonder if this outpouring of singing love will melt Vera and Dorothy and create a truce, if not a friendship.

As her fingers tap the rhythm on the arm of her chair, Vera smiles. Nudging closer to her, I chide: "Remember the day you told us how you socked that heavyweight champion, knocked him to the ground with your purse when he tried to kiss you in the park?"

Pleased, Vera laughs, relaxes in her chair, sings with me as I begin singing the *nigun* again by vocalizing "lai, lai, lai . . ." As our singing ends, it awakens one of Rebecca's deepest memories.

"I come from a family of fourteen children. We never fought." Rebecca smiles broadly and her eyes light up with so much joy it is contagious.

"How did you avoid fighting?" I ask.

"My mother. She disciplined us. It was very interesting. We never resented this. We got so much out of it. We respected her. Every morning before we went to school, she sat us children down, even the little ones, and we had to listen to her instructions—how to act, what to say, how to behave. She did all this with joy and had us laughing and joking. This was very hard to do because she raised all of us by herself."

"When I was little I wanted to be all by myself because my mother hit me," Dorothy says.

"Hit you? Very sad." Vera shakes her head.

"Our mother would never do that," Rebecca says with a smile. "She was from Poland. As a Jew, she went through plenty of suffering. But when she came to this country, she put it out of her mind, went right on."

"I can't put it out of my mind. I think about my mother hitting me all the time." Dorothy, often abusive to others, suddenly seems fragile.

"We didn't have enough to eat," Rebecca went on, "but that didn't deter mother. She gave us joy, made her life and ours happy."

"My, that's wonderful." Dorothy leans forward in her chair, an eager look in her eyes. Her agitation has vanished.

"Mother was our mentor. You know, even though we were poor, she always wanted to feel like a rich lady, an aristocrat. She never went out without wearing her hat. Nobody let on that she wasn't rich; we children never made fun of her. We hadn't the heart to spoil her illusion."

"We were poor, too. But we weren't happy." Soft words from Dorothy, when moments ago hostility had the upper hand.

"You weren't?" Vera turns to Dorothy.

"No, I tried to run away."

"Our mother never gave in to despondency." Rebecca glows as if her mother were right before her. "She taught us never to give in to defeat. Mother had the brilliancy to fight her way through life—and she did it through joy."

Picking up my four-stringed Indian tamboura from the

table, I cradle it in my arms and again sing the *nigun*. The melody seems to permeate the room, inviting Rebecca's mother to become part of us. Rebecca had spoken of her mother many times in the past, but now her recollections take on a new depth.

"Do you know where your mother got this joy?" I ask Rebecca.

"Oh, most certainly. We lit candles every Friday night. She did this spontaneously in her own way. She was so open-minded, vivacious." Lively and animated, Rebecca seems to become the very portrait of the mother she is describing.

"And did we sing!" Rebecca claps her hands in delight. "Even when we were very young and father was dying, she kept our spirits up."

When a singer sings a *nigun* with the intent of healing, praying, or praising, the music moves both singer and listener into a dynamic experience with the Creator. According to Hasidic tradition, if we pour out our hearts before the Creator while singing, our songs may be lifted to the highest heavens. Did our singing spark within Rebecca a deeper recollection of the influence her mother had on her, lifting her up into the joy we now see in her?

Suddenly I see a parallel between Rebecca's life and the Jewish tradition. Rebecca's family contained the same kind of joy the Jews had in Israel, a special joy that they experienced on the Sabbath—Sabbath joy and song, inseparable.

Just then a story comes to mind, about the triumph of another mother who celebrated the root of the Sabbath joy. I decide to share it with the group.

"It was sundown on Friday night and Anzia was coming home." Expectant faces look at me as I begin to tell this tale. "As Anzia approached, she noticed a pile of broken furniture in the street. Her mother was standing amid this pile—homeless, abandoned. Anzia's illness, the hospital bills, lost wages, unpaid rent—she realized they had been evicted.

"Anzia's mother was humiliated yet she seemed to grow in stature. There among her flimsy belongings, the people in the street stood watching her. Filled with faith and the pride of her people, she struck a match, lit the Sabbath candle, refused to relinquish her Sabbath joy."[2]

"She's just like my mother," Rebecca beams.

Anzia's story draws to a close. I sing the *nigun's* haunting melody, which weaves its way into the stories of both mothers. The beauty and pathos of their lives, and ours, is sweetened through song.

Reaching the Inner Person with Compassionate Song

Pale, withdrawn, uncommunicative, Andora refuses to relate to the story I read as we sit outside near an oak tree behind the nursing home. Her eyes, half closed, do not focus on my face or the tree in front of her. I think to myself: she isn't here. Is she finished with life?

Although she grunts when I ask if she likes the story, her body remains rigid and not a flicker of recognition shows in her eyes. I stop the story, and start a song. Andora stays in her stupor. Suddenly I act silly as I gently tap her shoulder, arm, and knee. Playfully moving between all three, tapping rhythmically, I sing:

"Andora, Andora, what're we gonna do? / Andora, Andora, this moment me and you? / Andora, Andora, wake up your eyes / Show me you're alive right now!"

A smile brightens Andora's face. She looks straight at me and says: "I washed it." I sing "I washed it" and continue tapping Andora's knee. "The trees wave in the summer air / The rabbits run in the bushes over there / The sky smiles as the clouds drift away / The shadows dance where the grasses lay." Andora cocks her head from side to side, lifts and drops her shoulders in time to the music, moves as if she were dancing.

Where had I learned to carry on this kind of musical bantering? From Rabbi Shlomo Carlebach. On the deepest level, Shlomo made the teachings of the nineteenth-century mystic Rabbi Nachman come alive during a gathering at the Ojai Foundation in Ojai, California: "To make all the harshness in life sweet, you have to sing . . . when you sing, you make beautiful garments for God's presence. When you talk without singing, you disconnect yourself from the creation of the world."[3]

When I sang with Shlomo and listened to these teachings, I found myself wondering what it would be like to be in the world before it was created; to be present at the very moment when, before my eyes, I saw the world come into being. Who would want to be disconnected from that moment—a moment of awe, delight, and joy, of experiencing life as new, fresh, and free?

In this same spirit as a Healing Companion, I wondered if I could bring a feeling of awe and delight into the lives of elders, not only through singing, but also through poetry, dance, art, storytelling, spiritual dialogue and prayer.

I began with singing my talk. I found inspiration for singing through Rabbi Shlomo Carlebach's humorous teaching stories.

"Will you please dry your hands? On the towel, what do you think towels are for?" The exaggerated irritation in the rabbi's voice hinted of humor.

"Stop eating with your hands, I've told you a thousand times, eat with your fork, sit on the chair!" Shaking his head in mock disgust, the Rabbi lifted his hands to the heavens, shrugged his shoulders, and paused.

His voice began to soften. Shlomo spoke of how Rabbi Nachman didn't talk, he sang. So did his mother. Instead of talking when speaking to her children, she sang her words. To illustrate this, Shlomo sang, "Would you please dry your hands on the towel?" This musical request in lilting melodious tones contained not a trace of irritation or nagging. How could the children resist doing what their mother asked?[4]

Children Teach Us to Lighten Our Spirits

To practice singing my talk as Shlomo demonstrated in his example, one Friday night I invited a group of children and their parents to my cottage for a Jewish Sabbath celebration, hoping to keep Shlomo's playful singing alive. I set up the following singing game—when dinner began, for the entire evening we would stop talking and sing instead.

"Will you please pass me the bread and butter?" I sang to the child next to me.

"Okay," a small voice sang amid giggles around the table.

"How about a knife?" I sang.

"Here's the knife, here's the knife," a delightful set of notes echoed mine.

Uninhibited, the children quickly caught on. They didn't want to stop, and neither did their parents who began to experience how to be a child again.

Our singing game was magical. It created so much delight and humor that the children still remember it years later.

Through these musical experiences, I recognized the need for childlike delight in eldercare. I sensed that personalized singing would draw playfulness out of elders by shifting their focus from physical and emotional discomfort to immediate joy and well-being.

But reaching an elder through singing isn't always about playfulness. Sometimes a more serious tone is called for, as it was one afternoon with Rosetta.

"Honey, come talk to me," she pleaded.

"I've only got a minute, Rosetta," I sing.

"You never visit me."

"But I *am* visiting you right now," my song continues.

"No, you don't visit me." Tears begin. Sensing this is no lighthearted situation, I stop and ask, "What's hurting you Rosetta?"

"My brothers, sisters, they never come to see me." As her tears flow, I realize another kind of song is needed, one that is deep and compassionate. I recall that Shlomo once taught: "A song needs joy, crying, and depth."[5]

Taking Rosetta's hand, I gently stroke it and softly sing: "Rosetta, I'm sorry that your heart is hurting / I will stay with you until you're peaceful / I am with you and I won't leave you / I will hold your hand."

I watch as the tension around Rosetta's mouth releases; her knuckles, white from gripping the arms of her wheelchair, have let go.

A few moments of music helped her cross over the bridge of suffering to experience an inner quiet. Not only is Rosetta relieved, so are the wearied nurses, doctors, and aides who have been listening to her uncontrollable crying. Through the act of compassionate singing, the singer can reach inward to a place where peace exists in spite of outer pain. This inner connectedness is an important facet of the role of Healing Companion.

How did I find the right song for Rosetta? To bring to her the healing art of song, I had to move away from the idea of singing to entertain. Instead, I had to become an instrument of love, to call upon the Creator through my singing to mend what was broken.

What would soothe Sarah? She not only screamed all night, she hallucinated, was severely demented, and so enraged she had to be removed from the dining room in the nursing home because of her violent curses.

Sarah's room is the color of sunflowers. I enter and look out her window. A gentle breeze stirs the magnolia blossoms and blows them to the ground, and a fountain flows into a blue-tiled pond that is surrounded by smiling cherubs gazing down into the water.

In a black cloud of rage, Sarah slumps in her recliner, her face ashen, her eyes reflecting furious and fearful thoughts. She mutters, "All is futile." Recalling the words of peace activist and Vietnamese Buddhist monk Thich Nhat Hanh, I begin to sing: "May I learn to look at myself with love and understanding / May I plant seeds of joy in myself every day."[6]

Sarah's wide, childlike eyes begin to smile. It seems as if a shaft of sunlight has entered her entire body. Shining with delight, she sways, sings, and begins making large sweeping motions with her arms, creating arcs and circles in front of her. As her arms reach above, Sarah is enraptured. In spite of extreme physical weakness, she "dances" for half an hour, captivated by a gentle flow of energy. Although Sarah is an agnostic, as the dance comes to an end she places her palms together in a prayer position and bows with reverence.

My next visit turns into two hours of joy. Elders in demented conditions are believed to have a ten-minute attention span at best, but Sarah's attention remains unwavering. I sing: "In the garden of my heart / The flower of peace blooms in beauty." The words are rephrased from Thich Nhat Hanh's teachings. Sarah is often irrational. Yesterday, she said to me, "There is food under my blanket and violins all over my body." Yet now she helps me create the appropriate words to fit the music. In this present moment, Sarah is well both mentally and emotionally.

The Transforming Power of Song

Nursing homes tend to emphasize entertainments rather than personal, transformative moments. Yet, how did elders live before they became old? Did they fill their days primarily with theatrical experiences? In their last years, is the central core of an elder's life meant to be a constant parade of entertainments?

Shlomo once taught: "Most people sing to entertain; they are running low on gas, the songs are not deep. But the other kind of singing is, you learn while you sing and sing while you learn."[7] Singing can become a communion with the Highest Source; bring a touch of heaven to earth. Such music may reveal hidden truths and can mean more than cheering people up.

Through the years, in various spiritual centers around the country, I received life lessons *while singing*. As I sang, it was revealed to me that jealousy, fear, and lack of forgiveness were blocking the love within me. The more I sang, the more I yearned for a pure heart, to sing and serve the Creator instead of indulging my own selfishness, arrogance, and pride.

If we are open to inner promptings, Healing Companions can become *inner singers*. Instead of focusing on musical expertise, an inner singer hears from within words, music, and wisdom teachings as a song is being born. This experience can become an abandonment to Love, which may bring forth a new kind of song. Such singing may purify and transform the singer into a blissful state of consciousness.

Inner singing requires training that may come at a Sabbath celebration where ecstatic Hasidic Jews sing and dance; at monasteries and churches where prayers are sung; at workshops to free the body and voice for spontaneous movement and expression of the inner self; or spiritual groups where chanting is done. In an atmosphere of devotion, our inner life is revealed, expanded, purified. Writing in dream and prayer journals can also open creative channels that may help to free the singing voice.

Through these means we can be awakened to an inner longing akin to that of Bengali poet Rabindranath Tagore:

> *I touch by the edge of the far spreading wing of my song*
> *thy feet which I could never aspire to reach.*
> *Drunk with the joy of singing I forget myself*
> *and call thee friend who art my Lord.*[8]

Mother Teresa said that it is not how much we do that is important; it is how much love we put into the doing. So with singing, it is not how many songs we learn or how much training we have, but how much love we put into the songs we sing.

A new dimension enters the musical experiences we offer our elders when we make our songs into an invocation, prayer, or thanksgiving; when we sing an elder's life story; when we hum melodies without words. Even familiar songs have a new purpose. I found that out when I entered Liberal Catholic Bishop Isaiah's hospital room.

Expecting him to be depressed over the news that he might not survive a cancer operation, the bishop's hearty participation surprised me as we sang "I've Been Workin' on the Railroad." Our singing also affected the man in the adjacent bed who begged for just one last song— "Amazing Grace." Not only did our singing touch the two men but relatives listening in the hallway later told me they felt greatly relieved by the music.

Elders, families, and health care staff can benefit from the relaxing effects of music on body, mind, and spirit. If more hospitals included music for inner healing, the staff could undertake their tasks with greater ease and less tension. Patients' fears could lessen and their sense of well-being, and health, might improve.

While for some elders singing may be an intrusion at life's end, as Bishop Isaiah's life came to a close singing was one of the last things he asked for. As we sang by his bedside together, the soothing musical journey helped Bishop Isaiah remain calm as he withdrew from physical life. A simple song of tranquility began. Soft lyrics sang of going home to the sound of subtle joy.

❧ Steps for Healing ❧

Insights that can help heal

- Singing brings you closer to the light in yourself and in others.

- Singing brings peace to the soul and evokes a playful spirit.

- Songs can unlock hidden meaning in our life stories.

- At the core of our complaints is a cry for love.

- At the deepest level, our true nature is joy.

Helping yourself heal

1. Look back on your day. Did you voice any complaints silently or aloud? Did your complaint include feelings of being unloved? Replay the situation, approaching it this time with feelings of love for yourself.

2. Practice singing at home. Select a chore like washing the dishes or dressing your child and begin to sing a few notes. It does not have to be a melody. When you feel ready, start singing words. Describe the chore you are doing in musical tones.

Helping your elder heal

1. When elders complain, respond with a generous heart, like a parent who continues to love, nurture, and protect even when the child is demanding. Help your elders take a self-healing action by shifting the focus away from complaints and guiding them to find something good in their life. You can do this with a song, a hug, a touch, a kind word, or a prayer.

2. Be unafraid to move others to tears or to be moved to tears yourself. When we touch another through tears, we reach into the depth of love and healing can begin.

3. Healing songs open the heart to receive painful truths. Sing your talk. If you feel uncomfortable making up your own melody, choose a favorite tune (perhaps from a children's song) and make up your own words.

4. Guide your elders into song by singing a description of the weather, the evening meal, anything that is part of their lives. Encourage them to sing back to you as if you were having a conversation.

5. When elders exhibit inappropriate behavior or are severely agitated, sing words of empathy and wisdom to soothe and rechannel their anxiety and confusion.

For your inspiration

I complain, but I am not my complaints.
My elders complain, but they are not their complaints.
On a deeper level, our true nature is joy. Even if I can't carry a
tune, I have a singing heart deep within me.
Every day I experience a different rhythm and a different mood.
In this, my elder and I are one.

TWO

Inner Reflections

> *Freedom is what you*
> *do with what's been*
> *done to you.*
> —Jean-Paul Sartre

> *Goodness of heart*
> *is always within us;*
> *buried, it needs only*
> *to be uncovered.*
> —J. E.

"CAN A PERSON yell and scream without saying a word?" Surprised at my own question, I look out the window of Mountain Pines nursing home. Colorful displays of begonias and pansies and a fountain splashing over seashells greet my gaze. The recreation room, where a fire dances in the fireplace, smells of sizzling pinecones.

My question reverberates back to me as I begin facilitating a discussion called "Inner Reflections." I wonder what "yelling without saying a word" has to do with Vera's behavior. The friendly flames do not seem so friendly as Vera smacks her thigh, jerks her head, and shouts, "Get her out of my way. I don't want to look at her." Is this the same Vera I often experience as warm, wise, humorous—even humble? Can her aggression be turned into compassion, a spark of warmth replace her hostility?

The new resident, Dorothy, has just been wheeled in to the recreation room and is positioned next to Vera. Heather and Rebecca have joined us, Rebecca coming around to the other side of Vera's chair.

As she turns to me, Vera thrusts her hand with disgust in Dorothy's direction. "She's stupid, take her away." Her usual objection: someone else is in *her* territory. Will the garbled tone of her speech impediment camouflage her insults, or will Dorothy understand every word and be devastated?

Vera shoves her wheelchair away from Dorothy, latches the wheel brake, faces the group, and sulks. But sulking doesn't override her regal bearing: proud, she sits more like queen than naughty child; her graceful emerald green gown flows around her legs, her silver hair cascades over her shoulders.

For years Vera has had a problem—she rejects every roommate. How can I relate to this current conflict? Is there some creative way to mention Vera's behavior without her feeling accused, threatened, rejected—some way in which she can see what she is doing and correct her negative responses?

Vera's aggressiveness creates tension in the room. How will I begin today's discussion? After thirty years of working with older people, I have come to trust an inner process where spontaneous thoughts, images, and questions arise. Within the unconscious part of our mind, a wellspring of creativity exists. Healing Companions can learn to tap into and trust their own inner process so that a meaningful connection can be made to the elders in their care.

Deciding to trust my intuition, which prompted the question I had asked earlier, I repeat: "Can a person yell and scream without saying a word?"

Vera, suddenly eager, leans forward in her chair. "Yes, it's possible. A person can scream without a word being said."

"Really?" I reply. "How can you tell if someone is yelling when they don't make a sound?"

"You just look at his eyes," she answers.

"How so?"

Vera, animated now, says: "His eyes—a person may look at you in a terrible way. His eyes are yelling."

"What would you do if you saw such a person?" I look around the room.

"I'd stuff a rag in his mouth!" Heather replies with a laugh. "And then I'd run sixty miles!" The sparkle in Heather's eyes probably hasn't changed since she was a child. I could just see her, pigtails and all, flashing across the fields behind her father's farm as she runs after her eight brothers.

"Obviously," says Rebecca in her usual calm tone, "he can't listen if he's yelling." A broad smile accentuates high cheekbones and huge round eyes.

"What would you do?" I ask.

"Ask him what he needs." Vera's response touches me; she always goes down to the deeper level, down where the truth lies waiting. What is *her* truth? Her aggressiveness and snobbishness aren't new, but today those traits seem stronger. Why?

"What do you think he needs?" I ask.

"He's lonely," replies Rebecca.

"What is the underlying desire behind loneliness?"

"The need to be heard," Rebecca answers. "Friendship."

"And what is the value of friendship?"

Dorothy, the new resident, responds: "Love, companionship."

"Security," Rebecca says. Hers is a keen perception revealing a depth of intelligence you feel just by looking at her.

Then Vera: "Friendship eases our heart's condition."

Once again I wonder where all this is going, how it might come around to what really bothers Vera. I know the discussion is having an effect on all of them, a handful of alert, cognitive residents who are living with thirty or more elders who would be unable to understand this level of communication.

For these alert residents, it is vitally important to have experiences that validate inner wellness. By mingling continually with those whose mental functioning is severely impaired, a harmonious balance between body, mind, and spirit may be endangered, lowering their capacity for well-being. Keeping the mind supple, flexible, and eager to learn enhances the joy of life. Right now all of us enjoy tackling this imaginary challenge, enjoy integrating the truth of our own lives and growing from what we learn.

"What does this person who is yelling really need?" I probe, hoping to go even deeper. "Suppose you or I do something which annoys others. Suppose we are nasty, demanding, aggressive, and blaming of others, always wanting our own way. None of us is perfect. What do we need?"

"We need God," Vera answers.

"I sure needed God today in my car." I laugh. "I was driving as if I owned the road. Everybody was in my way, and I was in a hurry. Couldn't they see I had to get there *Now?* I honked and swore. I'm glad no one was in the car with me! When my behavior is out of control like this, what do I need?"

"Ask God for help," Vera replies. I wonder, is Vera able to link this discussion with her own aggressiveness? Is she becoming aware of how disruptive her behaviour is?

"But . . . there's another problem," I reply. "I curse in the car. It has become a habit. I've been doing it for years. I hardly notice it anymore because my behavior has become part of me. I'm not aware I'm doing it or how it affects my outlook—I'm just acting without being conscious."

"I see what you mean,"Rebecca says with a laugh. "We could all be like that."

"If we look around us, we may notice someone who is yelling without saying a word. But their face, eyes, or body tells us they're angry or upset. What do we have to give them?"

"When I'm like that I tell myself I can't always be right and am open for correction," says Rebecca.

"We give them love," Vera answers.

It dawns on me. Vera's behavior is not the problem. The problem is her breaking heart. And that is not something easily corrected. This is the Christmas season. Her son is in prison, and she hasn't heard from him in months. She has lived in this facility for years, surrounded by people who are incoherent or withdrawn, unable to match her mental acuity. Vera is alone in her despondency.

What happens to a mind that is not stimulated? It loses its elasticity, its creativity, its ability to voice wisdom accumulated through years of living. When enthusiasm for life and learning flees, what remains? What does Vera have to live for? She acts out of jealousy and depression because she can't ask for what she really needs most: love. Vera is unable to say "please love me." How many people can?

"You're right, Vera, but we can only give love if we ourselves are loving. First we have to acknowledge our anger, jealousy, depression." I can sense that the residents are enthusiastically engaged in our discussion. "We have both a light and dark side in us," I continue. "When we're caught in the dark side, how do we return to harmony? All of us have moments of peace, of well-being. What ways do each of us have for finding peace inside of ourselves?"

"Peace," Heather says. "I used to love walking in the

woods. My dad always said our memory is our best companion. When I miss my husband and get depressed, I remember walking together in the woods."

"Yes, even in a wheelchair," I say, "we can mentally travel far away. We can go to the place where we once felt love and peace. When we reexperience this peace, our frame of mind is changed and then we have something to give the people around us."

"That's true," Rebecca says, smiling. "When I think of my mother I feel so peaceful."

"Psychiatrist Gerald Jampolsky tells us the essence of our being is love," I add.

"How beautiful," Rebecca replies.

"When we share experiences, we see how easy it is to get separated from the love we have within ourselves. We don't even know it's happening."

"Yes, that's right," Vera assents.

"In what way can we realize this separation?"

"The next time I think someone doesn't like me," Dorothy says, "I'll ask myself if it is I who doesn't like them." It's an astute comment coming from Dorothy, who seems more and more confused, not always able to grasp what is being said.

She adds: "I know what I can give. I remember a poem—it goes something like this: 'There was a lady bent and old / Shivering and shaking with the cold / But she smiled as the sun set red / "Thank you for beauty, God" she said.' "

It's another surprise. I wouldn't have thought Dorothy could retain not only a poem but the ability to apply it to our discussion. Today she is alert, although in previous visits her responses have been repetitious and contradictory.

"I find my peace by talking to God," says Rebecca.

"You mean the way the fiddler did on his roof?" I laugh.

Rebecca smiles: "Yes, it's very simple. I talk to him all day long."

"I find peace by praying and listening to music," Dorothy says.

"There are many ways of finding peace," I say. "Our challenge is to find a way to be aware of our thoughts and feelings, how they affect our actions—and our peace. If I'm unaware, how can I grow, change, be transformed? If I don't recognize that sometimes my behavior is harmful, what can I do to realize it?"

"Ask God for help." Vera has the answers, but does she live her own advice? I don't know, even though we have prayed together many times.

"One way I stay aware," I reply, "is to review what I said or did at the end of the day. I call it my inner view. Was the tone of my voice harsh? Was I inconsiderate? Did I feel anger, hatred, sorrow?"

Vera nods her head in agreement.

"I don't need to beat myself up, blame myself if I discover I acted in a negative manner," I continue. "I acknowledge what happened, ask forgiveness, desire to be transformed, let go of the incident, and return to peace."

Glancing over at Vera, I see a different person from the one who entered this room an hour earlier. Now calm and relaxed, Vera is no longer the aggressor but a person of wisdom, perception, insight. During the hour, she has become a purposeful giver. For now, her self-esteem is restored.

"We have an ability within us," I conclude, "that allows us to see and acknowledge how our thoughts and actions create trouble. Once we see it, we can begin to change."

Rebecca beams. "Because of my negative responses, it's my fault that my candle went out." Her face and eyes glow with sudden delight. "But as soon as I decide to look within, find the good in myself—I'm lighting my candle again!"

What's Missing in Eldercare?

Why did I introduce *inner exploration* in my work with elders? After visiting elders in nursing homes, assisted living facilities, and private residences where they lived with loving families, I discovered that something essential was missing in the care they were being given.

Some confided that, even though they were surrounded by people, there was great loneliness. One elder who lived in a scenic mountain community where she was surrounded by grandchildren, pets, and a devoted daughter, said: "I feel like I live alone on a deserted island."

I came to realize that by introducing a process of inner exploration, elders would be allowed to honor their feelings and longings. I have found that this process opens people to profound emotional and spiritual healing.

Few in the health care professions are available to listen to the deeper feelings elders experience, to evoke the wisdom elders have to give, to challenge them to think, explore, and expand.

With this in mind, I decided to assist elders in reconnecting to the inner vitality and curiosity I knew they possessed. It was then that the vision of developing my Healing Companion program began. As elders explored their true beliefs—not what they had been taught to believe by others, but what their minds and hearts responded to as truth from within—we embarked on an exciting journey together.

My intent was to help elders experience life as growing, not shrivelling. Vigorous discussions led me to believe that the enrichment of life has no end and is a gift we all deserve. As I set up guidelines for both groups and individual sessions, an atmosphere of trust was created. This allowed difficult moments to be eased, and an openness of heart to be expressed.

Anyone could say anything. Confidentiality would be maintained. No one would criticize what anyone said, even if what was shared was directly opposed to one's own beliefs. We would listen with an open mind, grow in goodwill, become a miniworld, a circle in which to find a common bond no matter how different each of us was.

We would turn this sharing of ourselves into an adventure. By seeing ourselves as a microcosm of the world at large, we would attempt to attain harmony. Our differences would enhance rather than threaten us.

The groups of elders with whom I met began to see that honesty begins with "me." Self-honesty became a pathway to convert negativity and direct positive feelings into constructive channels. As a Healing Companion, I realized that when I look at another person, I look into a mirror and see myself. Sometimes a person's behavior is grotesque or extreme. How could this be me? Perhaps I try to shrink away, refuse the connection. *"I've* never done or said the things I am seeing and hearing." I pride myself on being a gentle, soft-spoken person, but I am now called to look at others on a deeper level. There I find the human me, which is also in everybody else.

From this basis, I found ways to relate to elders who exhibited behavior problems. By prompting Vera to consider angry behavior as a plea for love, for example, she reconnected with her deeper self. She was changed, at least temporarily, from a negative, judgmental person into someone with equilibrium, dignity, and self-worth. It was the beginning of a very beneficial process for her.

Through self-reflection, my group of elders moved away from how humans *behave* toward what a human being really is and can *become*. We touched depths that brought us to the heart of a question that any person of any age might ask: "What do we as human beings need more than anything else in this world?"

❧ Steps for Healing ☙

Insights that can help heal

✦ At times we are angry or aggressive, but this is not who we really are.

✦ Underneath our anger, we are love. Our desire is to love and be loved.

✦ The energy of love is stronger than the energy of anger and hatred.

✦ Transcendent love has the power to heal.

✦ All of us are able to return to feelings of peace and harmony.

Helping yourself heal

1. To attune yourself to an elder who expresses angry, antisocial, or aggressive behavior, it is helpful to begin by acknowledging your own. Try this reflective exercise. Review your day. Did you reject anyone in your thoughts, your actions, your speech, or in a dream? Did you ignore anyone who needed your attention? Were you possessive of your territory, knowledge, position, or point of view? Did you have an attitude of superiority? Did you speak harshly or have vindictive thoughts? Were your emotions sometimes out of control?

2. Accept your shortcomings without blame. Forgive yourself and others, and affirm your willingness to grow and move on.

Helping your elder heal

1. Reassure your elders that we all have a dark and a light side. Tell them you understand their anger and aggressiveness, and that it is okay to have these feelings. Assure them of your acceptance and love.

2. Help your elders return to a healthy emotional condition by encouraging them to remember a time when they felt loved and at peace.

For your inspiration

I have a seed of goodness and wisdom within me despite moments
of anger, frustration, or meanness. This goodness
is my true nature, who and what I am meant to be.
In this, my elder and I are one.

THREE

Our Dreaming Selves

*And your young men
shall see visions,
and your old men
shall dream dreams.*
—Acts 2:17

"MY THIRTEEN-YEAR-OLD brother suffocated under the earth while digging a cave, and my mother grieved endlessly over his death." In the living room of Valley View residential home, seven elders listen to Milka's story.

"Mama believed in her religion. Through a dream, God let her know that he exists. She dreamt that my brother, Bajo, came to her, drenched in water. 'Mama, I am pleading with you—stop your crying. Can't you see how your tears envelop me? Because of them, I am clothed in water. I am overcome, Mama, I can't rest. It's good for me here—I am with God. *Ja sam sa Bog*, Mama,' Bajo said in Serbian, 'I am with God. You *must* stop crying.' "

Outside, the shadows of dark billowy clouds pass over the grass; they pass through our minds as Milka's story deepens.

"Only then did Mama's crying end. It was as if she turned off the tap water. Every day was so good. Before my brother died, my mama always used to sing around the house—after her dream, she began to sing again."

Was the telling of this dream giving Milka a new sense of self? While her story unfolds, Milka's being is infused with enthusiasm and openness. A Serbian woman of striking beauty, she has come here under bold protest. Threatened with police arrest, she was forced to give up her property, on which she had not paid taxes for ten years. Milka was angry. Would she make life miserable for everyone in this tranquil residential community?

The Humane Society had been called to remove fifteen cats and two dogs from Milka's house. Adult Protective Services had been notified that fire or disease could render Milka's living conditions unsafe. As soon as Milka arrived here, she was immediately sent for psychiatric evaluation. The results: paranoia and dementia.

Yet the depth of Milka's dream story presents us with a mystery more vibrant, alive, and loving than any psychiatric label. Psychologist Thomas Moore writes that when we listen to a life story, it reveals a greater scope of meaning than diagnostic evaluation or terminology.[1]

Still, I could appreciate the diagnosis. Years back, I had visited Milka's home. What confronted me was both genius and eccentricity. Along a pebbled pathway leading to her front door, large mounds of neatly arranged bottle caps adorned one side of the entrance. On the other side, piles of coat hangers leaned in tidy stacks against the trunk of an oak tree; dozens more hung from leaves and branches. On either side of the front door, magazines and newspapers formed two columns framed at the bottom with shells and rocks. On top of each, potted plants managed to create a semblance of order and balance. Inside, the stench stung my nostrils. Animals had made their home here; they had complete charge of the house, which was dark and cluttered. The backyard contained sculpted rock formations, in the center of which were empty cans and bottles of all sizes. Thin strips of wood with knotted and twisted old rags wound around them framed a base for empty milk cartons sculpted into a pyramidal design.

In her younger years Milka was the manager of a high-fashion women's clothing store. At her job she was used to taking control. Will she become domineering here and upset our group's emotional and spiritual balance?

As Milka's story comes to an end, all of us have been caught up in a sense of mystery. Through the window we watch rays of sunlight pierce the darkening sky. Nature's mirrored light seems to weave its way into Milka's dream story, into the clouded emotions of her life—and into ours. Her vibrant personality is quiet now. A hush settles over the room.

Having shared the memory of a dream, which, though not her own, has become hers through seventy years of carrying it, we are welcomed into the depth of Milka's heart, into the allegiance she pays to the gift of mystery and transformation. This deeper dimension tells us far more about her than eccentric behavior; it is the core through which we can relate to the best within her.

As Healing Companions, we can fine tune our perception through the stories elders tell and begin to honor a reality that cannot be explained but is deeply felt. By listening to elders' dreams, we gain entrance into something beyond diagnosis; we begin to touch the essence not only of who they are but who we are.

"Once I had a dream that also changed me," I say. Sometimes I share my own dreams as an impetus for elders to share theirs. Milka looks at me with great interest.

"Ten years had passed since my dad died, but I was still grieving. Then I had this dream: I saw my dad remarried to a vital, attractive woman. He was now an artist and experienced great satisfaction. In the dream he was thirty years younger than when he actually died. Freed from his old life—a job that bored him and a marriage to my mother that lacked common interests—my dad was finally fulfilled.

"When I awoke from that dream, for the first time since his death I felt gladness whenever I thought about him. The dream somehow released me from grief. At last, I could let my father go."

Dialoguing with Your Dreams

Dreams have a mysterious power; in the telling of them, we become witness to an act of transformation. Indeed, we may experience awe, surprise, insight—gifts that open us to life's fullness. For many elders who spend hours with nothing to do, this gift is worth pursuing. When we allow our unconscious dreaming self to speak—in other words, when we speak our dreams to others—we glimpse a deeper dimension of who we are and how we are evolving. We begin to connect to a meaning that enhances our existence, one that makes us eager to live with adventure.

Recently a dream brought me in touch with a deeper aspect of myself. In my dream I was with Mother Teresa in Calcutta and had a burning desire to ask her how she prepared for her own death. When I awoke, I felt great peace, deep fulfilment—the exact opposite of how I was feeling in daily life.

What was the dream telling me? Could it give me guidance in my current situation? I had been meditating for months on what to do in a troublesome friendship with eighty-five-year-old Darwin whose escalating demands alarmed me. The more I gave, the more he wanted. Trying to make me feel guilty for not giving more, he threatened to cut off the friendship. Angry and frustrated, I was losing the ability to love him. Could this dream help?

Some dream figures embody wisdom; if we honor their presence within us, we may receive valuable instruction. The figure may be a known person like Mother Teresa or it may be someone we've never heard of. Through dialoguing with this wise one aloud or in our journal, he or she may help transform our attitudes. Healing Companions may find new insights by dialoguing with an elder in a journal. Tensions, confusion, wisdom, or clarity may emerge to aid the healing process.

Inspired by my dream, I decided to have a talk with Mother Teresa in my journal. What would *she* have me do about Darwin?

"You must purify your conscience," she told me. "All thoughts of getting must give way to giving. Be a fountain of love and blessing. Be kind; smile. Die to show your love."

What did she mean, "Die to show your love?" Suddenly I knew: I had to let go of my selfishness, of my emotional reactions that had convinced me Darwin was too difficult to deal with.

While I saw the need to let my negative attitudes die, I didn't see what this had to do with my longing, in the dream, to know how Mother Teresa prepared for dying. She answered this in my journal: "Respond with your whole heart to Darwin, as if he were a child longing for love. Forget irritation, impatience, self-interest. If you do this, when it is your time to die, you will know the Lord is saying: 'Well done, I am pleased.' "

The message: If I love, my death will be good. Within me lived qualities of wisdom and compassion embodied in the dream figure of Mother Teresa, who now instructed me in how to prepare for my own death. That night I invited my friend Darwin to dinner. My vantage point was totally different.

Instead of seeing him through the eyes of my own needs, I began asking what would give *him* greater happiness and fulfilment—I began to love again.

By exploring our own dreams, Healing Companions become more effective in relating to elders. As we enter the world of the dreaming self, we connect to life as a river flowing without effort. Inside of us, this river has a life of its own. When we are moved by that flow, we begin to know what to do when elders are disturbed. We know not so much through our thinking mind as through our inner world, through intuitions and feelings that manifest in our touch and in the words we speak or sing.

Validating an Elder's Dream

A Healing Companion does not have to be a trained dream analyst to enter the mysterious realm of dreams with an elder or to encourage them to engage in dialogues with dream figures. When we listen to a dream as if through the ear of an artist, we seek not so much to literally understand it as to receive its creative influence upon us, to be taken into the mysterious unfolding of sight, sound, color, smell—into the mystery our lives are seeking to reveal. When Healing Companions relate to elders on this level, intimacy occurs, and with it our elders' sense of fulfilment that he or she has been embraced as a whole person. This happened with my client Gloria.

One day I received a frantic phone call. Would I come at once? In haste, I arrived at the nursing home where Gloria waited in the hall. A woman of great dignity, Gloria was intellectually, spiritually, and artistically astute. The other residents in the nursing home were not on her level; she rarely had anyone with whom to converse.

Gloria had been having nightmares. In one of them, she found herself hopelessly lost, wandering between old, dilapidated buildings. Everything was dank, dark, and ugly. She awoke in a panic. What was her dream trying to tell her?

Her life was ebbing away. At a rapid rate, Gloria's body was decaying and she knew it. Over the years, Gloria had committed herself to death with great calm; she was ready to die. But if, indeed, she accepted death, why was she having panic attacks?

My rational mind tried to seek answers to rational questions. But answers did not come. It soon became clear. Listening to Gloria's dream story in a deeply respectful way was enough. I honored her inner process; I let her know someone supported her as she entered into unknown, inner regions. I was willing to validate the flow of imagery presenting itself in her dream world.

How did Gloria feel about the nursing home? She told me that the place had no aesthetic charm, was often chaotic, devoid of laughter, and filled with rows of laconic elders sitting in wheelchairs for hours, staring at nothing. Even though the home oppressed her, I saw that she managed to cope. When I asked how she perceived her body, she confirmed that it was weakening daily. She wished to be free of this old life and was impatient to get out of it.

I asked Gloria if the decaying buildings in her dream portrayed her way of life and her decaying physical self. She told me the dream image spoke accurately of both. As she recounted her dream, the images began to merge with her feelings. The dream had become an artful canvas, which depicted thoughts and feelings she was now more clearly aware of. This awareness intensified her spiritual yearning. In the dream, she was caught in a place she did not want to be, a reflection of her waking desire to be free of the encumbrance of her body, to move onward into death—which for her meant a fuller life in spirit.

The images were not pleasant. But they gave a sense of wholeness to Gloria's suffering by connecting her to her daily life in a deeper way. Because she entered into her pain more fully, accepted it rather than rejecting it, Gloria found a measure of release.

When dealing with elders who do not have the psychological and spiritual awareness that Gloria had, or who experience varying degrees of dementia, it is enough for a Healing Companion to listen to the dream without discussing its meaning. Although there is potentially more depth in exploring dream content, by trusting in the mystery unfolding in the dream a Healing Companion accepts its creativity, wisdom, and intuition, its potential for spiritual and emotional healing. No elaboration of the dream is needed.

Dreams are a wonderful way to initiate communication. For an elder who is irrational or unresponsive, asking a simple question about dreaming may produce surprising rewards. Even if an elder doesn't remember an actual dream, pleasure in the sudden recall of the *experience* of dreaming lends dignity to an elder's lackluster life.

While Healing Companions might fear that discussing dreams which depict death or darkness will accentuate an elder's distress, such may not be the case. As night moves into day, so too "out of darkness light shall shine,"[2] out of the inner self may come resolution, light. Talking about an elder's dreams, and bringing to light the troubling thoughts that dream images sometimes call forth, may release anxiety and fear.

On the other hand, if a nightmare is severely disturbing it may be best to balance dream work with uplifting thoughts, images, and prayers. Elders who have limited stamina need additional protection from negativity. Still, it is important not to assume that because an elder is frail, he or she cannot handle the darker aspects of life. Some elders may benefit by becoming conscious of the dark side, intense feelings, and gloomy images, particularly if in their younger years they explored their inner world.

When the body weakens through aging, mental and emotional faculties may become unbalanced. Self-control may fail; negative feelings, held down in the shadow of the self for years, may suddenly rush forth and leak out in emotional outbursts, agitation, or anxiety. If Healing Companions become aware of *their own* shadow side by examining repressed anger, fear, and unforgivingness found in their dreams, it becomes easier to accept with compassion (rather than with criticism or annoyance) these same negative emotions surfacing in elders when they become aggressive, violent, or prone to excessive nervousness, nightmares, weeping, or complaining.

As Healing Companions, we can find an intuitive balance between too much emphasis on the dream world—and not enough; too much focus on darkness, heaviness, unresolved tensions—and not enough stimulation of joy, jubilation, celebration.

While many elders do not remember their dreams, creating a supportive atmosphere for the dream world to awaken within them may spontaneously trigger sudden, important memories or past dreams, as it did for Milka. Caregivers and family members should be aware that dreams can become a rich source of creativity, energy, and fascination, that they can validate our wholeness, offer insight and guidance, point the way to new beginnings for spiritual awakening.

Dreams Can Connect Elders to Their Spiritual Selves

A dramatic case history discussed by Jungian analyst Edward Edinger clearly illustrates the potential dreams have for awakening the dreamer's spiritual self. Edinger recounted the mysterious transformational quality within the dream journey of a middle-aged man who knew nothing about philosophy or religion. The man attempted suicide before his dreams began. Over a two-year period, the man recalled a series of dreams. Since the man had difficulty comprehending analytical interpretation, Edinger simply listened to the man's dreams and together they searched for their meaning.[3]

Through a series of thirteen dreams, the patient was exposed to unknown worlds and symbols. In one of them the man saw a darkness glowing with luminosity, revealing a golden woman with a face like the Mona Lisa. At times, these dream symbols guided the patient, released from the limitations of his ego, toward a spiritual awakening. A new dimension emerged, completely unknown to him before he became involved in considering his dreams.

In another dream he saw a green man made of grass doing a dance. This image gave the patient a sense of peace. Edinger comments that the dream, which occurred close to his patient's death, presents "a vivid and beautiful image of the eternal nature of life." With Edinger's guidance, the man began to experience peace in his life. His personality underwent a transformation; he gained greater insights and some of his daily frustrations ceased. Three months after the last of these dreams, a sudden stroke caused the man's death.

Can dreams prepare us for death? It is not clear whether the dreams of Edinger's patient prepared him. But even if they did not, unless his dream images had been made conscious and shared, he might have continued to have no connection with the spiritual wisdom and joy that his dreams sometimes revealed. He might have died never having connected to his inner self, his wholeness, or a transcendental reality.

"In elderhood, dreams are one of the preparations for death," says Jungian psychologist Don Sloggy. "In young adulthood, dreams prepare us to go out in the world, take our place, establish work, marriage, vocation, schooling. In the second half of life, dreams orient us toward an inner journey, the movement toward life's completion."

Sloggy told me that although some caregivers and Healing Companions may not have a psychological understanding of dreams, acknowledging the reality of the dream, listening to its story, witnessing it, can help an elder fulfill his or her hunger for a more meaningful life.

As Healing Companions we must attend not only to an elder's physical need for rest, nutrients, exercise, and mental stimulation but to the inner needs of the soul, the inner life of feeling, dreams, creativity, prayer, reflection, contemplation. These needs, as well as the needs of the physical body, make up the *whole* person, who needs our support and love. Giving this support brings us beyond traditional caregiving into the birth of a new role: the Healing Companion.

We can encourage elders to share their dreams with Healing Companions, other elders, family, or friends. Sharing dreams opens them to a rich inner world, to the treasure of mysterious events taking place within their dreaming selves.

Drawing Our Dreams

Our dreaming self draws pictures in the night. Painting them in daylight reveals a hidden wisdom seeking expression through our souls. That wisdom is reflected in one of Cambria's dreams: White horses pull a ship trimmed in gold across the sea. Cambria is the only one on board. When Cambria awakens from her dream, she experiences a profound sense of peace.

Seeking to gain greater insight into Cambria's dream journey, I consulted Jungian analyst Don Sloggy. "A ship trimmed in gold depicts royalty," Sloggy told me. "The dream is a sacred image of the self. When someone died in a Navajo tribe, the best horse was buried with the person. It was believed the horse would carry the deceased on his or her journey."

In the act of listening to dreams such as Cambria's, a Healing Companion inexperienced in the world of dreams can develop openness and reverence for dream events. Even if the Healing Companion does not understand the dream, he or she can accept symbols like Cambria's ship as powerful statements of the life within. Cambria's dream reflects her inner state of mind. Although her daily life consists of monotonous days at the Valley View residential home, her inner reality is regal and vibrant.

After my group listened to Cambria's dream, each member sketched the ship, entered into the dream, and expanded on Cambria's story by creating new ship stories born out of their drawings. Initially, these elders were reticent about drawing, but they soon became fully absorbed. Afterward, they wrote a few words on their sketches, describing their feelings. The sketches brought forth "ship memories" from each person's past, as well as their hopes for the future. For Cambria, the drawing experience heightened her inner reality, expanded its richness, and validated her sacred journey as she inwardly prepared for eventually leaving her body.

Since group participation added content to Cambria's dream that did not relate to the deeper, original dream image, this might have interfered with Cambria's inner process, causing her to be distracted. If she and I had shared her dream in a private session, she might have found a deeper connection to the images. Nevertheless, her experience in the group setting proved fruitful.

The group sketching experience convinced me that elders need more than drawing simply as a means of distraction from boredom and inertia. Although craft experiences are wonderful ways to relax, have fun, and produce something creative, sharing their hopes and dreams gives elders a deeper satisfaction than the activity itself.

When emphasis is placed on dream images as valuable messages for enriching life, elders can draw without worrying about talent and technical skills. This kind of participation enhances commitment to the unfolding of inner life, to growth in the deepest sense.

Dream Exploration for Healing Companions

Carl Jung said that we need to find the living, breathing soul in the stories that make up our lives. The story of who we are includes our dreams. Healing Companions can prepare to receive the dreams of elders by exploring their own dreams. They can keep dream journals, seek wisdom from their dreams, dialogue with dream figures, and contemplate the mysterious elements within them.

By sensitizing themselves to the inner world, Healing Companions may become more attuned to the inner needs of elders, to the dynamic interplay of the opposites that often characterize dreams. Healing Companions need to realize that dreams can be an unseen influence on our moods, actions, and thoughts. Visions, even prophecies, can come through our dreams and expand our consciousness. Elders deserve to be heard on this level.

How does the Healing Companion who is psychologically untrained relate to his or her dreams? Dreams can be received like the contemplation of an abstract painting or poem. We reflect on its meaning without having to know exactly what the artist had in mind. By simply allowing a poem, painting, or dream to enter us, we may receive them as musical tones. We may not grasp the entire or literal meaning, but as we open ourselves we are touched and moved in an inner way.

Like the rhythms in nature, dreams weave the opposites of life into one continuous circle; the seasons of birth/death, sorrow/joy, storm/calm, fear/faith. These opposites may pull at us, create conflict. But an awareness of this dramatic inner process can teach us how to live with these opposites in a harmonious way.

When we are open to the unique language and mystery within our dreams, we may experience more vibrancy, creativity, new spiritual awareness, and a depth of meaning in our lives. Dreams are our adventure into the unknown regions of our inner selves, regions both Healing Companion and elder can come to accept as gateways to a richer understanding of, and connection to, their own inner lives.

❧ Steps for Healing ❧

Insights that can help heal

◆ Dreams heal.

◆ Dreams deepen our insight into daily living.

❖ Dreams can reveal a hidden wisdom to help us through difficult passages.

Helping yourself heal

1. Keep a dream journal and write any responses you have when you wake up. The memory of your dreams may come sporadically. Open yourself to the possibility that the unconscious is a creative genius, sending you unexpected insights, ideas, and guidance via dream events, characters, and imagery. Honor your inner world. By doing so, you will have a greater appreciation for elders who live in the world of imagination.

2. Reflect on a recent dream. Close your eyes and, in your imagination, go back into the dream's scenario. Dwell at the place in the scene where it came to an end. Imagine something new developing. Wait to see what happens. Whatever words or images come, allow them to flow without analyzing them.

Helping your elder heal

1. Give your elders an opening to share their dreams with you by telling one of your dreams or making one up. Share the meaning the dream brings to you, or even your confusion about it. Then ask your elders if they have had a recent dream. Some elders are too shy to share. Be patient. Elders may not remember a recent dream but may recall one from the past. That is fine. By listening to their dream, you validate their inner life.

2. Ask your elders to reflect on their dream. Have them close their eyes and go back to the situation in the dream. Then ask them to imagine something new happening at the end of the dream. Have them describe the scene verbally to you or to the group. Help them by reflecting back to them what they've described.

3. If your elder does not wish to draw, you may draw, paint, or make a collage depicting imagery from your elder's dream. Have the elder watch as you do this, and ask for his or her suggestions or comments. In this way, they will become a participant instead of an observer and will be helping to give shape and form to the deeper meaning in their life. If the image is a negative one, draw the original image, then draw the opposite of the image, a positive, more inspiring picture. You can leave a portion of the image unfinished. Ask your elder to guide you in its completion.

For your inspiration

I have within me infinite worlds.
I am a gifted person with creativity to share.
My dreaming self hears stories, sings songs,
experiences adventures, and faces my demons.
My elders also have a world of dreams. In this, we are one.

FOUR

Dreaming in Daylight

I wandered lonely as a cloud
That floats on high
o'er vales and hills,
When all at once
I saw a crowd,
A host, of golden daffodils.
—William Wordsworth

"WE ARE DREAMERS dreaming a giant snowflake . . . it's floating above our heads in the living room. What is this snowflake doing in the house? What is it trying to tell us?" I ask these questions of the elders at Valley View residential home where we are off on a new adventure: *dreaming in daylight*.

My question stirs Milka, who puts down her newspaper and stares at me in anticipation. It also awakens Avena, as usual dozing in her chair.

"Boy, I can't wait! I'm going skiing!" Avena claps her hands to her chest, as excited as a young girl.

"Is our snowflake going to remain above us?" I prod, hoping to inspire them to enlarge the image.

"Look, the snowflake is as large as a cliff!" A man of few words, Terrance's lethargy is suddenly broken as he blurts out this sudden revelation. Normally, he sits in a quiet corner of the living room doing nothing. "I remember going out on our sled."

"Terrance, you're going to meet a lady on that sled," Milka says, looking over at him with mischief in her eyes.

"But wait," I add. "Now there is a shadow emerging out of our snowflake. It's growing, changing, turning—into a big, black cat. What is this cat telling us?"

Avena: "It's a warning, maybe misfortune. I shouldn't go skiing—I might break my leg!" We all begin to laugh.

"I'm planning to go on a trip alone," Milka says. "But now I'm worried. Maybe there'll be snowdrifts, I'll be marooned somewhere. But that could be good. Maybe somebody will come along, get me out of a rut, and I'd get a couple of nice dates out of it!"

When we began this session, Milka was slumped on the couch. She held her aching head in her hands, complained of a migraine. Now there is no evidence of a headache; wide-eyed and grinning, Milka leans forward in her chair.

"We are waking from this dream. Let's ask ourselves, what does the dream mean? What is the snowflake telling me about my life?" I look around at a group of eager faces.

Milka: "The snowflake has something to do with guidance: since it's summer here, maybe I should take a trip, go where it's cold."

"Makes me see my life is boring," Avena says. "I'm missing having fun." She settles back in her chair, suddenly quiet.

"The snowflake reminds me of my sled," Terrance says.

"Maybe I'll climb into it with you!" Delighted, Milka looks at Terrance who has not had this much attention for months.

"The snowflake tells me I want to go to Europe, meet a man, have an adventure!" Milka beams, waits for my reaction.

On an adventure myself, I started a group imagination exercise as an experiment. I wonder where it will now lead. It doesn't take long to find out.

"I've gone to Europe and met a Serbian man," Milka begins. "My husband wasn't Serbian though I loved him dearly. This man is the same nationality as I am; he fascinates me. I want to travel with him, but, of course, he has to be good looking and reasonably intelligent for me to be interested. And gentle. If he isn't, I'll punch him in the face!" Milka's eyes widen in playfulness. "Actually, I don't know what I'll do if he is terribly good looking—although I'd thumb my nose at him if I was still married!"

This desire to connect to a Serbian man has not surfaced before. What significance might it have? Milka is deeply drawn to her roots, to discovering her connectedness to her people, her country. This desire indicates an unfulfilled longing in her soul.

"Milka, I'm going to be this gentleman meeting you in Europe," I say. Settling myself on the couch so that I face her directly, I begin a dialogue:

"I'd like to show you around in my car. Would you come?"

"Absolutely. I'm interested in Yugoslavia. My grandmother and her husband died fighting the war in Bosnia. I'm hoping to see as much as possible of the country."

"I have a cottage by the sea, it's beautiful. Would you stay there with me?"

"I'm a widow lady," Milka says while wiggling her hips, and, in a coquettish voice, adds: "We'd have to have separate quarters. I wouldn't want the world to think I had a commitment . . ." she puts her hands on her hips, winks, and concludes ". . . to you!"

"But you might find out you like me. Why not let your hair down and see?"

"Well, I'll definitely pay my own way. I wouldn't want to be obligated to you. And I have no intention of taking advantage of you." Milka grins: "I have to watch that guy. After all, I want to meet a lot of people and don't want him to hinder my chances. What if I found some European I'd like to keep, take back with me to America?"

Listening to Milka, I almost see her as in days of old: a young maiden, long hair coiled in braids, lace dress flowing to the ground, giggling and flirting with the boys at the park, the barn, the dance.

"Are there other things you want to do in Yugoslavia?" Deliberately, I change the focus.

"I want to tell the leaders to stop fighting. If they stop battling, they'll have clearer minds, be able to concentrate on good things."

"But aren't you afraid to go where there is a war?"

"Why should I be? They can do no more than kill me. If they showed that kind of animosity, they would not be acting like human beings. I would say to them, 'You're acting like animals.' "

"Animals often have more sense," Avena says.

Time has run out; our imaging session is over. These elders whom I have known for several years have come alive in a new way. The use of imagination has brought out inner qualities that have not surfaced until now. Is there something more that might awaken in them through imagery?

The next session's dialogue with Avena brings back the memory of a boyfriend she had when she was in her twenties. Avena sees the boy clearly: blue eyes, sandy hair, tall, athletic. She begins to relive dinner parties, dances, sitting in the car with the radio on as she gazes at the stars.

Taking on the role of boyfriend, I ask: "Are you interested in marriage?"

"Heavens no!"

"No?" I am surprised at her answer.

"No, I don't want to be tied down. I'm not through living yet; it's fun being single!"

"What's fun about it?"

"I don't have to account to anybody for anything." Avena tosses her head over her shoulder. Smiling, she sinks back in her chair.

Stepping out of the role of boyfriend, I then ask: "How does this memory speak to you today, fifty years later?"

"I had a great time!" Avena straightens up, bounces in her chair like a schoolgirl. "Thinking back on it, I'm having fun all over again!" With a broad smile, eyes sparkling, she concludes: "I feel like I'm there right now."

Living a second life: Is this what is happening for these few moments to Avena? The immediacy of that moment fifty years ago has now taken hold of her. In our institutions, even at home, do we encourage an awakening of imagination, creativity, renewal of the inner self? We believe it is important to exercise our bodies; why not exercise our imagination, recognize its benefits when used in positive ways?

Reflecting on these sessions, I began to wonder whether there isn't something more to *daylight dreaming* than reliving memories.

More Imaginary Adventures

One day, I decide to be a bit wild on our imaginary adventure. I begin to introduce images like these: a goat is sitting on my white shag rug in the living room watching television; a bag of mushrooms is tied in a knot to the steering wheel of my car; my husband is surfing with our five-month-old baby on his surfboard and accidentally drops her in the ocean. Where will such imagery lead us?

The surfer image takes hold.

"Stupid goon!" A jovial mood sets in. "I'd hold that husband of mine by his feet and drown him!"

Elders often find it difficult to initiate images; I embellish this scene in order to stimulate them. "Now my husband and I are arguing. I told him to keep watch over our child, but he didn't. My baby is in the ocean!" I wail. Laughter follows.

Our laughter can be heard throughout Valley View. In this mode of playfulness, everyone relaxes. A lively discussion ensues on a man's role in the care of children. Then we discuss the child *within us*, how we respond when we feel neglected, unappreciated, criticized. Do we care for and love ourselves?

This imagery session suddenly sparks the memory of a dream Cambria had last night in which four angels surrounded her bed. A few weeks back she had had pneumonia. Extremely weak, she seemed to have lost her joyful spirit. The reawakening of her dream image not only aids her healing process, it also creates a deeper capacity for reflection. A practical woman, Cambria is usually incapable of reflecting on abstract poetry, literature, or ideas. By involving her in the illogical aspects of the mind, a new gateway opens that enables her to respond to life's mysteries. Our playful imagery session sparks the memory of dream angels, now bestowing happiness and well-being.

To allow imagination to roam free is to awaken an inner act of poetry:

> *"The flowers of spring are winter's dreams*
> *related at the breakfast table of the angels."*[1]

We do not know what Kahlil Gibran was thinking at the time he wrote this poem. But when we guide elders to free their imagination, they enter into a poetic process. It is not to make poets out of people that we encourage elders to be imaginative; we do so to free their minds, so they can gaze with delight into dimensions beyond the ordinary.

"There's a bear on the plane! What are we going to do?" Another imagery session is under way. Jumping up from the couch, I wait for the group's reaction.

"Be quiet and pray." Milka shows us more of herself at each session.

"Stuff the bear in a suitcase!" I plop back down on the couch. My image makes everybody laugh.

"Tie him up—open the door and let him out!" Avena giggles. She is back to being young again.

"I'd rather he stay where he is!" Milka says with a laugh.

"I'm suing the airline," I say. "Look at my baby. She's turning blue." Everyone roars with laughter. "What am I going to do?" I look around. Who will pick up from here?

"Don't worry, I'll sit next to you, hold the baby, stick her in my jacket. We'll just be quiet and everything will be all right." Milka becomes a comforting presence in this scene. I didn't know she could be calm, nurturing. Was she like this when emergencies occurred?

The dream image shifts. "We are now on a ship." I wait to see what they will do with this. The dimensions of the scene grow as the members of the group create it: the waters are turbulent, people dine and dance, and then suddenly—the ship leaves the ocean, travels by air.

How do they feel about the possibility of going to outer space? Are we on a UFO? Does anyone want to go to the moon? Avena visualizes herself swinging on a star, free, happy, unafraid.

How often do we encounter carefree elders over the age of eighty? Why can't they feel free more often, have fun defying the gravity of aging by lifting their minds into flights of fancy?

In our culture, we prize maturity; we value rational, "intelligent" responses to events, people, things. We are supposed to be sensible, reasonable, safe and sane, rather than buoyant, delighted, carefree, filled with wonder. If we dare to burst out with childlike abandon, we are considered immature.

I recall the time I forgot myself while teaching an exercise class in a retirement community. As the exercises progressed, I led them in playful motions, phrases, rhythms, and sounds that became increasingly spontaneous. I felt like a delighted child. When the session was over, an elder came to me, and, in cautious voice, said: "Have you worked very long with older people? Do you usually work with *children*?" Although I had worked for fifteen years with elders, this person clearly thought I hadn't quite "matured."

As adults, we seem threatened when another adult expresses a youthful spirit. And yet it is just such a spirit that can revive, renew, and heal. Spontaneity is a genuine way to express playfulness, to create an authentic, lively experience, which lightens the spirit and soothes troubled minds.

From Imaginary Image to a Real Memory

One day in an imagery session I began to play with this dream image: In the corner of my living room, I tend a garden. Now that everyone is used to this irrational *daylight dream* world, the responses are immediate.

Avena imagines tomatoes in the garden; we are picking and canning them. Suddenly Janeen interrupts. A plain, prim, intelligent woman, she begins to tell us her story:

"Every summer in Wisconsin, I was sent to my aunt's house for cherry picking. It was wonderful. She would pack us girls a good lunch, and we'd set out in a big wagon pulled by a team of horses. We'd spend all day in the orchards. One summer, toward the end of the season, we girls took a boat trip after our picking and then went to town. Down the street we heard music. Instead of going back to my aunt's, we went into the ballroom and danced till late.

"When we finally got home, we banged on the door. My aunt heard us but ignored our knocking. She locked us out of the house to punish us. We crawled into the woodshed, tried to sleep on the steps. The house didn't have a bathroom. At 5:30 in the morning my cousin came out to use the outhouse. He left the front door ajar, and we barreled into the house, went to our rooms, lay down, slept through an electric storm.

"My aunt was so angry the next day she wouldn't say anything to me. Because of my aunt's mood, I decided that when my brothers came, I would leave her and go home with them."

I suggested to the group that everyone enter into Janeen's story as if we were all dreaming it. "Here we are picking cherries, having a great time. But now we've angered Janeen's aunt. We've stayed out too late. The dream is ending. We are given this choice: Are we going to stay with Janeen's aunt even though she is angry, or are we going to go home?"

"Pee on you, aunt, I'm going home!" What happened to Milka's headaches? They are completely forgotten. "Who do you think you are? I'm just a kid having a little bit of fun—an old-fashioned kid to boot. I would have wanted to spit in her eye!"

Aghast, Janeen says: "You wouldn't say this to my aunt,

would you? We showed her a great deal of respect."

"I'd tell her off. I'd say, 'Who are you to judge me? You don't even know me.' "

"But my aunt was right for being indignant."

"My mother would have defended me! She wouldn't have allowed your aunt to put me down. 'Leave my child out all night? Never!' She would have trusted me in the dance hall; she knew her child. She would have said (in Serbian), 'Day is day, night is night—you should get home earlier.' But she wouldn't lock me out."

Janeen didn't flinch. "We were guests in my aunt's house; she worried about us. When you're in someone else's house, you try to uphold their habits. I believe my aunt was justified because we disobeyed her."

It's a good-natured disagreement. Tolerance for each other expands as we see how lives have been shaped by different values, attitudes, and beliefs.

"If it were I," says Milka, "I'd stay and talk, straighten things out with her aunt."

"Not me. I don't want to feel upset; I don't want any more problems—I'd go home." Avena responds just like she normally is; shy, nervous—whenever a disturbing event occurs, she removes herself.

The session is over. It turned out to be more than simply recalling a memory. What made this group experience so dynamic? Memories have deeper significance when we observe our responses to them, seek the meaning, the lessons, the essence within them. When group members add their imaginary endings onto Janeen's memory scenario, she is inspired to revisit that memory on a deeper level.

As for the overall benefits of our *dreaming in daylight* sessions, elders found that they were awakened to their gift of creativity. Once they were released from dreaming themselves old and useless, having spent too many hours in boredom and inactivity, they experienced a new vitality springing from their own fertile imaginations. I recall what Dr. Thomas Moore once said: "When imagination is allowed to move to deep places, the sacred is revealed."[2] And so is creativity. These elders enjoyed being playful and dramatic, weaving stories, dreaming dreams—experiencing moments of pure delight.

❦ Steps for Healing ❦

Insights that can help heal

◆ Cultivating playfulness lightens our burdens.

◆ Delight is the key to a joyful spirit.

◆ Imagination is a gift everyone has and can activate.

Helping yourself heal

1. Spend time imagining an outlandish image in an unexpected place. Project yourself inside the image and allow the image to take you where it will.

Helping your elder heal

1. Elders have fun with the following exercise. Picture two unrelated objects doing something you would never expect them to do: the moon is climbing up the kitchen ladder. Help your elders create what comes next. To start them off, ask "Where is the moon going?" You can use any image you choose, and you may want to incorporate making a mural, poster, or collage into the exercise.

2. Begin with an imaginary story, leaving a sentence in midair with the words suddenly, fortunately, or unfortunately. For example: "Sharon's husband rushed out of the house, got into his car, and unfortunately . . ."; or "A young girl with pigtails falls off her bicycle in the middle of a rose garden and suddenly . . ." The next person goes on with the story from there.

3. Introduce your group of elders to an imaginary family gathered during a holiday. Set up the story by making it catchy. For example: "Remember last Christmas when Uncle Joe tripped over the toaster and the chickens flew into the house?" Ask your elders to continue this imaginary story.

For your inspiration

I have within me the gift of delight, playfulness, and spontaneity.
This gift is infectious; it awakens the same quality in all of us.
In this, my elder and I are one.

FIVE

Hearing What Elders Mean

*Once we learn to accept
the symbols that well up
within us we are made
aware of an invitation to
live life at a deeper level
than it is lived every day.*
—James Roose-Evans

*Listen, oh my son . . . incline
the ear of your heart.*
—Proverbs 5:1

"I DON'T BELIEVE IN 'OLD.' " Although he lives in a nursing home, Atwood is a fifty-year-old paraplegic. He sits in the recreation room in his wheelchair as we talk about the meaning of growing old. "I am as young as the universe itself—this shall be for me for all eternity." Atwood is new to our group, which has been meeting for several years. Thin, muscular, graying at the temples, Atwood's liquid brown eyes seem to see beyond the confines of the room.

"I don't want him to get out of my sight!" Heather's flirtatious response makes me chuckle, but it is lost on Atwood, who doesn't respond. Sitting in her wheelchair, Heather twirls the end of her thick, white braid while watching Atwood with her penetrating hazel eyes.

"I was holding the hand of a nurse,"Atwood says, "and I said to her: 'Upon this hand I hold is the seed of life, which has lovely grown.' "

"I don't want to hold hands. I want to pet his face!" Heather winks. "I'm not ninety-six for nothing!"

Heather, feisty as ever, recalls a poem she heard as a teen:

> *I love you little*
> *I love you mighty*
> *I love your pajamas*
> *Up to my nighty.*
> *Now don't be offended*
> *And don't be misled*
> *For I mean on the clothesline*
> *And not in the bed!*

Heather laughs. "We didn't dare let our parents hear us kids say this so we said it behind the barn!" Heather sneaks a look at Atwood; still no response. Will Heather entice him into a friendship with the markings of romance, as she did Emerson, the young man she met some years back in the nursing home? Back then, Heather's enthusiasm didn't last long. Underneath chiding and jokes lives another Heather, one who has never been healed:

"My husband used to grab me as I walked by him into the kitchen—kinda rough-like. He'd pull me by the neck, kiss me hard, and then let me go with a pinch on my behind. I liked it! That's what I had for sixty years,"she sighs, "but not anymore. He's been dead eight years now." Heather's tone becomes solemn, her head drops.

For years she has dwelled on the memory of her husband; she idolizes him. Friendship with Emerson didn't fully release

Heather's grief. What will happen if she starts a friendship with Atwood?

One afternoon some weeks later, Heather surprises me: "You know, I'm going to have my own horse again, and I intend to ride it! I'll get on that horse and I'll be riding off anywhere I want!"

An emphatic toss of her head, a smile of pleasure—Heather's confident tone begins to echo over and over in my mind. What is she really saying? Is there more to her declaration than simple fantasy?

A sense of exhilaration grips me. Profoundly stirred, I find myself visualizing Heather and her horse galloping through the fields. At her age Heather isn't going to mount a horse and ride off into the horizon, but something must be deeply shifting within her. Certain that Heather isn't aware of this shift, I wait to see what unfolds.

Symbols Speak an Inner Truth

Healing Companions have the capacity to develop an intuitive sensitivity, to become guided on deeper levels, and to trust their inner responses when elders tell their stories. It is easy and natural to become impatient, bored, exasperated by repetition. Yet when stories are repeated over and over, and symbols recur, these loose strands, woven into the tapestry of what their lives have been, reveal a deeper sense of meaning. When Healing Companions are aware of such symbols, we can often use them to help us guide the elder's process of self-acceptance, so vital in the last years of life.

Throughout the years I had known Heather she had experienced life without her husband as empty. This was the first time she had expressed enthusiasm over something other than being with a man. Pleasure in life suddenly didn't seem to depend on her husband.

Was Heather beginning to accept herself as her own person, apart from her husband? Many marriages mirror this dynamic: the mate gives over to the wife or husband the finest human qualities. Then when the mate dies, so do these qualities, and with them, self-worth and depth of personhood. Was Heather taking back qualities that had once belonged to her, including the quality of freedom, symbolized by the horse?

As I listened to Heather, I wondered—could she be reverting to the young, courageous, independent girl she once was? Was she unconsciously experiencing a kind of rebirth, carrying the joyful part of her past into a now hopeful future?

When I consulted Jungian psychologist Don Sloggy about Heather's journey, I described her desire for this new horse. Pondering Heather's scenario, Sloggy reflected that perhaps Heather had been thrown from her horse—the horse being a symbol for a life of her own. I wondered if Heather could have disconnected from her sense of self by giving up her ability to enjoy life independently from her husband. Had she projected her happiness as only being possible with him, the one for whom she lived?

Sloggy offered further insight: "Heather's horse could be a symbol for carrying her through the transition into the next world. The horse as symbol may act as a connection between this life and the life to come."

Heather's inner self ingeniously drew upon a meaningful symbol—a horse—to express an essential aspect of where life was taking her. Perhaps this horse was more than simply a pleasurable memory of her days on the farm.

Concrete, earthy, practical, Heather lived, spoke, and acted with directness. She had a "no nonsense" approach to life and would likely not be interested in inner, symbolic meanings. Yet her psyche had a wisdom of its own, producing an image that deeply expressed the spiritual growth taking place within her.

Sloggy believes elders need someone to witness both the inner and outer unfolding of their lives even if, as was the case with Heather, they are not aware of deeper levels of meaning and mystery. When a Healing Companion acts as witness, he or she becomes a mirror for the circle of completion taking place within.

"In the last stage of life," Sloggy told me, "the most important thing before crossing over is the awareness of, and coming back to, the living reality of the soul. From this return comes a returning home, a peace and acceptance of what one's life has been."

How does a Healing Companion facilitate this deepening experience? "Our culture places an overemphasis on training and education,"Sloggy said. "If Healing Companions draw out their own depths, they will help draw out the depths in others." This guidance helped me trust the question that continued to haunt me. Even though I saw no outer signs, was Heather's end near?

When Heather first told me of her new horse, she was healthy; indeed, she appeared to be a long way from dying. Yet I felt an immediate, almost urgent intensity. Was her horse symbol indicating that she soon would be carried away as swift as the wind on a creature preparing her for leave-taking?

It wasn't long before I found out. Two months later, I entered Heather's room and went to the side of her bed. She smiled at me, nodded her head—and died.

Listening with Our Heart

When we listen with the ear of our heart, we hear a pulse beating within words, images, and symbols. That pulse is a living essence within us, an essence that takes on many tones.

One day Flavia, who had been living in a residential home for ten years, took me aside and told me that Mary, Mother of Jesus, had tea with her that afternoon. Drab, overweight, with eyes dull and puffy, Flavia was usually mute. But now her cheeks were flushed with excitement and her eyes glowed with an inner radiance.

When I shared her story with the administrator of the home, he remained unimpressed. Clearly, his mode of listening was from a suspicious, judging mind. He quickly reminded me that Flavia had a history of mental illness; often she had been aggressive, domineering, controlling. I couldn't blame him for viewing Flavia's meeting with Mary as another "wild, paranoid, inflated ego trip." Yet in my mind Flavia, for a few moments at least, was a woman transformed.

How then was I to listen to her tale of Mother Mary? Was I to take it as a hallucination? Did Mary's presence come to her in an authentic vision? Whether Flavia experienced an actual or imagined reality, she had quite clearly been illuminated. As Healing Companions, we need to listen with awe to the inner events shaping the lives of elders.

We cannot shun those rare moments when an elder expresses a vision of health, even if a major portion of that elder's life is unbalanced. The more we encourage an inner place of inspiration, the more we provide a sacred space for wellness. For Flavia, this event was a moment of great solace, comfort, grace, and hope. It framed her face in a halo of joy, enhancing what might have been the one place within her that was healthy and whole.

Joy is an expression of well-being; coming from Flavia, it was a religious expression of her faith. I chose to listen to Flavia as if she were completely well, honoring her spiritual focus without questioning its validity. Was it this openness that encouraged Flavia to join our group?

She came hesitantly, and it was months before she expressed herself. Later, she told me that all of her life she had been shy, finding it impossible to express herself in front of people. As time passed, Flavia began to speak in our group not only with conviction but expressing qualities of wisdom, peace, and assurance. These qualities gave the rest of us courage and inspiration, which sometimes seemed to surpass our own.

I came to see that listening to an elder's history, taking in the "facts" that make up their lives, is only one aspect of the truth about who they are. We must also begin to confirm what an elder presents as a healed portion of the self; we need to listen to the call of their soul and seek to encourage its enhancement.

One day I appeared at a local nursing home to find Henry sitting in his wheelchair weeping. He was so distraught he could barely speak. I walked behind the chair, put my arms around him, and held him as he cried. When I asked him what was wrong, he told me that he feared he had insulted his daughter—she hadn't been to see him for weeks. He wanted to ask her forgiveness for anything that he might have done to offend her.

Henry's daughter was a lovely woman; I knew she would not reject her father. Puzzled, I asked the nurse what happened. "Nothing," she replied. "Henry's daughter was here an hour ago; she comes on a regular basis." Her counsel? "Just forget about him, don't get sucked in."

"Sucked in?" To what? My ear heard only a cry of longing, a cry of hunger. Henry's need for love, warmth, and connectedness was not being met. Even if it seemed his suffering was unreasonable, Henry was a human soul, calling out for love.

As Healing Companions, we need to realize that logic is not the only criteria for listening to our elders, for giving tenderness in times of pain. When we read a poem, we look at it symbolically. We can do the same thing with life—look at life as a poem.

Although some of the needs that elders express are reminiscent of infancy, we must recognize that *any* cry is an authentic, desperate request, a symbol of emptiness that needs our care. As death may draw near at any time, it is imperative that Healing Companions make every effort to fill an empty heart with love, so that love may become an ever-flowing fountain in life's last hour.

Our task is to "give until it hurts," as Mother Teresa of Calcutta would say—to become, in our giving, a light in the midst of darkness.

❧ Steps for Healing ❧

Insights that can help heal

+ The inner world is a gateway to wellness.

+ Even in the midst of emotional instability, the fleeting moments of an elder's radiant joy are treasures to be honored.

+ Symbolic images carry meaning for the soul.

Helping yourself heal

1. The following reflective exercise will help you establish a deeper rapport with an elder by connecting you to the wisdom figures within you. Become quiet within. Close your eyes.

Think of someone you admire who radiates deep love. Invite this person to be present with you. Recognize that this person's insights are actually inside of you. Sense his or her spiritual presence and ask for guidance. If you intuit an answer, you may want to write it down for later reflection.

2. The following exercise may help you crystallize and express your feelings concerning your current life situation. It will give you an experience of the significance of symbols in your life. Then, when an elder expresses a symbol, you may be alerted to its potential meaning.

Close your eyes. Focus on one particular aspect of your life, such as your health, an important relationship, your child, or your job. Wait for an image to come that symbolizes your situation. Reflect on the meaning of the image that emerges. Do not be concerned if an image does not arise. It may take time before you can cultivate an awareness of symbolic images.

Helping your elder heal

1. You may want to honor an image your elder is expressing by creating an object that reflects this image. Try using modeling dough or clay for making pots, free-style shapes, or any object of your preference. Engage your elder in your creation by conversing about the pot's size, shape, and color, and what may be put in it. Is the pot to be used only for special occasions?

2. Trust the healing potential within an elder's imagery. Even if the imagery seems irrational, allow your elders to teach you their way of gaining closeness with an infinite source of peace and well-being.

3. Listen attentively when elders use images in their speech. Be alert to the symbolic meaning of these images.

For your inspiration

*My elder and I speak a similar language through the pictures
alive in our minds. We have within us a vast panorama of ways
to view our daily reality. At any moment we can be given
the gift of radiance. We have the ability to receive this radiance
and to experience a deep abiding peace.
In this, my elder and I are one.*

SIX

It's Never Too Late to Be Yourself

*Self-esteem and self-love
are not sinful.
They make living
a joy instead of a chore.*
—Bernie Siegel, M.D.

OUR SONG SAILS out the window, singing its joy into the rainbow arcing across the mountains:

"I am a worthy, wonderful person / The light within me is shining bright / I am a worthy, wonderful person / And everything is gonna turn out right!"

The song concludes. Five elders are seated in a circle in the living room of Valley View residential home. Self-esteem is essential if elders are to fully honor themselves. I ask them: "Do you think getting old rattles your self-esteem?"

"I've got so many drops I forget where to put them! Nose, eyes, gargle, teeth! One day I put my nose drops in my eyes—this could end up being serious!" Milka's eyes sparkle. Her vivid turquoise barrette, tucked into her thick white hair, gives her hazel eyes a youthful glow.

"Here's Tim Hansel's version of getting old," I say. "He writes, 'You know you're getting old when:

—Your back goes out more than you do.

—You get winded playing chess.

—Dialing long distance wears you out.' "[1]

"I know I'm getting old," laughs Milka, "when I don't want to walk because I'm wobbly on my pins! Today I got so tired after breakfast I went back to bed!"

"Did you get your energy back?" I ask.

"I don't know. I'll have to look for it!"

"Maybe you should write your own joke book, Milka! Okay, let's quit joking. When you're old, what really starts to happen to your self-esteem?"

Cambria: "Even if we're old, it's like the song says—we're still worthy, wonderful persons!"

"We're worthwhile?" Avena shifts forward in her chair. "To whom or to what?"

"To my grandchildren," Janeen replies with a laugh. "They say, 'So glad you're here, Grandma—where's your pocketbook?' "

"Mine say, 'So glad you're here so we can say we love you.' " Cambria fumbles in her jacket pocket, brings out a photograph of five grandchildren, and passes it around.

"I don't know about being worthwhile," says Janeen. "We're not that important at this time in our lives. At one time we were—but now? We've been put away where we're safe!" She laughs, but is she joking?

Before Janeen came here, she lived in her own apartment. One day she left her shoe in the oven and forgot to turn off the stove. Her son walked into the kitchen, smelled something burning, and immediately made arrangements for Janeen to move to Valley View. Although she has been here for several years, she still hasn't forgiven her son for taking her away from home.

"I'm here waiting to die." Suddenly Janeen isn't laughing.

"If I passed away tomorrow," says Avena, "no one would care. Who needs us?"

"Nothing matters anymore," Janeen says, suddenly pale.

"If it wasn't for you," Avena looks at me, "we'd have nothing to look forward to."

This sudden mood shift is shocking. These elders are happy, eager to learn. They live in the best assisted living facility in town. For years they have gotten along well together, and they often participate in classes at the senior day care center. Yet while they enjoy life, their inner selves reveal another story—feelings of abandonment, emptiness, lack of worth.

When family dysfunction, divorce, unresolved grief occurred in the past, these elders had access to psychological or psychiatric counseling. But now that they are old, lack of funding in institutional settings, high fees that many families can't afford, and the tendency of many counselors to reject elders as clients have left them with scant support.

Having realized that one of the difficulties in coping with aging is often a poor self-image, I decided to offer a series of self-esteem classes.

Opening Up with One Another

In one of our first sessions, in a lighthearted vein I jokingly begin: "Of course, none of us have had any of the following attitudes:

'I'm so stupid. I never do anything right!'

'It's always my fault.'

'She does everything better than I do.'

'Something is wrong with me!' "

"I feel all those things," Avena says with a laugh.

"So do I," Cambria says, nodding.

"Avena, is there anything you wish you could have done—and didn't do?" I ask.

Her hands fidget in her lap. "I don't know what it is—I have children, a husband, everything, yet I feel empty inside, like something is missing." Usually a perky, happy person, her voice drops.

"There are other ways to achieve a good life," Milka says. "Through the Supreme Being, that's what Mama taught me."

"Avena, when you were young, what were you good at?" I ask.

Avena looks down, flushes. "On the stage at the school assembly, I used to make hundreds of kids roar with laughter." Suddenly Avena's hips wiggle girlishly in her chair. "I ad-libbed, felt real good. Then I was asked to enter the state humor contest. I was so bashful I clammed up. From that day on, I cut it off, never got on stage again."

"But you say you enjoyed standing up in front of everybody."

"Yes, I enjoyed the attention."

"What stopped you?"

"I was afraid my mind would go blank, I would forget what to say. That was the end of my life, right there. I should have entered the contest. I haven't been the same since."

Reflecting on what Avena shared, I wonder if we clothe ourselves so well outwardly that underneath no one really knows who we are. Do many of us live inwardly isolated, alienated lives, fearful of what we might become if we dared expose our inner feelings, talents, thoughts?

"My family doesn't care about my feelings." Avena nervously twists the beads she wears around her neck. "I might as well stay here till I die."

"Why, honey, that's not true," Cambria smiles over at Avena, who is sitting opposite her chair. "Your son adores you, he visits every week."

"No he doesn't." Avena squirms. Not only is she unable to remember when her son was here, she can't even remember what she had for lunch an hour ago.

"He *does* visit you, honey. He just brought you that wonderful plant. You should be thankful."

Cambria's idea that Avena "should" be thankful isn't going to be helpful. Her good intentions are often tinged with judgmental overtones. Knowing this, I ask the group: "Could we listen to Avena without opinions—just listen deeply through the ear of our hearts?" Hoping to encourage Avena to be herself, I add: "Even if Avena's son does come, and brings presents—let's honor her real feelings. Let's shed light on our style of listening, broaden the way we hear, receive, and relate. If we do, maybe we'll be with Avena on a deeper level."

Avena's son loves her, comes to visit her often—but inside her, something hurts. I have found this in other elders, too. Their inner reality doesn't match the outer one. This disconnection creates confusion, which may breed feelings of inferiority. Healing Companions need to relate to feelings as an authentic reality no matter what is happening outwardly. Trying to impress upon an elder whose mental recollection is severely impaired that something really happened even though they deny it—like Avena's son coming every week—may create stress and inhibit open communication with that elder.

Cambria says: "We're fortunate we can talk like this—we can't with our families."

"My family doesn't realize how awkward I feel. They always try to get me to perform for them," Avena says.

"How does that make you feel?" I ask.

"I just feel sad."

Entering the territory of sadness does not sit well with the owner of Valley View, whose instructions are to keep my classes "cheerful." As I listen to Avena, I sense unresolved, unhappy memories. What would heal them? Could the opportunity to express and face her feelings be a beginning for releasing the past, developing greater self-esteem, becoming free to move toward the future with more peace?

Poet Maxine Kumin wrote: "That man may be free of his ghosts / he must return to them like a garden."[2] Is it possible to safely return to the ghosts of our pasts, find beauty even in our griefs and disappointments, experience transformation by looking our ghosts straight in the eye with the faith that, by facing them, we may be healed of their power to hurt us? Would our self-esteem be enhanced by doing so? And might we develop a new sense of courage and hopefulness about our future? Is it wise for elders in the last phase of life to ignore their fears and hurts, and instead spend their days relating only to what is pleasant?

The theme of staying away from sadness, keeping a "cheerful" outlook, exists in many long-term care facilities. One day in a nursing home, I asked the residents if they preferred being cheered up. Did they want to explore only happy subjects or themes that sometimes made them cry? They all answered "We would rather have our tears."

Today my intuition guides me to focus on joy. If Avena continues to express her sadness, this may become problematic. After I leave there is no one who has the time to support Avena through her feelings or guide her toward choosing a constructive way to review her past, to find the good in it rather than the bad.

I begin to lighten our mood by singing. Avena taps the

rhythm with her fingers. "I am a worthy, wonderful person / No matter what I've done in the past / I am a worthy, wonderful person / And I deserve some happiness!"

Turning to Avena when the song ends, I tell her: "You're a worthy, wonderful person, even if you made some wrong decisions, even if you ignored your beautiful talents!"

"God has a big eraser! You're not a failure if you don't make it," Cambria says with a laugh.

The others nod in agreement. Avena smiles.

"You're a pleasure to be around," Cambria says as she reaches over to hold Avena's hand.

"No, I'm not important," Avena shrugs. "I don't think I have anything to say. The other members of my family are more important than I am," she sighs. "All I ever do is listen to them."

"You know about things only *you* can express, things that nobody else knows." Cambria pats Avena's hand. "Some people are introverts; they can't express themselves. I used to walk a mile out of the way just to avoid meeting someone."

"You did?" says Janeen. "I'm shy too."

"Yep, it used to hurt to talk," Cambria reveals.

Avena's mood changes. Her voice, suddenly lighter now, seems to reflect the comfort of knowing others have similar feelings.

The discussion reminds me of a poem called "Ed," which I now begin to recite:

> *Ed was in love with a cocktail waitress,*
> *but Ed's family, and his friends,*
> *didn't approve. So he broke it off.*
> *He married a respectable woman*
> *who played the piano. She played well enough*

> *to have been a professional.*
> *Ed's wife left him . . .*
> *Years later, at a family gathering*
> *Ed got drunk and made a fool of himself.*
> *He said, 'I should have married Doreen.'*
> *'Well,' they said, 'why didn't you?'*[3]

Fearing what others might think of him, Ed denied his heart. Fear of failure prevented Avena from being herself, expressing her feelings, thoughts, and talents. My friend Gerry Gladstone, at age eighty-four, told me her view of regretting the past: "The only power we have is in the 'now.' We can't change the past; we have to let it go." But before we can let go of the past, we may have to become aware of our reactions to what happened, how past events may still affect us today. How can elders do this unless they are given the opportunity to focus on their feelings, to express and release them?

"Whatever you believe, have the courage to believe it, say it, and do it." Catherine, a tall, bright woman with large mischievous blue eyes, a broad smile, and long white hair hanging in a ponytail down her back, joins us as the poem concludes.

"My mother came from Ireland," says Catherine. "It was heretical if you married outside your faith. I defied the whole thing. I married a Jew." Catherine tilts her head with pride. "Even though we had moved to America, which was a freer country, my mother said she would poison herself if I did it. I told her, 'You don't mean what you say; you're trying to scare me. This is not Ireland where marriages are arranged. I don't have to ask for your permission.'

"Although my mother didn't approve, I made my decision and stood by it," concludes Catherine. "What I'd like to leave behind as my legacy is the ability to be your own person."

Catherine has no problem with her self-esteem. "Not all of us are so courageous," I respond quickly, in hopes that Avena won't be tempted to compare herself with Catherine, which may increase her feelings of inferiority. "Whether we have courage or not, use our talents or not, make right or wrong decisions, please other people in order to get their approval while denying our own inner truth—all of us are loved. We are still worthy, wonderful persons!"

I add: "Did you know that when he was a young boy, Mahatma Gandhi was afraid people would make fun of him? He was terrified of the dark, had to sleep with the light on?"

"It's hard to believe," answers Cambria.

"He failed in every class in college, was clumsy and tongue-tied. After Gandhi became a lawyer, during his first case he was unable to utter a single word during his cross-examination. Ridiculed, he fled the courtroom."[4]

Studying the lives of great people can be a beneficial influence on our attitudes, transform our feelings, and expand our potential. Would it be so for these elders?

Suddenly the class is interrupted by a new resident, Helga. Placing her walker by the side of an empty chair, she sits down. Quickly, she is up again, jiggles her walker, sits down. She looks around anxiously, begins to mutter. Helga's mental agitation is felt by our group. Everyone is distracted. What can I do?

Many elders who live confined lifestyles find their minds easily distracted when there is the least change in the environment. My class is no exception; they all stare at Helga. If I am able to move their attention back to the subject, they may gain some measure of self-control. By doing so, their self-esteem may increase.

"It was because Gandhi was a failure that he had to turn inward," I continue. "And that's where he found peace and the power to finally help the poor. Even if he couldn't change a difficult situation, he was determined to change himself—each seemingly unresolved conflict became an opportunity to seek honorable solutions.[5]

"In life we can be like a piece of seaweed, allow ourselves to be pulled, dragged, slapped, lifted, pushed down by the ocean waves of events—all kinds of interruptions." With Helga's situation in mind, I continue: "Or we can allow the waves to wash over the shore while we stand aside, remain calm. Because Gandhi turned inward, found God within himself, he developed this capacity to be unaffected by outer disturbance. So, instead of emotionally or mentally being dragged through turbulent waters, we too have the capacity to simply observe what goes on, remain calm, choose to stay centered on what's important, all of which strengthens our self-esteem."

Helga gets up again but now all eyes are riveted on me instead of her. Helga walks out of the living room into the hallway.

"Gandhi had this ability to concentrate with great intensity. When challenged with adversity, he stood his ground, unafraid. Through prayer, scripture, and meditation, his inferiority was transformed. He went forward to meet life anew. Putting the past behind him, he developed self-control; he chose to focus on what he was called to do in the present. As he was dying, the calm he cultivated throughout his life resulted in his last act of greatness: with dignity and peace, he forgave his assassin."[6]

"Mama taught us that the greatest power comes through God," Milka beams. "He forgives all our weaknesses. He loves us so much we can never be inferior. You are his wonderful child, honey," Milka says, looking over at Avena.

"Gandhi found that truth also," I say. Turning to Avena, I change the subject: "Can you find anything good about your decision not to be a comedian?"

"I don't see what."

"If you had become one, maybe life wouldn't have been as good as having a family, home, and husband?"

"Definitely. I have a good life and a wonderful family."

Looking around at everyone, I say: "As we review our lives, we might want to develop new thought patterns, change our emotional attitudes toward old events and find new dimensions. Do you want to try?"

They nod.

"Susan Jeffers writes: 'An affirmation is a positive statement that something is already happening.' She goes on to say, 'positive words make us physically strong; negative words make us physically weak.' She gives some examples of affirmative ideas we can repeat to ourselves when negative thoughts come up: [7]

'I am now handling all my fears.'

'Mental pain is . . . a blessing . . . it is a sign that something needs correction.'

'Let's see what good will come from this situation.'

And this last comes from my ninety-year-old friend, Gerry: 'I let go of the negative parts of my past and am free to live a beautiful life in the present.' "

"Yes, we have to live for today," Avena says, nodding with a smile.

Seeing everyone react with enthusiasm, I go on. "Self-esteem consultant Marilyn Grosboll tells us we can say to ourselves: [8]

'I am fine; I just *thought* I wasn't.'

'I can handle it; I always have choices.'

'The fact that I think or act differently from others does not make me wrong.'

'I am not this body; I am the worthy person inside this earthsuit.'

'I do not have to perform perfectly.' "

I conclude with Marilyn's comment, " 'I get excited reading the newspaper—I'm not in the obituaries today!' Marilyn inspires people to be excited about life no matter what is happening. She advises us to start positive self-talk *before* we feel like it." I go on: "Often we let our emotions take over our lives instead of disciplining ourselves to take charge of them. Since we go to great lengths to exercise our bodies, develop muscle power, why don't we give energy toward developing our will, train it to strengthen our thoughts for expressing joy, strength, courage?"

Then I begin to laugh at an incident that happened last week, making it clear I haven't done so well developing my own will: "As I was leaving my friend Gerry's house, I complained: 'I'll be utterly exhausted if I make that extra trip to the bookstore. It'll be horrible driving two hours in the heat. When I finally get home, I'll be too tired to accomplish anything.' " Her back riddled with pain, Gerry leaned on her cane, looked at me with clear, warm brown eyes and said: 'Why don't you tell yourself: I'll be so inspired by this new book I'm going to buy, my work will improve! I'll have more energy because I'm inspired! New ideas will open up my enthusiasm! I'm looking forward to driving home with joy!' "

To my group, I shrug jokingly: "So why didn't I?"

Everyone laughs, eager for more. But it is time to go. Getting up from the couch, I reflect on today's lesson. Although I respect the process of correcting negative thinking, I wonder how deeply self-esteem can be repaired, restored, and rejuvenated by simply correcting our thought patterns. The use of affirmations, developing healthy thoughts, taking courage from the lives of great people, and finding consolation and strength from sharing with friends are all valuable tools, but they may not be deep enough. What will help Avena love herself? What will heal her discontent and inspire her to embrace all that she is, all that she has done, and failed to do?

I recall what a Christian friend once said: "If you realize the Kingdom of God is within you,[9] you are confident you have all the abilities you need." She went on to reflect on scripture and said that God makes his home in your heart through faith. He roots and grounds you in his love.[10] If you accept this, you realize your self-confidence and sufficiency come from him.[11] You rely on God to transform you into his image;[12] and you trust him with your self-esteem.

She continued: "Your self-confidence grows, not simply by your own efforts or by the good things others say about you but by deeply receiving and believing in God's love. To base your confidence on the love people give you is not enough. Human love can change by mood and circumstance; God's love is eternal and unconditional." And then my friend added: "Do you know why I'm somebody? Because God made me—and God does not make junk!"

Walking down the steps of the residential home, I pass through the garden into the driveway. When elders enter the last season of their lives, shouldn't they be encouraged to gather their experiences, both good *and* bad, into a whole, and find a way to rejoice in the totality of what they have known? Shouldn't one of our final experiences be to reflect on the way events, relationships, and yearnings became lessons in our lives and shaped us into the people we were meant to become?

Opening the door of my car, I climb in. I realize that to love ourselves, we must touch the core of love itself, go beyond our minds into our hearts, into the heart of the Creator—to experience the unconditional love that created all that is. Will Avena experience this love, the fullness of true joy, before her life cycle runs out?

❧ Steps for Healing ❦

Insights that can help heal

◆ Our self-esteem is secured by our belief that our presence in this world is essential.

◆ Our presence changes the world around us.

◆ Our presence is a gift to the universe.

Helping yourself heal

1. Set aside time to listen to your thoughts. Write down any thought that threatens your sense of well-being. Note the times you criticize yourself, as well as any positive thoughts you have about yourself.

2. Affirm the ways in which you are valuable to others.

Helping your elder heal

1. Listen for your elders' negative statements. Ask if they have heard these statements from a parent, spouse, teacher, or friend. Help them to see that these negative statements are not authentically theirs. Encourage them to give up these statements since they come from someone else. Help them rephrase their negative thoughts into positive ones.

2. Ask your elders to recount the good deeds they have done. You may want to record their stories to preserve for family or friends.

3. Whenever possible, affirm your elders' goodness. Be genuine and avoid artificial compliments.

For your inspiration

*I overflow with joy when I live every moment knowing that
no one can destroy my birthright: to be myself without apology,
criticism, or embarrassment. If my self-esteem is threatened,
it is due to allowing negative thoughts or negative responses from
others to overwhelm the blessing I am meant to be.
I am a gift to the universe. In this, my elder and I are one.*

SEVEN

Is There Anything Funny About Getting Old?

When I was a little girl,
I ran after the pigs in the
clover fields, shouting,
"You'd better watch out or
I'll kick you in the bacon!"
—Martha, age eighty-four

Since I've gotten old and can't put
on my pantyhose, I ran an ad:
"Wanted, male or female
to put on my pantyhose."
No answers!
—Cambria, age ninety-two

IS THERE LIFE without laughter? Research shows four and five year olds laugh five hundred times a day, whereas some adults laugh only about fifteen times a day. Norman Cousins, author of the bestselling book *Anatomy of an Illness,*[1] helped cure himself of a serious disease by adding large doses of laughter to his doctor's treatment. Can adults expand their lives emotionally, physically, and mentally by laughing more?

What evokes laughter in elders, ages eighty to ninety-six? One day I found out at Valley View residential home. A group of educated, dignified women, all of whom had been active church members and committed to community service, discussed the ideal marriage and the advice of a Presbyterian minister. He had suggested that wives dance in front of their husbands to allure them. I am stunned by Janeen's response:

"He wants us to do the dance of the seven veils? We could—with six of them in the wash!" Prim Janeen now joking about sex, imagining herself naked with only one veil to cover her?

Ninety-six-year-old Catherine slowly rises from the couch. Bent over, she holds onto the table for support, unsteadily edges her way toward Janeen's chair. Suddenly she straightens up, lets go of the table, and stands facing us in the center of our circle.

"Did you ever see this?" She bends, tries to touch her feet with her hands. While bending, she recites: "Sally Rand has lost her fan!" Straightening her back in an upright position, she lifts her hands toward the ceiling while saying: "Oh don't you look, you naughty man!"

Everyone laughs as they recall famous Sally Rand, a stripper known as a fan dancer. At the end of her act, Sally would "lose" her fan, nothing was left to conceal her naked body, and the curtain would come down.

Satisfied with this humorous demonstration, Catherine returns to her place on the couch. Our discussion continues. We talk about biblical principles concerning marriage as outlined by Ed Wheat. I read aloud from his book: "Rejoice in the wife of your youth . . . let her breasts satisfy you at all times; be exhilarated always with her love."[2]

Finding another version in my Bible, I read: "Let thy fountain be blessed: and rejoice with the wife of thy youth . . . let her breasts satisfy thee at all times; and be thou ravished always with her love."[3]

"Do you think your husbands were always ravished with

you?" I ask.

Janeen, the oldest of our group, laughs: "As the years go on, it's not as wild and passionate. If we had the same feeling we had when we were first married, it would wear me out!" Usually serious and proper, what is happening to Janeen?

"It didn't wear *me* out!" Neila, who usually doesn't say much in our discussions, laughs.

"I can't remember, it's too long ago," says Avena.

"I'll *never* forget," says Neila.

"The word 'ravished' in Hebrew means to 'reel and stagger as if intoxicated, to be enraptured and exhilarated.'⁴ Is that how your husbands felt about you—and your breasts?"

"They're a nice handful, my husband said," Neila giggles.

"Mine liked it, too." Cambria laughs with Neila. They have become like young women sharing a mutual secret.

"Wine out of one breast, milk out of the other!" Catherine laughs so hard her head collapses on my shoulder. Earlier in the hour she was on the edge of a fainting spell. Now the color has returned to her face. Her eyes are bright.

Janeen becomes somber, her lips taut. "It isn't right to make jokes."

"We aren't talking dirty, it's just life," Neila says.

What can be done about this sudden discord? "Often I'm embarrassed by such talk," I admit as I continue the book discussion. "Dr. Wheat helps us to look at sex on a spiritual level. Through him we see that when we commit our spirit and will to 'do the best for the beloved at all times,' we give expression to spiritual qualities through our sexuality."

Asking Janeen if she is offended, I am surprised that she eagerly wants the discussion to continue.

To clarify, I go on, "Dr. Wheat reminds us that the Bible advises we should not deprive our mates from sexual intimacy unless we both agree to stop for awhile."[5]

Catherine: "You mean, we can't say we've got a headache?"

Janeen smiles. "You mean we have to have a 'love session' even if we're too tired?"

"The Bible says we can give it up for a season," I continue. "But what is a season? A summer?"

"That would be terrible," Neila laughs.

"What if your husband would like sex twice in the same night?" I ask.

Dawn says: "Twice a night—for the birds!"

Janeen: "Try somebody else!" Janeen is clearly enjoying herself now.

Dawn: "Every day he came home for lunch. Expected bed, wanted to be in the nest all the time." Laughing, she goes on: "He worshipped the ground I walked on. He'd hug and kiss until I gave in."

Janeen: "He'd say: 'How can I sleep?' He'd talk some pretty persuasive language, try to make me feel sorry for him."

Milka: "If he says 'every night,' I'm in trouble!"

"Shall we go on with this next week?" I ask.

Janeen, now all smiles, replies: "What've we got to lose? It's part of life."

Joking Around Is Good for the Soul

In the weeks ahead, I decide to find out what else elders laugh about. One day our group got into a discussion about burials. I was surprised to hear the following:

"When I die I'm not worried," Cambria tells us. "I've got an abundance of choices: in a grave next to my first husband or in a grave on top of my second one!"

I hadn't expected laughter over this topic. Everyone roars. I go on to the next. Is there anything funny about getting old?

Janeen has this joke to tell: "An old man lived in a nursing home. He was hard of hearing and constipated. When the nurse asked how he was feeling, he said, 'Not very good.' She said, 'Why have you got that glycerin suppository in your ear?' He replied, 'Oh, now I know where I put my hearing aid!' "

Milka has other ideas: "Old people get tired quicker—they lie down on their job!" Laughing, she leans back on the couch with an exaggerated flare, props her feet on a stool.

"I'll tell you what else is funny," she says. "Old people have trouble in the wee wee department." An elegant, keenly intelligent woman, I am surprised to hear Milka's expression.

"Imagine being in the park at a family picnic," she continues. "You have to go to the bathroom. It's too far to walk. There's only one thing to do—raise your skirt front and back, and wee wee. You'd think they'd realize we're too old to march across the grass, but they don't!"

"What do you do for toilet paper?" I ask.

Squeals of laughter. "One time I went to the restroom," says Catherine. "When I came out I noticed some people staring at me. I wondered what for. Turning around, I suddenly saw a trail of toilet paper stuck to my skirt!" Catherine clutches her stomach, laughs so hard her face flushes.

"You're lucky you had toilet paper!" Neila wakes up from her doze. "In Russia I went into the ladies room and a woman hands me a square of toilet paper—only one square!"

These elders found the capacity to laugh—at sex, death, and aging. Ossie Davis, actor, director, and producer, believes that humor is divine, one of God's greatest gifts: "It enables us to . . . understand that we are very large and yet also very small, and to make the adjustment, one with the other."[6]

Humor enabled our group to go beyond our anxieties and fears about aging, and to replace them with laughter. The next day we continue laughing as I present a monologue I wrote, a caricature of an old woman with a whimsical imagination:

"I don't see why it's so tough getting old. True, my hearing isn't so great, but when I think of what I've been listening to all my life, it's kind of a relief to be deaf."

"I know just what you mean, there's plenty I don't want to hear either," says Avena.

My monologue continues: "I mean, who wants to hear the neighbors squall and bawl, the tax collector bang on the door, the snores of the old man creating a hurricane on my side of the bed—and even worse, my mother-in-law's prophetic announcements? And do you think I mind that I broke my hip?"

"I mind that I broke mine. It hurt!" says Catherine.

I go on. "After all, I've been carrying, stooping, lifting, scrubbing, going and doing all my life. Why go on being a workaholic? I don't mind a bit if somebody helps me up and down. I get to have company every time I move. Now that's an accomplishment.

"Listen to this. I've gone to the bathroom alone my entire life. Don't you think it's time I deserve some company—at least as far as the toilet?"

"I'd be a dead goose without my aide!" exclaims Milka.

Returning to my monologue, I say: "Nope. I don't mind in the least that I have to have someone to lean on. Why not? Everybody leaned on me most of my life, it's no wonder my hip went out.

"It's high time people realize leaning is a first-class occupation. We elders need a training course: 'Learn how to pick the right partner to lean on.' God forbid we should pick the wrong one.

I can see it now. I get a leanee who doesn't appreciate my leaning, turns the other way, and leaves me stranded in the middle of the street.

"What would I do with one hip higher than the other and a god-forsaken cane? If I lift the cane to swat that squealing dog (which is all the cane is really good for), I'll get off balance and oops, there goes the other hip.

"But on the other hand, there's a good advantage to losing my leanee. I can sit down in the middle of the road. I need a break from standing, which is downright tiresome. Besides it's a good spot to snack on Sally's terrific cookies. Why is it a good spot? Because sitting there will do the traffic a lot of good. They need a break, too. Speeding so fast, rushing about, now they can sit still and have time to think, by golly, while I finish my cookies.

"What do you all think of this lady?" I interrupt my monologue to ask.

"She's right," says Janeen. "A little lounging doesn't hurt anybody. The world needs to lounge more and rush less!"

My whimsical old woman continues: "Now about leanees. If they don't answer the ad, they'll miss becoming a pillar for old people. Just think of it. A leanee gets the delight of squishing my soft flesh. I mean soft like feather down, I'll have you know.

"I'll tell you what else is good about me. It's my chicken soup. I held up the world with it. That's why I deserve to have leanees hold me up; it's an even exchange. But I'm not going to exchange my recipe."

"I'll tell anybody about my Irish stew recipe. I got it from my grandmother," Catherine says.

I continue: "Well, only a Jewish mother knows how to make chicken soup, and I'm not giving away the secret. No, I'm not saying a word. Why? Because if you think I'll say a word, you'll be after me for another word. You'll be asking me to make decisions about my coffin and *your* inheritance. What, you need me to sign something?

"I'm telling you, my brains don't work any more. Didn't I just sign a check last week? Was it for my haircut or your birthday? I could have sworn your birthday was last week and we just ate your birthday cake. Let me tell you something: I would consider it a great sweet if you would stop waving that checkbook in my face. I'm not signing another check. Can't you see my hand is trembling at a rate of speed faster than the pen can write?

"I can't change getting old. There's nothing I can do about my hearing, my speech, legs, and hips, that's all. And if I'm not careful something else will go out—though I'm not sure what else is left."

"I'll tell you what is left—my hair! It's falling out," Catherine interrupts, "and I don't like it one bit."

"I may be old but I haven't given up the ability to be adventuresome. Some people go skydiving. Why can't I sail out this window and become the first flying grandma in history? I ask you, have you ever known a grandma to jump out of a window for the sake of an exciting lifestyle?"

"That's going a little too far—*hoisting* my legs out of a window?" laughs Milka.

I conclude: "Believe you me, I'm going to laugh my way out of that window yet. If you're ever awakened in the middle of the night to the sound of laughter coming from the stars, you'll know I skydived my way upwards, climbed an invisible ladder to the heavens, and from there I'm still directing everybody's life.

"What? You don't think I belong in heaven? Whatever gave you that idea?"

❧ Steps for Healing ❧

Insights that can help heal

◆ Laughter is a healer.

◆ Cultivate the freedom to be silly—it's good for the soul.

◆ Laughter counteracts the tendency toward rigidity
   and inflexibility, which are often seen in the aging process.

Helping yourself heal

1. Cultivate spontaneity. Learn to trust your ability to express yourself freely and openly.

2.   Review your day. Create a character that makes jokes; it might be a clown, a Jewish mother, or a rabbit with a squeaky voice. Allow this character to talk out loud about something mundane that happened to you that day. Speak in this character's voice, exaggerating his or her tone and gestures. You may want to write down your monologues to use later with your elders.

Helping your elder heal

1. Present your monologue to your elders as an example of how to laugh at the mundane. You may not think you are good at this, but be willing to surprise yourself. In the mood of laughter, anything can happen.

2. Bring humorous poetry, jokes, songs, or stories to your elders. See what makes them laugh.

3. If you hear laughter arising spontaneously in your elders, go with their themes and let your elders lead a humorous session.

For your inspiration

*Laughing is a wellspring for my healing. I
am a spontaneous jumping bean of joy. My elder and I are free
to play, to be silly, funny, and absurd. All of our self-criticism flees
before the sound of our laughter.
In this, we are one.*

EIGHT

The Need to Be Needed

Every tree is dependent
on air, wind, rain, sun;
so, too, we need
to allow ourselves to be
dependent on one another.
—J. E.

Instead of doing something
for someone, do something
with someone.
—J. E.

WHEN I ENTER the nursing home my mind is more on my own troubles than on my client Suzanne. I guess my face shows it. Suzanne is sitting alone, as usual.

"How are you?" she asks as she pats my hand.

Against the rules of my training, I blurt out, "A bit blue."

"Tell me about it, honey."

"I'm afraid if I talk, I'll cry."

"Go ahead, cry, honey. It's good for you." She gives my hand a squeeze.

And so I cry. And then I feel immediate guilt. I think—as a geriatric specialist, I'm not supposed to cry in front of my clients, I'm supposed to help them. But suddenly, Suzanne's voice takes on a different tone. She begins confiding problems she has never before shared. Is she doing this because I have exposed mine?

I ask her if I have burdened her with my tears.

"Oh, no, honey. When you cry it makes me feel I have something to give." Her response reminds me of psychiatrist Gerald Jampolsky's comment that we can be teachers for each other.

Just now Suzanne has become a teacher for me. She shows me I have something important to give besides mere listening. I can give her the dignity and importance of helping me. I begin to see that the new role of Healing Companion involves more than deeply caring for an elder; it includes being deeply cared for *by* an elder.

Former assistant secretary general of the United Nations, Robert Muller, tells of a conversation with Father Pierre, a French priest.[1] The horrors of World War II had weakened Father Pierre's body. He had been ill for a long time, and his parish, situated in the poverty-stricken outskirts of Paris, had used up his last reserves of courage.

One day, while visiting a former criminal who had attempted suicide in a shabby hotel room, Father Pierre broke down. He told the criminal he was in such despair that he couldn't imagine helping anybody.

"Father," the criminal replied, "do you mean to say that there might be on this earth someone more miserable than I, someone who might need my help?"

Hearing this, Father Pierre recognized that "man's greatest need was to be needed by others." He then hastened to confide his sufferings to the criminal. Through this incident Pierre later became inspired to create the first Peace Corps.

How can caregivers and Healing Companions create inspiration for our elders? The usual professional answer focuses on the help we give. But relationship involves *two* people in dynamic interaction. If one, the elder, is passive, and the other, the caregiver, is actively doing all the giving, where is the balance that makes for a mutual exchange of ideas, insights, and respect? Why do we, as professionals, deny our humanness, turning ourselves into a blank screen? Taking on the role of a "nobody," we actually mask an attitude of a "superior somebody" constantly giving to the elder in need. We encourage helplessness. Can we admit we are often in as much need as they?

Can Those Who Need Healing Be Healers?

On another day, I decide to admit my need to Suzanne, whom I had been visiting for five years. Other than her grandniece, a teenage girl, who comes once a week when she is able, I am Suzanne's only weekly visitor. Today I want to talk to Suzanne about Fred, a nursing home resident who is dying of cancer. His suffering is almost more than I can bear. Could Suzanne give me guidance? Often after our talks, I feel emotionally and spiritually healed.

But not today; on the way to her room, I am shocked by the scene I encounter in the corridor of the nursing home.

"Get out of my way!" Suzanne shrieks, slamming the metal footrest of her wheelchair into the woman's chair in front of her. "Get away!" I am horrified. Is this the same woman I know, the one who is always lucid, humble, quiet spoken? There is no way I can speak with Suzanne now. She is completely irrational, might not even recognize me.

Seeking the nurse, I ask what happened to Suzanne.

"She's almost always like this," she replies with a shrug.

But she has never been like this with me. Her mind is always clear. The medical staff relates to her outer condition, disorientation, confusion. I relate to her inner wellness.

The next day I find Suzanne subdued; her round face is slightly pallid. She tells me she feels exhausted, can't talk much. I assure her I won't stay long. I ask if she has the energy to show me a better way to be with Fred in his struggle with death. Since the nurse told me Suzanne has almost no attention span, I wonder how she will respond.

"When a person is dying of cancer, honey, he must believe God is the most beautiful thing there is, and that God will finish his job. Sometimes it takes a minute, sometimes a thousand years. Death is really the beginning. We don't realize how wonderful it is." Suzanne's voice suddenly becomes vibrant, her cheeks flush. "I just thank God for a beautiful death. God can do all things if we place ourselves into his hands. He'll make our death, and our living, happy. This is what I'm looking for—God the father and Jesus the Son, to make the home going beautiful."

"Suzanne, why is Fred so agitated? He's a religious man."

"Honey," Suzanne leans forward, her long, thick white braid trailing over her shoulder, "to overcome fear we have to trust and obey. There is no other way to be happy." Taking my hand, she continues, "Trust that heaven is a place of reality, where love and warmth abide." Feeling the warmth of Suzanne's hand in mine, I suddenly relax.

"Suzanne, what do you mean by obey?"

"In your thoughts. If you think of yourself as being sick, you are not obeying God. Obeying is when you don't think about the cancer, it's not in your mind. You think about the lovely skin where the cancer *was* and isn't there any more.

When you get to the place where you know you don't have cancer and you can say, 'My Lord has taken it away.' "

"Even if the cancer is still there?"

"That's right, honey, you obey him by saying it is done."

Over the years, when I needed peace and strength to get through a difficult day, I came to Suzanne. I never understood why I always came away feeling renewed. Until today, Suzanne was too humble to tell me that for years she has been involved in a healing ministry.

"Nothing is incurable," she continues. "God can perform anything. There was a woman who had cancer that severely disfigured the side of her face. One day while cooking, something fell. She got down on the floor, found the diseased skin, and said, 'Oh, Father, forgive me for my weak faith, for having to see with my own eyes what you have already taken away.' "

"I'm not doing much to help Fred with his faith," I say.

"Yes you are, honey. When someone is dying, just by listening you help renew his trust. It's like a mother who has a lot of work to do. When her child asks for something, and the mother says, 'Go away, I'm busy,' the child has to trust that the mother will ultimately give him what he wants—because she loves him. But until she does, he has to trust—waiting is the hard part. You have to believe that healing is just around the corner. You can't see it because the corner is in the way."

What is Suzanne teaching me? I also need to trust God's will in Fred's dying, even if Fred is in agony. I must accept my inability to take away his suffering. Suzanne's diagnosis is organic brain syndrome. Yesterday her behavior was bizarre; she was unapproachable, incoherent. Today, she is my mentor. For forty-five minutes she has been clear, completely focused. Could it be that when a Healing Companion reaches the depths of an elder's heart, goes beyond superficiality, attention span is no longer a problem?

"I believe that as I am dying, I am being changed," Suzanne says as she shares her spiritual views on dying. "I want to come into a beautiful relationship with God *now*. Otherwise, I won't know him when I get to him after I die. When I come to the Father, I'll be one with him." Joy animates her face.

Silence fills the room, and Suzanne lifts her hands to the sky, closes her eyes. Peace settles over us. When her brown eyes open, they are warm and glowing. Her drab cotton smock does not mar the beauty of her inner light.

I recall the times I found Suzanne alone in this room singing with joyous abandon, her arms lifted to the heavens. She seemed so complete. During such times, I wonder why Suzanne says she needs me. Assuming I am needed only when there is sorrow, I forget life is often richer when there is someone to share in life's joys.

"Right now, the people here don't like me." Suzanne's comment brings me back to our discussion. "But there is nothing impossible with God. I just look to Him and say, 'You know how I am Lord and I don't want to be this way.' I don't waste my time struggling, trying to change myself. I know the Lord is eventually going to change me—into a likeable person."

No one except me has time to draw out Suzanne's wisdom. Her family and friends have all died. The staff is too busy. Did Suzanne show her deeper self because, as a Healing Companion, I tried to love her as my closest kin?

The next time I come to see Suzanne, I ask her if she might offer her wisdom to Fred. To be needed is a sacred aspect of being human. My intention is to honor Suzanne as a wise and esteemed elder who is capable of deep sharing in spite of severe dementia.

Suzanne agrees to visit him. Fred's experience of dying has

become a torture. As we enter his room, Fred is yelling, "Where's the train, I want to get on the train, the bus, I'm on the bus, Linda, Linda . . ." Fred's voice trails off.

"You don't have to be afraid," Suzanne places her hand over Fred's. "You're going home. So am I."

"Home on the bus, I'm waiting for the bus, home, where is it? Hey, Linda!" he screams, "when's the bus coming?" Fred is delirious. Suzanne remains calm.

"The bus is coming when the Lord is ready," Suzanne says. "Meanwhile, we have to wait patiently. No use worrying, the Lord has the time and the place all fixed up for us. We're going to a beautiful home." As Suzanne softly begins to sing "Goin' home, I'm goin' home," Fred becomes quiet and drops off to sleep.

❧ Steps for Healing ❦

Insights that can help heal

- ✦ Intimacy opens the heart and promotes healing.

- ✦ When you allow an elder to help you or someone else in need, you bestow an important gift.

- ✦ Our relationships are deepened when we share through our hearts, our aspirations, and our feelings.

Helping yourself heal

1. Intimate conversation is often absent in an elder's life. To be intimate with your elder, you need to discover how you feel about your own vulnerability. Are you able to open your heart to the people you love? Have others accepted you when you exposed your deeper feelings? Do you fear vulnerability?

Helping your elder heal

1. Your vulnerability is a key to allowing elders to give on a deeper level. You can share your vulnerability on two levels. If you're uncomfortable being too open, start by sharing a small concern about your life with your elder. You can share on a deeper level by telling your elders about a fear, a weakness, or a longing. When doing this you give them an opportunity to feel they are needed.

2. When talking to your elders, try to draw out their achievements, no matter how small. Help them recall the times when they felt appreciated and loved. Reinforce this on a regular basis.

3. Counteract your elders' feelings of uselessness by engaging their assistance in some aspect of your daily life. Think about solving problems in the areas of chores, hobbies, child rearing, or household duties. Within the limits of your elder's energy, ask for advice. When you honor your elder's wisdom and are willing to share your needs, healing may pass between you. Be sensitive. Some elders do not feel comfortable giving advice. If you discover this, respect their reticence and refrain from seeking guidance.

4. Even if your elders are confused, forgetful, emotionally distraught, or wildly demented, believe that they still have something to give.

For your inspiration

My true nature is to give and to receive.
In this, my elder and I are one.

NINE

Making a Home Wherever You Are

*When life requires
giving up almost all
of what makes you happy,
there is always one small thing,
a touch of love, which is a key to
the remembrance of past joys.*
—J. E.

*It takes so little
to give so much.*
—J. E.

JOHANNA HAD JUST settled into her room at St. Andrew's nursing home. Going to the table by her bed, I opened the drawer to make sure the scripture meditations I had typed for her and the meditation cassettes were there. They were. But where was the stone?

Phoning the assisted living facility where Johanna had been living for the past two years, I asked the administrator where it was. She didn't know. In the haste of transferring Johanna to the nursing home, who would think there was anything significant about a stone?

Maybe when they removed it from her drawer, they hadn't noticed the gold cross embedded in the stone? Yet the stone was polished and was obviously more than a simple throw away rock from someone's back yard. Johanna was too ill for anyone to ask her if the stone was special. Why didn't someone try to find out from friends or caregivers?

After returning from a hermitage in Big Sur some months back, I had given Johanna the stone as a gift. Polished and carved by the monks, the smooth "worry" stone, when rubbed or held, was said to exude a calming influence. At a time when Johanna was close to dying, it might have brought her comfort.

When moving an elder from one place to another in the rush of emergency care, small things easily go unnoticed. But often it's the small things that make a room in a nursing home feel more like home.

One day I visited my friend Gerry. Her home was filled with art treasures collected over a lifetime. I asked her what art objects she would take with her if the time came for her to move to a nursing home. She told me she would feel "completely alone, utterly isolated" without her art. As we walked through her house, she pointed out the things she valued most.

"I'd want the sculpture Bernie did of a mother and child. This painting my father did when he was very old. That wall hanging my husband and I brought back from the Caribbean." To Gerry, it wasn't only the art that was important; it was what the art represented—family and friends.

After twenty years of visiting elders in nursing homes, rarely have I enjoyed the ambience in their rooms. Fear of losing precious items can inhibit elders and their families from creating an aesthetic atmosphere. But isn't it worth the risk of beautiful treasures possibly being misplaced to allow elders to enjoy beauty day by day? In Gerry's case, the pieces she chose were small enough to fit in a small room. More important, her art would give her consolation, brighten her days.

Marion's family also believed in preserving a beautiful

environment, even though Marion had Alzheimer's disease and didn't appear to enjoy anything. The family placed a tiffany lamp on the table by her bed. Gazing at the shelf above it, I saw lovely, well-tended plants, their healthy green leaves trailing down the wall. Above Marion's bed was an attractive oil painting of lavender lilacs. By creating a feeling of home in Marion's room, her family made Marion and those who visited forget they were in a nursing facility.

As I left Marion's room, I met Orleta's daughter, Donna, in the corridor. She told me she had brought her garden azaleas to her mother: "I don't know whether she realizes the flowers are here, but it's a joy for me to bring them. It's something I've always done—bring flowers for Mom. It makes me feel she is still alive. I believe the flowers watch over her like guardian angels."

I was reminded of the flowers I used to place on a portable altar I created in my cramped room in India. A cardboard box covered with a gold silk cloth, a candle, and a photograph of a saint was the only beauty in my otherwise bare room. It doesn't take much to beautify your personal space. Even in a nursing home room, it's easy to cover an end table with a special cloth, add battery-operated candles or a small lamp, and, if desired, a small object representing an important aspect of an elder's life.

To Johanna, a portable altar wouldn't be important. Yet she might have received an added blessing, a touch of intimacy, a reminder of my love for her, if someone had thought to bring her the stone.

❧ Steps for Healing ❦

Insights that can help heal

◆ Beauty in the environment brings vitality to the soul.

- ◆ Creating a meaningful atmosphere around us enhances our self-respect.

- ◆ Sacred objects reflect comfort and peace.

Helping yourself heal

1. Sit quietly and think about the important people in your life; the significant spiritual symbols you relate to; the art you find pleasing; the things in nature you admire. Look around your house for meaningful objects you would take to brighten your world if you had to go to a nursing home.

2. If these objects became unavailable, consider what other things you could take with you that represent the meaningful aspects of your life.

Helping your elder heal

1. If your elder's room is not aesthetically pleasing, an alternative is to create a portable altar. Listen for the meaningful people and experiences in your elder's life. Find a special cloth, photos, battery-operated candles, significant objects, books that are representative of your elder's experiences. Arrange them in a harmonious way on a table, tray, or shelf.

2. At appropriate times when your elder needs emotional or spiritual healing, sit together before this altar in silence, play music, pray, or share experiences that validate the life your elder has lived.

For your inspiration

I am able to assist in creating a gentle, healing environment in the place where my elder lives. All around me the world reflects beauty. This outer beauty inspires the inner beauty of my soul. In this, my elder and I are one.

TEN

Transitions: Stepping Stones to Joy

> *The heaviness of darkness*
> *gives birth to light, just as*
> *dry wood bursts into*
> *vibrant flame.*
> —Carole Marie Kelly

> *Having nothing*
> *and possessing*
> *all things.*
> —2 Corinthians 6:10

"HAVE YOU EVER tried to control the universe—make it do what you want?" My question causes laughter to light up the faces of five women sitting in a circle in Valley View's living room.

"Is there anything in this life you can actually hang onto?"

"My son is trying to take away my property!" Milka says and then viciously bites the skin under her fingernails. "He has already dispensed of my china, my antiques, and my books. I'll fight him to the end." Her angry tone turns suddenly into that of pleading child: "I have such a lonesome heart, all I want is to go back home just to get some happiness in me."

Milka has just expressed anger and bargaining for happiness, two of the five stages of grieving that Dr. Elisabeth Kubler-Ross first discovered in people who were dying. Those stages apply to any kind of transition. Soon Milka will express the other three stages: denial, depression, and finally, acceptance.

"I don't even have my Bible," Janeen says. "My brother brought me here, just left me—didn't even ask if I wanted to stay."

I knew Janeen's son, a kind, caring man. Her Bible was in her dresser drawer, this home was the finest in town, and she had new companions on her own wavelength. Yet this outer picture didn't match her inner feelings of loss, grief, anger.

"Is it possible for you to force the universe to get you out of here?" I ask, looking around the circle.

Cambria laughs. "I don't even have a car—and there certainly aren't any trains!"

Janeen adds: "I don't have a bicycle!"

"All I've got is my walker—and that won't get me far!" Avena chuckles.

"I've lost not only my home but my sister," Milka says, tearing at the skin on her fingers with her teeth. "I'm grieving. I tell you it's not worth living without her."

Milka feels depressed, another stage of the grieving process.

"But we don't own people," Cambria says and turns toward Milka. "God puts them here for us to enjoy only for a little while."

"Well, I guess that's so," Milka shrugs. "God can't let us live forever." A brief smile brushes her lips. "I'm grateful I have two wonderful nieces. That's why I'll be going home soon." Milka stops biting her fingers, looks at us expectantly. She has entered another stage, the stage of denial.

We all know she isn't going home, but no one says anything.

Milka chews her lip, eyes turned inward, looking at some unseen thing inside her.

"You'd like to control your life, wouldn't you?" I ask Milka.

"You're damn right!" Milka slaps her hand on her knee, holds her head high. A hint of defiance: "I'm going to—make no mistake about it!"

Facing Milka, I ask: "But what happens if you can't control what happens to your house," then turning to the others, "to your car, your bank account? Should you keep telling yourself 'I'll defy what life is giving me by trying to do the opposite' or 'I'm overwhelmed' or 'I can't handle this' ? "

"No, that's not what this class teaches!" Cambria's blue eyes shine. "Soon I've got a big decision. Should I sell my home?" Leaning forward on the couch, she adds: "I really don't know what I'll do. But since I've been meeting with this group I'm not worried any more. I'm using Marilyn's affirmations: 'I don't know what to do *yet*, but when I do, I'll do it!' Next I tell myself: 'Out of confusion comes clarity.' I'm no longer afraid to wait until I get my answer—I'm living in my diamond essence!"

Last week I spoke of the *diamond essence*, a concept created by self-esteem consultant Marilyn Grosboll.[1] This diamond essence is the aspect of our personality that is the perfect, nonphysical side of ourselves, the place where nothing is wrong. This essence, our true self, contains joy, love, power, peace, wisdom. Our diamond essence is always available; we have only to turn to it, acknowledge it, and live it.

Put Off the Old Self, Put On the New

The following week, Cambria's diamond essence is shining. Glowing with a warmth I haven't seen before, she tells us: "I can't believe what's happened. At the beginning I fought it, but suddenly I realized there was no use resisting." She pauses, gently presses her hands against her heart.

"I went over to my home and gave it up—just like that." Cambria snaps her fingers, spreads her palms to the sky. "I was really surprised. I did it without crying! It was a relief, I feel great—and it was because this class helped me live in my diamond essence!"

"No one is going to take away my home!" Milka blurts out.

"Milka, listen to what Alesandra just told me at the nursing home." Hoping this story will release Milka's anxiety, I continue. "Alesandra insisted her family admit her to a nursing home; she *wanted* to give up the warmth of her family life. They protested: 'But you were always here for us, you were our inspiration. You must promise you'll come home as soon as you're strong enough.'

"How do you think Alesandra responded?"

Milka stares at her hands.

"Alesandra told her family: 'I've always been there for you; now I'm going to a place where I'm most needed—it's time to give to other people.' "

"That takes real inner strength—to *choose* being in a nursing home," Cambria says. "She must have a deep relationship with God."

"Alesandra cried when she told my class: 'The All-Seeing Eye saw I needed to be with others. It was wiser for me to give up my old life than to stay with my family, never growing. Maybe I had a stroke because I was always thinking of myself, had no time for anybody but me.' With tears in her eyes, she concluded: 'I've never told anyone this story till now.' "

Seemingly oblivious, Milka vehemently scratches her leg. "Milka . . . Milka!" Rather loudly I try to distract her from scratching. "How about one of Marilyn's best affirmations: 'I will find value in every unwanted situation!' "

"How dare my son touch my property without telling me?" Ignoring my comment, she continues to scratch until blood dots her fingertips.

What will calm her? Knowing religious topics can be controversial, I decide to take a chance, meet Milka on her own familiar territory, and use the Bible as an avenue of wisdom.

"Scripture tells us to put off the old self, put on the new, to be 'renewed in the spirit of your mind.'[2] 'The old things have passed away, behold; they have become new!' "[3] Milka suddenly looks at me intently.

I continue: "Putting off the old self might inspire us to give up old ways of reacting like these:

'It's my family's fault I'm living in this place.'

'I'll never forgive my son for taking my Bible.'

'What I own is mine and nobody's going to get it!'

'No one can stop me from getting out of here!'

"If we put off these old thoughts and reactions, put on our new self," I continue, "find value in every unwanted situation, accept that the Supreme Being, the Higher Power, the Source of Wisdom dwells within us, we may be freed from destructive ideas. We may realize this Supreme Source isn't trying to get even with anybody, tell anybody off, hold onto possessions and resentments, or feel depressed. If we live in this new self—we may have peace."

Milka now looks at me eagerly; she has stopped scratching.

"Preacher Kenneth Copeland says we can choose to keep rehearsing our problems—or move on to rehearse the solution. In his terms, the solution is to put our minds and hearts on the Supreme Being."

"You mean—put off the problem, not focus on it twelve

hours a day, focus a little on the Supreme Being?" A playful smile suddenly brightens Milka's hazel eyes. "Put the problem in a reserve box and fight it out later by yourself?" Pleased, Milka sinks back on the cushions and sighs: "My family was very religious. They taught us to rely on God." Milka snuggles deeper into the cushion. "You know, honey, I was fighting you like mad, even though I knew you were trying to get through to me—and now you did!" Milka winks at me. She has finally reached the last stage, acceptance. "I'd like to take you home with me. I sure wish you were my daughter."

Relieved, I reach over to hold her hand. I had been worried our discussion would provoke her compulsive tendency to dwell endlessly on the worst. Later I might let Milka know that the five stages she has gone through are normal responses. This will validate her feelings.

Our society thinks that to keep peace between people, we shouldn't talk about religion or politics. We fear if we encourage elders to discuss comparative religions or contemplative spirituality, arguments about religious beliefs will arise. Yet knowing my group is fascinated with the spiritual traditions of other cultures, I decide to risk reciting a verse from the Hindu scripture, the Bhagavad Gita:

> *When you keep thinking about sense-objects*
> *Attachment comes. Attachment breeds desire,*
> *The lust of possession which, when thwarted,*
> *Burns to anger. Anger clouds the judgment*
> *And robs you of the power to learn from past*
> *Mistakes. Lost is the discriminative*
> *Faculty, and your life is utter waste.*[4]

"I'm angry all right!" Milka says, a joking lilt in her voice. "But . . ." she pinches my hand playfully, "it isn't really getting me anywhere, is it?"

"What does this verse mean?" I ask them.

"It means being free of our possessions—God is our only security," Cambria says. "We can't be attached to anything other than God."

"We have to start thinking a little more about our blessings," Milka says.

"Do you remember the story of Abraham and Isaac in the Book of Genesis?"[5] I ask. "God told Abraham to surrender his beloved son, to kill him. Abraham was in agony; God tested him. Do you love me more than your son? Are you willing to give him up for me because I asked you to?"

"What a terrible test!" Milka's eyes widen. "Mama taught us to honor God; if we put him first, we'll be happy."

"We definitely can't expect our families or our homes to be the source of our happiness," Cambria says. "The source of our happiness is the miracle of living one day at a time." Cambria is wise. She has learned to retain her humanness while at the same time refusing to cling to people and possessions as the primary source of peace and contentment.

Hoping to draw the group into a deeper discussion of inner life by pondering the kind of question that has an endless depth to it, I ask, "What is the source of true happiness?"

"The source of our happiness is to know and believe in God. *"Bog je moja moch,"* she says in Serbian, "God is my strength." Milka's eyes glow with satisfaction.

Joy after Loss, Joy in the Present

At our next meeting, I ask the group to further ponder the same question: "What is the source of true happiness?"

A lively discussion ensues with talk of marriage, children, and their own childhoods.

"Are the ones we love the source of our happiness?" For the next hour and a half, I prod them: "Where does our happiness go when we no longer have families or spouses?"

"Our happiness becomes different," says Cambria. "My husband and I were so close—we were married forty years. Our wedding day was July sixteenth. On the sixteenth of every month, my husband used to send me an anniversary card."

"Life is definitely not the same as it was," Avena says pensively. "We have to find a new contentment."

Dawn, the new woman who moved in three days ago, joins us. The sweep of her auburn hair braided into a long ponytail gives her a youthful air. After her hefty frame settles into the soft cushions of the couch, she begins to tell us: "My relationship with my husband wasn't based on superficial, physical attraction. Our love was spiritual. When my husband was dying, he said, 'I don't want to be no other place in this world but with you.' 'Same with me, Arnold,' I told him. I stayed by his side and saw there was no struggle, no gasping for breath like other people do—he just died. It was the most beautiful moment of my life."

Her brown eyes fill with tears. A warm silence encircles us. Although we have just met her, Dawn has given us the deepest essence of her life. She has communicated clearly, even though she has Alzheimer's disease. Through her poignant sharing, we are knitted together—in awe.

Cambria fumbles in her pocket for a Kleenex, dabs her eyes, and says softly: "As he was dying my husband said to me, 'I don't know how I can get along in Heaven without you.' " A gentle smile plays around her mouth. "Even though he died ten years ago, I think of what he said every single day."

Tears that transcend sorrow: at this moment, both Dawn

and Cambria have gone beyond grief, accepting the event of death with gratitude and love. Will they, and other elders like them, remain destined to find their greatest happiness only by reliving the joys of the past? Or will they also find joy in the present?

For the next few weeks our discussions continue. The group is shaken out of complacency, drowsiness, dullness. Usually half asleep when I arrive, within moments these elders wake up, become intensely alive as they consider healthy ways to relate to loss—by embracing sorrow rather than getting rid of it, by honoring pain and trusting in its transformation.

Giving birth to an attitude of acceptance and release, can they experience happiness in spite of what they have lost? Sometimes the emotional effects of transition—whether from the death of a loved one or from giving up everything that had brought them happiness and security—surface years later, after an elder has been living in a residential facility or nursing home. When this suffering occurs, who is present for elders to help work through these sorrows?

Caregivers and Healing Companions may be afraid to listen to feelings that they think might be too heavy to handle. Will hurts be unveiled that we don't want to face in our elders or in ourselves? Are we concerned that emotions might be stirred up, possibly increasing the difficulty of our caregiving tasks?

To dwell endlessly on negative feelings is unhealthy, yet to bypass them is also unhealthy. If Healing Companions and caregivers can approach our tasks as adventurers, willing to take risks, allowing fear, anger, anxiety, and grief to be expressed, and giving elders acceptance, encouragement, love, and trust as their inner truths emerge, won't it be easier for our elders to surrender what they cannot hold onto and discover a new joy, grace, and serenity at life's end?

I began to think so after several visits with my client Nora, an accomplished artist who had studied in China. On our first encounter, Nora is curled up like an abandoned child on her bed. Her eyes are glazed, her hair disheveled. When she sees me she sits up, and gestures to the clothes hanging in her closet.

"See those clothes? No one lives in them anymore." Nora has just moved into Golden Pines residential home and is experiencing the loss of her former life. She feels empty, confused, and dissatisfied.

"I pay a lot here. I didn't get my watermelon this morning. An emergency happened with some woman. I resent it. Now my daughter is pressuring me to paint. I'm not interested in ever painting again. I'm not interested in your visits either. You don't care about me. I'm definitely not number one in my daughter's life either. Believe me; don't mistake her visits for caring."

Nora's feelings are a normal part of the life transition process. Hoping that she will feel more at home within herself if she realizes the value of this temporary state of emptiness, I tell her that as changes occur in health, lifestyle, or relationships, it is normal to feel upset.

"I'm reading this wonderful book by William Bridges,"[6] I say. "He wrote about transitions and the disorientation that happens when things that used to be important are suddenly meaningless."

"Yeah, they sure are—meaningless." She gazes at the floor, her torso slumps.

"He writes that these are times of opportunity. Instead of trying to make your distress and disenchantment less disturbing, if you surrender to this mysterious gap in your life between your old ways and the new way germinating through this discontent, something good will come out of it. It's a matter of faith in being reborn."

"Very, very interesting." Nora suddenly sits erect, looking intently into my eyes.

"Can you honor your feelings, and begin to see the potential in them for new beginnings? William Bridges writes that our culture has 'forgotten the importance of fallow time and winter and rests in music.' If you can go through this waiting period accepting that a new season of life is coming, then it's really okay not to do anything, even paint, or to know who you are just now. It's okay to let go of the expectations people have of you."

"Yes, okay, I see. I could never measure up to what my father wanted from me, even though I went to college and got my degrees. I was never able to be as good as the brilliance of my brother's mind."

"Maybe this transition will help you become your own person, not the one your father or your daughter expect you to be."

"It's frightening not to know what's coming."

"Of course. It's normal to be fearful about the unknown."

Nora's eyes are eager. "You know, I need to give up living in the past and set new goals for myself."

A few weeks later, Nora tells me the roses in the garden are beautiful. "But I'm not going to paint them."

"Well, maybe you're just supposed to look at them."

"Oh, I wish I could convey the beauty of a rose and everybody would be drawn to it . . . the most beautiful rose ever painted."

"You know, Nora, you need to own your passion, your aspiration to create beauty. Not many have this gift. And you say you're not spiritual. But to create beauty is one of the heights of spirituality. Some people think that beauty is God."

When I return the next week, Nora greets me affectionately

and hands me a painting. Surprised, I look down at the paper. Nora has come home to her new self. I hold before me an exquisite rose.

❦ Steps for Healing ❦

Insights that can help heal

+ Uncertainty, doubt, and confusion are normal in times of transition.

+ Confusion can lead to clarity and growth.

+ The seasons help heal; they mirror the changes we all go through.

Helping yourself heal

1. Reflect on the transitions in your life. At times, a transition may include feelings of grief. Of the five stages of grief, do you recognize your passage through anger, bargaining, denial, grief, and acceptance? Are you in one or more of these stages now?

2. If you are in the stages before acceptance, honor your anger or sorrow by finding a creative outlet for releasing them. You may want to try expressing these emotions in some form of art, or read books on grief and life transitions. Reach out to a friend who can help you find ways to express your feelings.

3. After you have experienced the five stages, create a closure ceremony. Visualize or actualize going to a sacred place in nature or at church. Offer something to commemorate your lost relationship, job, or home. It could be a poem, song, drawing, shell, rock, or flower. Leave your offering in that sacred place.

Helping your elder heal

1. When your elders are in the grief process, discuss the five stages. Listen attentively. Afterwards, guide them through a closure ritual or encourage spiritual acceptance of their situation. For some elders, it might be satisfying to include in the closure a ritual object that signifies the person or thing or state they are giving up. Use a photo, a magazine clipping, or a meaningful object, and place this before your elder. Contemplate together, uncovering feelings, meanings, and memories.

2. You may include drumming and rhythm instruments as a way of communicating. Everyone has an internal rhythm. Give your elder a drum and allow him or her to explore spontaneously. Instruct your elder to drum the rhythm of his or her name. Create a rhythm and encourage your elder to repeat it. Discordant, uneven rhythms may represent anger; soft, slow rhythms may express grief; and underneath sorrow you may find a joyful pulse wanting to be expressed.

For your inspiration

My life moves and shifts like all of nature. I resonate with the movements of the seas, the rivers, the storms, the fluctuation of the moon and the sun. Like the seasons, my elder and I go through changes. Sometimes we resist; we feel angry, sad, lost, confused. Sharing these challenges, my elder and I are one.

ELEVEN

In the Midst of Tears, Joy

*You and I were created
for joy, and if we miss it,
we miss the reason for
our existence!
Only the heart that hurts
has a right to joy.*
—Lewis Smedes

As SOON AS she sees me, her eyes fill with tears. Last night Janeen's brother suddenly died. Dragging my chair close to hers, I caress her hand for a long time as Janeen pours out her love and grief. Will we be able to shift our intimacy to the group that is about to begin? Will Janeen want to be part of it?

Surprisingly, she consents to join. As I sit on the couch, I realize I am unprepared to deal with this sudden death. Taking part in superficial chatting during a time of grieving will be meaningless for Janeen. Wondering what to focus on, I scan through a book of Tagore's poetry and begin reading aloud:

"Is it beyond thee to be glad with the gladness of this rhythm?" I read. "To be tossed and lost and broken in the whirl of this fearful joy?"[1]

As Janeen hears the words "gladness" and "joy," I wonder whether I was foolish to select this passage. Will focusing on joy be too painful for her? The verse trails off. No one is able to speak; there is a stunning silence. The poet's words have met us in our deepest places.

Glancing out of the window at a sudden swirl of leaves caught in a gust of wind, I break through the silence: "Can we be glad with the rhythms of our universe? When we watch autumn leaves fall, where do they go? Once part of the tree, they mix with earth, become part of a new creation. Although they die, they don't leave the universe; they become transformed. Like the leaves, do we ever lose anyone or anything in the universe—even in death?"

This tone of questioning seems to have soothed Janeen. She now looks at me calmly.

Watching the amber sun die behind jagged peaks along the mountain range, I add: "The one thing we can depend on is change. The sun setting and rising, the ocean's waves emptying and filling, migrating birds coming and going—all of life shifting and changing. Can we be glad with the gladness of this rhythm?"

Janeen's body relaxes, her face is soft. Smiling, she gazes out of the window.

"Where does a person go when he or she is no more?" As the sun splays its last rays along purple crests jutting into the evening air, my question hovers in the silence. A feeling of awe; no one answers. Following an inner flow prompting this impromptu lesson, I recall aloud an experience I had some years ago:

"One summer in the Sierras I took a workshop on Attitudinal Healing.[2] The leader asked us to think about someone we deeply loved—even if that person was no longer alive. My friend Mary came to mind. I imagined sitting with her under the shade of the pine trees.

"Although she had died five years ago, suddenly Mary became very real. Inwardly I shared with her my conflicts, my loneliness, my dreams—and there she was, caring, loving, supporting—just like she always had been. In those moments, I felt her love and was certain it would always be with me." Tears fill my eyes. Janeen has tears in her eyes too.

"That's when I knew—love is eternal, it never leaves. I can't lose Mary, she's still here. Whenever I call her, she'll be with me."

Clouds of sorrow have cleared from Janeen's eyes, now serene as a blue sky.

I continue: "What does it mean 'to be tossed and lost and broken in the whirl of this fearful joy'? What is fearful joy?"

"People are afraid of joy," Janeen says. "Not long ago my nephew took me out to dinner. We had a great time; we couldn't stop laughing." Her eyes dance with delight. "When I got back I came into the living room bursting with excitement. I started telling the aides about it. They looked at me like I was nuts." Janeen laughs, the glow of that happy memory still shines in her face.

"You are still caught in the excitement of that joy, aren't you?" I ask.

"Sure am. We met the most fabulous man that night—we laughed till we cried."

Leaning over, I place my hand on Janeen's shoulder. In the midst of loss, she has experienced a touch of joy. Tagore's poetry did what no amount of my trying could do. Her healing has begun, a scant twenty-four hours after the death of her brother. My objective is not to skim the surface of sorrow, avoiding its arrow of pain, but to open a space for Janeen's healing, knowing that for some people grief takes years to release. Janeen's moments of joy will later be interspersed with sadness.

Tears Are a Tribute of Love

Veronica's husband had died a year ago, but due to memory lapse Veronica couldn't remember. Asking for him the other day, she was told he was gone. Sobbing uncontrollably, in grief and in anger, she had demanded: "Why didn't someone tell me my husband died?"

"Someone *did* tell you a year ago," I had answered.

Gathering a small group of elders along with Veronica, I begin a discussion on grieving. Veronica's sobs are soon subdued. Rather than try to insist that she recall her husband's death, I relate my own recent loss.

"Any of us can forget about a death, and a year later it can come back like it was yesterday. Tears are a tribute of love. Some tears are so deep, they last forever."

Out of the depth of my own desire to weep, I confide to Veronica that I sometimes hold my tears back for fear they will never stop.

I ask the group, "Have you ever known someone you felt you could never live without?"

All six women reply that they have. Some of them, usually incoherent, now listen and respond with intent alertness. Without knowing it, are these elders starving for something real, hungry to share life's passion and pathos? Is that why they have come out of withdrawal into vivid aliveness?

Veronica turns to me: "Your silent tears may be deeper than if you cried aloud."

Moving from tears to joy, I read from chapter ten in this book. Absorbed in listening, Veronica stops trembling. At peace now, she seems able to carry on with life.

My attention returns to Janeen who waits for me to speak. "How do we know there is joy, the 'gladness of this rhythm,' as

Tagore writes, during times when we don't *feel* joy—when our feelings are actually the opposite?"

Avena: "If we look for gladness, we'll find it. If we don't, we won't."

Cambria: "I know when gladness is there—something bubbles inside of me. All of us are gifted with gladness. We should continue to develop it, even when we are feeling low and sad . . ."

"And full of grief," adds Janeen.

Avena: "We can be happy, joyful—or despondent. We have a choice."

Milka: "It's up to us!"

"When we choose joy, everything is all right," I say. "No worries, no grief. We experience only this moment. What do we have right now that is joyful?"

Janeen: "We have each other."

Milka: "We're sane, not crazy."

Avena: "Contentment."

Cambria: "We're alive!"

Their responses ring out into a much brighter room than the heavy grief that had hung like a shadow over us an hour ago.

"Some people are afraid of gladness. I remember a Sabbath celebration at my house," I say. "My friend Lilly was almost giddy with laughter, drunk on joy, singing, telling stories. I had never seen her this way. But she never came back. Months later I asked why. She said she couldn't stand so much joy—it overwhelmed her." Turning to Janeen, I add, "Maybe the aides rebuffed your joy because they're afraid of it."

"Maybe that's it."

"Another time," I add, "I brought the Sabbath celebration to an old couple in their apartment. The wife was Jewish, the husband was Catholic. He always wanted to experience the

Jewish Sabbath. As I began to sing, I felt joy rise up in me. I looked at them both. They seemed bewildered, hesitant. I thought, if I let my joy spill out, it might be too much for them. So I held it in. Is this how many of us live our lives, holding in our joy? Afraid of what people will think? Unable to find joy in the midst of sorrow?

"A friend once told me," I conclude, 'never be ashamed of laughter that's too loud or singing that's too joyful.' "

"I was once afraid of what others would think," Avena says with unusual frankness. "I never told anybody but I was ashamed of feeling joyful when my mother died."

"You don't have to be ashamed here with us, Avena," I reply. "The real thing is not what people expect us to be, but what we are. I had a similar experience. An unexpected joy came over me soon after my best friend died."

"Really? What happened?" asks Avena.

"After she died, nothing seemed to matter, nothing made sense. I lost my enthusiasm, even at the outdoor Greek Festival where I love to dance. I went through the motions of getting to the festival, watching the dancers, and even dancing myself. But I felt uninvolved, like I was looking and listening from a distant place outside of myself.

"Then all of a sudden, while I was on the dance floor, the music, the air, the happiness of the people vibrated within me; a panorama of love embraced my body. A sudden exuberant energy swept me into the dance with a full abandonment into joy. I was twirling like a teenager!"

"Oh my," exclaims Avena.

"With great gusto, I cried out in joy. It was my thanksgiving for the great dance of life. This time my joyful dancing was authentic. Two weeks earlier, I had danced around my friend's open casket with a sudden lightness of spirit. But when I began singing and playing my tamboura, all I really wanted to do was cry."

"I don't see how you could feel joy just two weeks later at the Greek Festival," says Avena.

"I don't either, really. After all, I had lost my closest, long-term friend. Gerry introduced my father to my mother, loved me unconditionally, and understood all my sufferings. She left me, and there I was singing. How could I possibly dance in the midst of my grief?"

"Yes, how could you?" Avena looks at me incredulously.

"The message seems to be: joy is an unseen gift. Underneath sorrow, joy is waiting, joy is alive. The late Rabbi Shlomo Carlebach knew about this. Darlene Rose, a devoted student of his, told me about the essence of the rabbi's teachings on the Holocaust. She recalled the rabbi saying that, yes, you keep tragedy in your heart, but it has to be on the outside of your heart. The inside of your heart is so divine it's like God. If you don't fill your heart with joy, you'll never make it."

"Joy can be real deep," Milka says. "Our Serbian people had many hardships and they didn't lose their joy."

"That's what Rabbi Carlebach was talking about. Darlene said the rabbi also taught that you can cry on one side of your heart and laugh on the other. He said that to bring people back to life takes strength. And strength comes from joy. You can't make it on sadness. The rabbi said that if you're very sad and God sends you an angel to give you everything, you wouldn't be able to receive it. But if you're filled with joy, you can carry the whole world on your shoulders."

"The rabbi's teachings remind me of how Liuba Levitska carried her suffering," I go on. "She tried to sneak some food to her mother in the concentration camp. Caught by the Nazis, they punished her with twenty-five lashes and put her in the ghetto's prison tower for a month of solitary confinement. She was known for her beautiful singing. You know what she sang?" I ask, wondering if this story is too intense for the group.

"No, tell us," says Cambria.

"She sang a song about 'two loving doves who were torn from one another by an unknown evil force.' Her song was heard by the other prisoners. She became known as the 'nightingale of the Vilna Ghetto.' Her song comforted the prisoners and became a symbol of their feelings about the Nazis.

"One day the Nazis drove her to the killing ground and asked her to take off her clothes. She refused. They told her if she didn't, they would pierce out her eyes. Liuba never stopped singing in the car as they drove her to her death; she never stopped singing as they shot her.[3]

"Does this story depress you? Would you rather not hear it?" I ask.

"We *want* to hear it, to be reminded," answers Milka. "We want to be sure nothing like that ever happens again."

"It gives us courage," Cambria says.

"It tells us we can find a glimmer of joy even in our grief," says Janeen.

The following week Janeen is the first to be waiting for my group. I begin by reading from the diaries of Etty Hillesum who died in a concentration camp: "And I want to be there right in the thick of what people call 'horror' and still be able to say: life is beautiful . . . And now here I lie . . . dizzy and feverish . . . If I could only be there to give some of those packed thousands just one sip of water."[4]

"She wants to help people," says Milka, "just the way my daddy used to do. Many people would come to him with their troubles and to me also."

"When we help others, we forget our own suffering," Cambria says.

Janeen looks at Cambria with a smile, and says, "God wants us to help others and when we do, we feel joy."

"Only when we live from our highest, deepest self, the 'diamond essence' that Marilyn Grosboll speaks of, are we able to connect to joy in the most difficult circumstances. Etty responded to life from her highest self. Imagine being able to feel as she did when she writes:

" 'The misery here is quite terrible and yet, late at night when the day has slunk away into the depths behind me, I often walk with a spring in my step along the barbed wire and then time and again it soars straight from my heart . . . the feeling that life is glorious and magnificent, and that one day we shall be building a whole new world.'

"Her story reaches beyond sorrow, shows how she turned the deepest losses into gains." Janeen smiles as I conclude: " 'Against every new outrage and every fresh horror', writes Etty, 'we shall put up one more piece of love and goodness, drawing strength from within ourselves. We may suffer, but we must not succumb.' "[5]

❧ Steps for Healing ❧

Insights that can help heal

- ❖ There is no such thing as permanent loss; the natural rhythms of the universe permeate our lives with a sense of continuity.

- ❖ Love never leaves when a loved one dies; our memories keep alive the vitality of that love.

◆ Hope is rekindled through wisdom teachings.

◆ Resiliency and courage reside in the human spirit. Underneath sorrow, joy exists, even when it is not felt at the moment.

◆ Joy comes as a spontaneous moment when, despite outer circumstances, suddenly all is well from within.

Helping yourself heal

1. Look within for joy, as well as for the tears that heal. Think of something you love and have lost. Be with the lost person or thing in your imagination. Invite a dialogue, a touch, or a sound—invite something special to come into your heart. If sadness arises, accept your feelings. You are making an eternal connection with your love, and that love will heal you.

2. Assure yourself that tears and sadness do not have to overwhelm you. Your tears are a tribute to your capacity to love.

Helping your elder heal

1. Gather poetry, essays, or stories that passionately inspire you. These may help heal an elder who grieves.

2. Dancing is a way to integrate feelings of sorrow and joy. Some cultures dance feelings of grief and mourning as a way of honoring a loved one who has died. Such dances often have the component of joy. You may spontaneously create a dance or choreograph one for your elders. After showing them some movements, ask them to help you create the beginning or the end.

For your inspiration

Within my soul I am endowed with an infinite container of strength, courage, and joy. This joy is sometimes submerged in sorrow. Yet joy is the essence of my being. Joy is the healer and carries the power to see me through all losses.

My elder has this same gift. In this, we are one.

TWELVE

Depression: Is There a Way Out?

God is faithful,
who will not let you be tempted
beyond what you are able,
but will with the temptation
make also the way out,
that you may be able to
endure it.
—1 Corinthians 10:12

"OLD AGE IS the death of enthusiasm." Abraham's words hover between us like dark clouds, diminishing any joy he once knew. "I'm not kidding, hell is now."

Watching Abraham's depression grow, I am convinced his crisis is spiritual, not physical. The medical staff hears his physical complaints. I hear another story: Abraham once loved God and has lost a vital relationship, which could help him now.

As a boy and into manhood, Abraham faithfully attended church. He loved ritual and devotion. But this didn't help him apply spiritual principles to disappointments, challenges, hardships. When his minister approached him with homosexual overtures, Abraham left the church—and God.

Yet through his sister, Rene, Abraham still remains linked to spiritual life. Proudly he tells me Rene not only knows the

Bible, she lives it: "Even in emergencies, Rene's peace never leaves her." But Abraham does not accept Rene's religion. Although her influence has inspired him, it doesn't penetrate his depression.

"I'm telling you, I'm not afraid of death, it's not cowardly to want to die—I'm afraid of living."

Moving my chair close to his bed in the nursing home, I reach out, hold both of his hands, and begin gently massaging his forearms in rhythmic strokes.

"What's so painful for you, dear Abraham?" I look into huge brown eyes, seemingly larger than usual through his thick glasses. "You have so much to give."

"That's a laugh."

"Is it? You've given me so much by knowing you."

"I don't believe it." Leaning forward in my chair, I scan his intelligent, distinguished features: wide forehead, square chin, thick white sideburns, and neatly trimmed wavy brown hair.

Suddenly, he exclaims, "When I was young, people said it was impossible to climb the mountain near our house in less than two days—I did it in two hours—without any food."

"Lucky you have such strength."

"Had. Now I spend my time envying those cleaning girls. They sweep the floor—I can't even do that."

Equating strength with physical rather than spiritual power, Abraham is becoming a passive victim of aging and death. What can I do for him?

"Dr. Bernie Siegel understands you," I reply. "He says: 'Helplessness is worse than the stress itself.'[1] Do you think there is something you can do?"

"I can't do anything, that's the whole problem."

"You *are* doing something—you're sharing your feelings."

Abraham stares at the ceiling. "Look, I know you're trying

to help me. But what I need most in my life is death—it's something to be thankful for—it's not dreadful."

"Life also might not be dreadful . . . would you consider options?"

"Options? The only option I want is to be able to get dressed by myself, make my own bed, walk down the hall, and help some of those poor unfortunate people. And I can't do any of it."

For over a month I've listened to Abraham's complaints without imposing my views. Now it is time to intervene. If Abraham can see the effects of his unrealistic expectations, his resistance to aging, will a shift in attitude take place?

"Abraham, can you imagine what would happen if you jumped into a raging river determined to swim upstream? Your whole body would struggle and strain against the surging waters. Wild currents would force you downstream, yet you'd keep trying to swim against them. Do you think you'd make it?"

Abraham leans toward me in his bed, his eyes suddenly eager.

"No!"

"The more you go against the flow of the river," I continue, "the more frustrated and exhausted you become. Isn't that true?"

"Yep, that's right!"

"So you're confined to a wheelchair, you have arthritis, and you're getting old. You'd give anything to get out of it. But the river refuses to change its course. The more you try to force the situation to yield to the way *you* want life to be, what's the result?"

"I'm wearing myself out. You've got it!" Abraham says with a laugh.

"Do you like the results you're achieving by trying to swim

against the current?"

"You've got me there!" Smiling broadly, he adds: "Will you stop making me laugh—it's fattening!"

Abraham's restored humor is a good sign. Last week, worried about his deepening depression, I phoned Marilyn Grosboll. Our conversation showed me my frustration was similar to Abraham's. I, too, have been thinking I have to *do* something to help free Abraham from depression—or become a failure, a feeling many caregivers face.

Marilyn counseled: Allow Abraham to express grief over the loss and betrayal of his body; give up the notion that it is wrong to be depressed; offer Abraham new options for relating to life; accept Abraham's choice to remain depressed and refuse the options if he so desires. Most important, love him unconditionally as he is, without trying to change him.

Her advice relieved me. I no longer had to take responsibility for Abraham's healing. Abraham was free to continue his misery or opt for change. As the weeks went by, Abraham experienced brief moments of release, and I was more relaxed. Still, his complaints continued: "I am old, useless, a burden to my family."

Our culture doesn't help heal these kinds of feelings. We are taught that self-worth is attached to what we *do* rather than who we *are*. When aging forces us to stay at home, our extroverted culture continues telling us that our happiness is based on material achievements gained through physical and mental agility. We are not taught how to do nothing—and do it with grace. Except for retreats in Catholic monasteries and relatively few retreat centers across the country, the average person has no way to learn to *be*, to contemplate without being required to *do* something. Having no graceful way to live through the deterioration of our bodies, we drift through old age like a boat without a rudder, aimless, without purpose.

Several months pass. Dissatisfied with Abraham's continued lack of self-acceptance and his barrage of complaints, I decide to seek the guidance of author and spiritual director Valerie Stevens, whose freedom from twenty-three years of depression has been an inspiration to many.[2] After I described Abraham's frame of mind, Valerie responded: "In the eternal perspective, even depression can have a good result if it draws us closer to God."

I wonder: Would Abraham be willing to accept the idea that his depression might lead to something good?

Valerie continued: "When we're happy and well, we take all the credit. We think we don't need God. But later, when we're not so well, from our self-centered perspective we try to deny sickness and oldness. But sometimes becoming sick and old is the only way we'll come to God. It's his means of preparing us to leave this world. In our culture, we think pain and suffering are to be avoided. We want life to be perfect. When it isn't, we get depressed."

As Valerie speaks, I wonder: Is Abraham's connection to God strong enough for him to want to deepen it?

"If God's purpose in my illness is to prepare me to look forward to my eternity with him," Valerie continues, "then when I see I'm no longer any good for this world, I have a different response. I can't wait to leave this body!" Valerie's blue eyes, brilliant with joy, startle me. How can she be so radiant over the prospect of death?

"My oldness becomes a gateway to an expectancy for my death. I look *forward* to living with the Lord in joy and peace." Valerie's happiness overflows. Her faith is a gift. At his age, can Abraham develop this? Would he even want to?

What Is There Left to Praise?

The following week, I return to visit Abraham. I am in a dilemma. Out of respect for privacy in religious matters, I desist from imposing religious beliefs. But knowing his spiritual history, his admiration for his sister's spiritual devotion, the degree and length of his depression, I decide to take a risk.

"Abraham, how would you like to climb a new kind of mountain, bigger even than the one you had at home—right here in this wheelchair?"

"Honey, what're you up to now?" Abraham takes my hand, looks at me quizzically. "I sure admire your perseverance. No one has talked to me this way. I might have lost my enthusiasm, but I'm enthused for yours!"

"Tell me, Abraham, what would give you joy?"

"Hah! I told you, I'm a burden. There is no joy." About to slip into discouragement over this habitual response, I suddenly recall my talk with Valerie. "You know, my friend Valerie Stevens was depressed for twenty-three years."

"Worse than me!"

"She's cured now."

"What's the rub?"

"Valerie's husband was a psychopath—which led to divorce and single parenting of four small children. A hoped for second marriage ended with the death of her fiancé. She had little money, no job . . . and her house burned down. Her depression began to change when she asked God: 'Are you allowing me to suffer because you want me to get closer to you instead of focusing on myself? If that's what you want Lord, I'll choose to praise you!' Abraham, would you be willing to try praising?"

"Praising when I'm like this?"

"Do you like the result of not praising, of being depressed?"

"Of course not!"

"If you keep basing your joy on what you want to *do*, you'll be depressed when you can't do it. Why not base your joy on who you *are* instead?"

"Who I am . . . an old man, a burden to my sister . . . base my joy on that?"

"I'm a burden, I'm an old man, I'm useless. Valerie told me her depression didn't change until she shifted her emphasis away from 'I.' She had to stop thinking about what *she* wanted and begin to seek and accept what *God* wanted for her."

"Does he want me to be useless?"

"No. He wants you to find him in spite of, and in the midst of, this difficult situation. Until you have peace with him, what will you have to give to the other residents you say you want to help?"

"You've got a point there." Abraham smiles, gently rubs my hand. "You're doing good work, honey."

Squeezing his hand, I smile into his warm brown eyes and go on: "Do you know what the symbol for 'crisis' in Chinese is? The symbol combines two words: 'disaster' and 'opportunity.' It doesn't take much to figure out the message, does it?"

"I get it all right!"

"So did Valerie. She experienced oneness with God when she began praising him in *all* circumstances. So we can train our will, choose to praise, even when we don't feel like it."

Small moments of light pass between us as the weeks progress. Abraham's negative attitude, ingrained over a lifetime, is not easy to deal with. But there is always hope no matter how much suffering occurs. It might be easier if he had begun a spiritual discipline in his younger years. Also, would his spirit now be revived if, in this nursing home, he was exposed to scripture in a way that was vibrant and applicable to his daily problems? Would his depression lessen if he had access to daily prayer, praise, and joyous celebration of the life of God?

Abraham needs access to his spiritual being; spiritual life has to take hold of him on the inside. Who will be committed to helping him awaken to the possibility of transformation, of inner healing? It becomes clear to me that the new role of Healing Companion might be an aid in that process.

Although I do not have the expertise to journey through Abraham's lost faith, to guide him into a deeper understanding of who God is, to unravel the shadows cast on his soul, I do what I can: turn to the inspiration of a man whose life resembles Abraham's, in the hopes that it will strengthen Abraham's yearning to grow in God, deepen his prayer life, and enable him to find courage and purpose in his disability.

"Abraham?" Softly I place my hand on his shoulder.

Abraham awakens with a jerk.

"Sorry I startled you."

"Oh, I'm full of startles!" His joke impresses me; in spite of depression, he still maintains a sense of humor. Cranking the mattress to a sitting position, I rearrange his pillow. Abraham puts on his glasses, lifts a glass from his bedside table, sips water from a straw, sets the glass down, and contentedly folds his hands on his heart.

"I apologize for being late—I stayed too long with the other residents."

"Are you kidding? If you help all of them, you're helping me. After all, I live here, and they're my family."

Touched by his response, I begin where we left off last week: "Are you ready to climb a mountain today?" I ask.

"Sounds good—what's the catch?" Abraham's head settles back onto his pillow.

"Believe you can still climb mountains—that you're not a victim of circumstances, that you can overcome freezing rains, winds, boulders fallen onto your path—that you can climb over despair, get to the top of that mountain and be free to start a new life at last."

"Boy, this next part better be good!" A light seems to have gone on somewhere inside; I see a sparkle in Abraham's eyes.

"Tim Hansel, who is in his forties, is reduced to life in a wheelchair. Do you want to know why?"

"All right, honey, give me the story." Abraham puts his hands on the bed railing, pulls his bulky frame closer to my chair.

"Tim is founder of Summit Expeditions, a Christian wilderness school near Yosemite. He went camping on a glacier, climbed to a height of fourteen thousand feet—and fell on the way down. He's never going to climb mountains again. His spine is permanently injured, and he expects continuous pain for the rest of his life.

"Tim was forced to find joy on the inside because he lost it on the outside. And he knew he couldn't do it without God. You want to hear what he's written?"

"Go ahead."

"He writes that he had 'to choose either to break down or break through'; that he couldn't wait until his circumstances got better before he was joyful; he had to choose joy now."[3]

"That takes a lot of guts! How's he going to do that?" Abraham inadvertently lifts his head from his pillow, inches his body closer to the edge of the bed.

"He comes to the conclusion that 'pain is inevitable, but misery is optional, and that joy . . . is not a feeling; it is a *choice*.' "[4]

"He just decided to be joyful?"

"He knows he can't do it without the continual renewal of God's presence and help. He writes: 'What a test of character adversity is. It can either destroy or build up, depending on our chosen response. Pain can either make us better or bitter.'⁵ What do you think it means to choose joy?"

"I wish I knew."

"Joy is beyond happiness—happiness can be snatched away at any minute. Today I'm happy because my sister came to visit, I feel well, the food is good. Tomorrow I'm miserable when no one comes to visit, the food is lousy, and I feel rotten!"

Abraham laughs, reaches his hand over the bed rail and playfully taps my hand.

"What's joy?" I ask. "It's deeper than happiness; it's the meaning I find *within* my circumstances; it doesn't depend on what's happening on the outside of me. Joy is the bright side of my heart; it's where Tim lives deep down with God."

"You mean I can beat the rap, beat the circumstances by overcoming them?"

Suddenly Abraham seems to have awakened from his sleep of passivity. It may not last, but in this hour together, each moment has become intensely alive.

"I still maintain change isn't possible. I'm in a trap. I'm responsible for my family and sometimes I wish they didn't come."

"I maintain, dear Abraham, that *God* is responsible for your family, not you. Tim writes that 'nothing robs one's strength and vitality so much as self-absorption. There is no greater waste of time than self pity . . .' "⁶

"That's true."

"I believe all things are possible with him—he can even change you! Do you believe there's hope?"

"Now where would we be without it? Tim's book is about belief and hope and who knows? One sentence could bring back my belief. I've never let anyone read to me till now." Abraham pats my hand.

"What have you gotten from it?"

"God has to take the rap—I mean, my situation." Unconsciously, Abraham lets out an audible sigh, verbally admitting for the first time his need for God. "Because the bottom line is . . ." the words come slowly, deliberately, "there's only one thing . . . " There's a glimmer of light in his eyes, a smile shining through his words. "One thing that matters . . ." he pauses, shakes his finger at me, and ends emphatically: "the Almighty!"

☙ Steps for Healing ❧

Insights that can help heal

◆ There is always hope even when our lives seem hopeless.

◆ We have the capacity to choose joy.

◆ It is possible to transcend feelings of helplessness.

◆ We can be helplessly unable to do anything and still be at peace.

Helping yourself heal

1. Before you can have an affinity with an elder who is depressed, you need to discover how depression operates in you. When you feel depressed or downcast, observe what brings this on. How frequently do these feelings occur? How do you express them? Do you allow yourself to prolong these feelings?

2. What would you like to have happen when you are depressed? Are you able to ask someone to be your companion? Can you ask for what you need?

3. Identify the feelings underneath your depression, such as anger, grief, or anxiety. Find a creative way to express these feelings.

Helping your elder heal

1. Does your elder have any spiritual resources to turn to? Ask your elder and also ask his or her caregivers. Use this information as a framework for healing.

2. Listen compassionately to your elder's story of depression. Realize, however, that, at some point, continuing to attend to his or her depression may prolong or accentuate it. Guide your elder into momentarily transcending depression by sharing poems or stories of others who have triumphed over adversity. There is no need to burden your elder with guilt or with the expectation that he or she must overcome suffering.

3. Share your discouragement or moments of depression with your elder. Trust that your own story may help relieve your elder's loneliness.

4. You can inspire hope and the capacity for change. Elders, as well as most of us, are not able to access their will or inner strength when they are very depressed. You can help them to access it by offering them inspiration in nature, Bible phrases, prayer, art, or music.

For your inspiration

Sometimes I am depressed, but I am not the depression. When depression threatens to overshadow me, I know it is a passing shadow. Eventually depression dissolves to reveal my healed and joyful self. Both my elder and I move through darkness and reach toward the light. It is this movement that connects us at the center of our common humanity. By this connection, we are one.

THIRTEEN

Facing Our Shadow

What in me is dark
Illumine.
—John Milton

In the dark
I lost sight of
My shadow;
I've found it again
By the fire I lit.
—Soiku Shigematsu

I SIT IN VERA'S room in the nursing home, where I have just made a fool of myself. Humility was the last thing on my mind when I told Vera of my latest discovery.

My closest friend's father had just died. His wife made a cassette tape for their children, expressing her love for each child, as she described her deepest beliefs about life and God. She ended the tape with her favorite song.

After knowing Vera for eight years, I am convinced she will be inspired to make a similar tape for her son.

"Who cares? I'm not interested at all. When I die I want my son to forget about me, get on with his life."

Her reaction makes me realize I have been carried away by

my enthusiasm, have projected my own interests onto her, assuming I know what is best for her. This self-centered perspective is a shadow aspect of myself, an immature part of me that, until now, I have never acknowledged. Is my perspective distorted with other elders as well?

Jungian psychiatrist Adolf Guggenbühl-Craig writes about health care professionals who act as if they have all the answers, who force their values on patients or clients.[1] Like them, have I been unwilling to admit that I don't always know what's best for a client?

Guggenbühl-Craig also reveals possible hidden motives in professionals that may be harmful to their patients and clients. Haven't I secretly hoped that no one else would develop an intimate bond with Vera, so that she won't want any one else but me as her Healing Companion? This possessiveness is an aspect of my shadow side, which could impede Vera's health care, make her dependent and unable to relate to others.

Psychologist Carl Jung believes our shadow side is submerged below the threshold of our awareness. When we shed light on our shadow, and make an attempt to see what is hidden, by paying attention to our dreams, moods, and feelings, we may discover rage, fear, or evil impulses, as well as our highest aspiration for love, compassion, and spiritual vision.

Whether health care professionals relate to evil forces as being within, or believe in the religious view of the devil or "evil one" attacking from outside, acknowledgment of the need to heal and overcome such forces may lead to creating a healthy completion at life's end. By acknowledging that darkness and impure motives exist and being courageously willing to face them, darkness may be transformed and wholeness and inner healing may occur.

When Dark Emotions Are Unacknowledged

"My family thinks I'm strong, can cope with anything," Natasha told me. "They don't know how soft I am on the inside, how much I cry. When I was a teenager I never told my parents I had contemplated suicide. One day I even had one leg out of the window. The only thing that stopped me from jumping was that I didn't want to hurt them. Now I think of suicide every day. Should I take these pills? But my family is so good to me. It would kill them if I did."

During the two years I visited Natasha in her home, she confessed a lifelong secret: At age eight she was molested; at age eighty-five, she still has nightmares. But it seems her daughter didn't want Natasha to dwell on anything negative. "Mother should be cheerful, forget the past, live in the now," she said. Natasha's daughter tried to ignore Natasha's continual anger, a clue something was wrong. Something deeply upsetting to Natasha had been left to fester, unacknowledged and unresolved. Instead, Natasha's daughter provided her with more visitors, outings, and house parties to distract Natasha from dealing with her inner self.

Henry's family was likewise unwilling—or unable—to help him deal with his volatile emotions, his shadow. "If I had it to do over again, I would never have married that domineering woman," he said, his shoulders hunched over in defeat. So in need of the comfort he wasn't receiving from family members, he pleaded with me, "Please, sit here beside me, hold my hand for God's sake, and don't even talk to me! I'm so desperate. I just need you to be close."

Married for sixty years, Henry diligently played the role of the devoted family man. But now his anxiety attacks unmask his true feelings. His son, busy with church affairs and professional commitments, does not have time to listen. He assumes Henry is upset solely because of an inability to accept living in a nursing home. Because his son and his wife are unable to   recognize the full spectrum of Henry's suffering, at the end of Henry's life he is alone with his grief.

Joan Chittister writes that it is up to each of us to face our inner self so that we are free to truly love: "Life is not what we see happening on the outside. Life is what goes on inside the quiet, murky waters of our souls."[2] Author Morton Kelsey tells us that "nearly all of us have our own inner monsters." If we do not face them, the "effect is uncreative and hostile to love and growth."[3]

Shedding Light on the Shadow

Is facing emotional pain intolerable? Is it safe to open a door to sharing secrets of the past? Can anything good come of it? Unintentionally, I found out one day at Valley View residential home. I was so upset with two people in my life I could barely think of anything else. Should I reveal my secret sorrow to these elders?

I chance it. Their response startles me. Avena immediately responds to my story with one of her own. As a young girl, while her father was at work, she found her mother with another man: "I think of this every day and have never told anyone."

Catherine, teary-eyed, reveals: "I was six years old when my uncle came to visit in the winter. I sat on his knee; he gave me candy. I remember him touching me where he shouldn't. I couldn't tell mother because he threatened to kill me."

Stunned, I wonder how this sudden admission would affect

the members of my group. Would they feel depressed or embarrassed about sharing these memories?

"I'm grateful to break open my heart, express my feelings, and let go of anger, fear, and shame. I always felt guilty for something I hadn't done. Somehow, I think I'll find more peace after sharing this." Relieved, Catherine sinks back in her chair.

Janeen adds, "It's a great privilege to hear a secret that has been kept for years." Glancing at Catherine, she goes on. "You bring us into your heart and soul. We appreciate it."

I wonder if there is anything more to do. "Would you be willing to bless these events?" I ask.

Incredulous, Avena and Janeen stare at me in disbelief. "We can't do that," they say.

I persist. "I don't mean for you to believe what happened was right. But, did the event teach you anything, change your life for the better?"

Silence. Thinking it over, they begin to see the events in a positive way. After Avena married, she determined never to repeat what her mother had done. Catherine's suffering led her to develop compassion for the suffering of others; she became a psychologist. Although they still felt the pain of the past, instead of dismissing the events as horrible, they recognized the beneficial aspects and blessed the learning they received.

Making peace with events of the past belongs not only to elders but to health care professionals as well. Facing sorrow, regret, and anger can cleanse thoughts and emotions, and increase joy, love, and gratitude. Such inner peacemaking can become the root from which effective caregiving grows.

The Magic Towel

I found out how I needed to make peace as I began reading aloud "The Magic Towel," a Japanese tale about a jealous, old mother-in-law, to one of my groups. No matter how mean this old mother-in-law became, her beautiful daughter-in-law remained kind and sweet. The old woman became so abusive that the daughter-in-law sought the advice of a monk. This monk gave her a magic towel and told her to wash her face with it.

The daughter-in-law did as she was told, and as she washed, she became more and more radiant. The nasty old woman became enraged. As she saw her daughter-in-law becoming increasingly more beautiful, she stole the towel and began washing her own face with it. Instead of becoming beautiful, she became extremely ugly.

First, her face turned into that of a horse, then a monkey, and lastly, a demon. In agony, the old woman writhed on the floor, beseeching her daughter-in-law to find a cure. Taking pity on her, the daughter-in-law went back to the monk to ask for a remedy. The monk advised her to have the old woman wash her face again, this time using the other side of the towel. When the old woman did this, she was restored.

From that day onward, the mother-in-law became kind and generous. She begged forgiveness, promising never to harm her daughter-in-law again.

Allan Chinen, psychiatrist and author of the retelling of this tale, comments on the significance of elder fairy tales in the development of elderhood. Interpreting this story, he writes, "The towel wipes away outward appearances, and reveals the face of the soul."[4]

Chinen reminds us that in youth we learn to wear masks and take on roles in order to behave appropriately in school, on our jobs, or at a party. In Jung's terms, we put on a "persona." But in the second half of life, we have the opportunity to let go of these roles, to become who we are without wearing masks, without trying to impress anyone. By using the magic towel, the old woman came face to face with the evil acting within her. Until then, she didn't realize how ugly she was. But when she saw the dark, shadowy side of herself, she was transformed.

This tale has lessons for anyone. It worked on me one day in a nursing home.

"Get my purse. Where the hell did you put it?" A resident screams to no one in particular. "My glasses, I want my glasses!" she yells.

"Shut up!" Her roommate swats the air as if to attack the yelling woman.

"I want my newspaper. Get it now . . . now!"

The cacophony is deafening, the chorus of voices unrelenting. How can the nurses stand this?

Engulfed by hateful emotions, I am repulsed, and wish I were out of here. Then I hear myself ask: Do I want to be like them by hating my mother? Suddenly their rage is my rage; these elders and I have become one. We are all crying for love.

I hadn't recognized my hatred until the week before, when my sister informed me that my mother was coming from out-of-state for a rare family visit. My sister did not include me in planning the activities, and no mention was made of celebrating my birthday three days away. For a crazy moment, I wished I had never been born into this family.

As the residents go on screaming, I want to scream too. Like them, I remember feeling unloved, lonely, abandoned. Facing this shadow in myself dissipates my anger and stops me from blaming my family. The error is mine, not theirs. I cannot change the way they are; I can only change the way I am. Instead of becoming a victim of rage as these elders are, I can take responsibility by cultivating a change of heart. Now I no longer separate myself from the residents. I consciously approach them through my own brokenness.

Author Henri Nouwen believes that healers who discover their own wounds of loneliness and pain are able to have compassion for others. No one "can be led out of the desert by someone who has never been there. Who can take away suffering without entering it?"[5]

Compassion grows in us through transformation. Chinen's Japanese tale mirrors this potential transformation; any elder or caregiver can use the magic towel, wipe off rage, frustration, self-hate. Purifying and healing wounds of the past may take a lifetime, yet we need not remain victims of the past forever.

The vocation and lifelong journey of healing and purifying ugly parts of ourselves brings with it this discovery: light overcomes darkness once darkness is revealed and the desire to change is awakened. It is then we can become messengers of light.

The Healing Power of Silence

How do we become messengers of light for one another? How does transformation occur? One way is to make silence and solitude part of our daily lives. Joan Chittister writes: "Silence is the beginning of peace . . . The fear of silence and solitude loom like cliffs in the human psyche. Noise protects us from confronting ourselves, but silence speaks the language of the heart."[6]

Our culture needs to balance outer activity with inner

quietude, extroversion with introversion. Our institutions tend to be unconscious of the needs of elders who require solitude.* For instance, at Valley View residential home, Cambria and Gloria are deprived of the solitude they took for granted throughout their lives. Now their mornings are rushed and interrupted, without enough time for meditation, reflection, and prayer.

Required to submit to the schedule of their aides, they can no longer give priority to their spiritual life. Believing meditation is most effective in the early morning, they used to meditate every day. But now the morning begins with physical care, which reverses their life rhythms, starts the day in a wrong spirit.

By afternoon, entertainments, visitors, and aides continue to intrude on their solitude. An aide may walk into the room and rummage through their drawers without saying why. A roommate may watch TV for hours, yet Cambria and Gloria find TV repulsive. How can creativity, inner perception, spiritual growth be possible for elders like Cambria and Gloria, whose wellness depends on silence and solitude?

Unfortunately, there are surprisingly few eldercare homes that take into consideration an elder's need for silence and meditation. Surprisingly, ninety-five-year-old Brigette found silence and solitude in an unusual way, one that eventually had a profound effect on her.

Always bragging about her talents, famous friends, and success as an actress, Brigette exhausted me. Repelled by her self-centeredness, I tried to avoid her. But one day I can't. Brigette paces the busy hall of the nursing home, furiously

---

* Institutions may consider asking, as part of an elder's history: What spiritual habits and rhythms did this elder have? How much time did he or she spend in prayer, meditation, or study? Where was this done? Did the elder keep a journal?

yelling, "I want to die. Why doesn't God take me? I'm a 'has been,' no good any more!"

Guiding Brigette to a couch facing a garden, I sit down beside her. "Who do you think you are?" I surprise myself talking to her like this. "Do you think demanding your end from God will force God to do what *you* want?"

Startled, Brigette shakes her head, her voice suddenly quiet. "No. You're right, it doesn't work. You're very wise."

"It's true, you're not an actress now. But your life is not a 'has been.' Why not ask God to show you his purpose for this new phase of your life?"

"I never thought of that. Thank you, you've given me a new idea." She smiles.

Brigette's openness amazes me. I go on: "Others in this nursing home have no life at all. Many of them can't talk or walk. But because you're older than I am, when you speak to them you reach them in ways I can't. They trust you."

"Me?" Brigette's intense agitation and depression seems to subside.

Wiping tears from her eyes, she places her palms together as if in prayer. Looking upward, she exclaims: "Thank you, God, for saving me for this."

Shocked at Brigette's sudden humility, I am further surprised as she warmly embraces me.

"Every day I sit here in silence," she says, gazing up at a crystal cross hanging in the window in front of us. Framed by trees and flowers, the cross glimmers in the sunlight. Taking her gaze as a cue, I begin gazing too. Although Brigette does not follow any specific religion, she now sits in total absorption, communing with the cross, oblivious to people coming and going in the hallway.

Neither of us moves; a deep stillness overtakes us. Fifteen

minutes pass, an extraordinary amount of time for a nursing home resident to commune in silence without falling asleep. How is Brigette able to concentrate on the cross this long? Does she try to contemplate its meaning? Is she a mystic? In this inner quietude, Brigette's anger and restlessness have abated.

Breaking the silence, Brigette turns to me with a look of wonder: "Thanks to you, this place is different now. It has new meaning." As we face each other, silent joy passes between us.

From that day on, Brigette and I have an inspired relationship. Because we shared peace in a world without words, we experienced serenity together, opened ourselves to God's presence. In those brief moments we transcended anxiety, grief, and despair.

In our culture, we need to be conscious of elders such as Brigette, Cambria, and Gloria who are drawn to spiritual life, who long for privacy and quiet for their souls. A "peace room" or sanctuary, big enough for one or two people, could provide silence, solitude, and privacy. Are we willing to create a space of beauty to refresh the soul, to encourage elders to seek peace in the midst of emotional pain and the suffering of the physical body?

❧ Steps for Healing ☙

Insights that can help heal

+ No other process so confirms the value of our interior life as the uncovering of the shadow within us. This profound process is a pathway for healing.

+ Facing painful shadow feelings can cleanse our thoughts and emotions, increasing joy, love, and gratitude. This is a lifetime process.

+ The grace of releasing the power of our shadow comes spontaneously. We cannot force it.

+ Embracing our shadow deepens our empathy for others.

Helping yourself heal

1. The negative side of your shadow self is revealed when your heart shuts down and you can't feel love or forgiveness. Befriend your shadow. Acknowledge hidden feelings of jealousy, anger, fear, or possessiveness.

2. Some caregivers at times are possessive. Are you? If so, how do you keep your elder bound to you? What is the tie that binds you? Becoming aware of this possessive tendency will allow you to be less possessive, and still maintain a close connection.

3. Projection is an aspect of your shadow self. You may project your views and feelings onto your elders or friends, not realizing that these are yours and not theirs. Examine your responses in a close relationship. If you give advice, does your shadow side insist you must be right? Can you admit you might be wrong? Humility is essential for effective caregiving. Become aware of, and respect the wishes of others, even if you do not agree.

4. One of the ways to experience a release from the grip of your shadow is to allow solitude into your life and to seek peace.

Helping your elder heal

1. When your elders seem overcome with negative shadow emotions, encourage them to admit their feelings. Be still and hold the peace your elders do not have at the moment. Breathe in peace, breathe out peace, and imagine a peaceful stream of light pouring from your heart into the hearts of your elders.

2. Help your elders connect to their peaceful center within. Play music, sing, hold hands, massage hands or feet, and help your elders appreciate their blessings.

3. There may be times when you think you know what is best for your elders' spiritual and emotional well-being. You may gently offer a suggestion. Then completely let go of the outcome. Entering into reflective solitude will help you release your attachment to your elders' reactions.

4. Look for ways to provide your elders with solitude.

For your inspiration

The beautiful soul that I am is sometimes clothed in shadows,
feelings of fear, anger, and possessiveness. When I have these
feelings, I remind myself that these shadows can never be stronger
than love. Love brings me the joy of who I really am.
My elder and I have our shadow side.
We also have love and beauty of soul. In this, we are one.

PART TWO

Enhancing our Spiritual Life

FOURTEEN

Why Can't We Talk About God?

Every soul that uplifts itself
uplifts the world.
—Elisabeth Leseur

"TELL THE OLD folks about your recent trip to Disneyland, and stay out of religion!" That was Cynthia's advice to me. She is the owner of Valley View, the best assisted living facility in town, and yet she is a person who clearly denies the value of spirituality. How was I going to stay away from discussing what these elders got so excited about, which was not religion but the spiritual side of themselves? Was I to ignore the fountain of joy in Milka's eyes whenever she spoke of God? Was I to change the subject from divinity when an intangible light, a deep sense of peace, seemed to embrace Gloria as I read the words of mystic Thomas Merton aloud?

Cynthia had her eyes on me that day when I quoted from Merton's *Seeds of Contemplation*, and I could sense her skepticism: "It is God Who breathes on me with light winds off the river and in the breezes out of the wood." Cynthia comes into the living room, pauses in the corner and listens. "His love spreads the shade of the sycamore over my head and sends the water-boy . . ." Cynthia walks through the living room and stops at the entrance to the hall as I continue reading "along the edge of the wheat field with a bucket from the spring, while the laborers are resting and the mules stand under the tree." [1]

Finished with the reading, I ask my group of elders: "When do we experience awe, connect ourselves to the wonder and mystery of creation?"

Cambria says, "It happened yesterday. We were in the dining room at dinner. I was admiring the new tablecloths, place mats, the vases with our garden flowers, and suddenly I felt a presence; it just came. It's like when I'm watering the flowers outside; it's awesome to see them grow. Who else could make all this growth happen? It gives me an appreciation of majesty, beauty, of who the Creator is."

Cynthia returns to the living room, rustles the newspapers on the coffee table, takes some pages, and goes back into the kitchen. Dawn says: "I remember when I was in Italy. I was about nine years old, and I'll never forget looking at the Stations of the Cross. When I saw Jesus carrying the cross, I cried."

All heads turn. Cynthia is approaching our circle, hands mail to Avena, Dawn, and Cambria. After she leaves, Dawn goes on. "I thought I saw God's lips move. He was speaking to me." She stops, her eyes misty with nostalgia. "I loved going there. After everyone went home from the sermon, I wanted to stay with God's love so I stayed in the church, slept in the pew." Dawn's tears touch us. Although she has Alzheimer's disease, for this moment it doesn't exist; Dawn is lucid, clear.

"Dawn, what a beautiful memory," Catherine says.

A loud thump causes heads to turn toward the bookcase. Cynthia scoops up some books that have fallen off the shelf. Restoring them to their places, she kneels to snip frayed carpet with her scissors. Is she doing this to hear more of our conversation? What am I to do about her nervousness over this spiritual discussion? Before I can decide, Gloria says:

"When I was in the hospital trying to walk after a fall, I experienced intense joy." Gloria's smile is almost rapturous. "It was practically impossible to walk, yet I was walking. I knew I couldn't do this alone; Jesus was helping me."

"The most awesome moment of my life," Janeen says, "was when I was eighteen and my brother was born. He was soft and smooth. The nurse put him on a towel roughly, and I thought he shouldn't be handled that way. I saw those small hands and legs playing against my mother's thigh. I couldn't believe this was a real person. All day I kept going back to the crib; it was such a wonder, like heaven on earth."

"Gosh, I wish she wouldn't keep going back and forth, it's driving me crazy," Catherine interrupts Janeen's story as Cynthia passes through the room for the tenth time. Like at a tennis match, heads turn back and forth. Her pacing has gone on for nearly twenty minutes.

"Yeah, it makes me nervous, too," Avena says.

"The baby comes out perfect, and there's a big overflow of love you didn't know you possessed," Janeen continues, oblivious to Cynthia's disturbance. "In moments like this, you know God has touched you. No matter how much Sunday school I had, it was the first time I ever felt God."

From my reading of Merton has come a sharing of spiritual roots. Contemplative moments now come alive in which a timeless sense of beauty and oneness brought splendor into these lives. Recalling such moments reveals important clues about these elders' spiritual connectedness. As caregivers, hearing about these important moments in our elders' lives can provide us with hints about how to reach them when they're going through difficulties. Redirecting fear, anxiety, and pain by focusing elders on spiritual moments, past or present, may aid mental, emotional, and spiritual healing.

As I get up to leave, I realize that to deny elders the natural outlet of spiritual dialogue is to impose a kind of spiritual repression. As it now stands, in facilities such as this, if some elders want more opportunities to talk about spiritual subjects, the staff may remind them that a minister already provides Sunday services. If elders want to ask for more spiritual involvement, they might feel too vulnerable to do so, fearing the risk of being thrown out of the only home they have. What choice is left but to keep quiet and endure?

Offering Elders a Spiritual Outlet

Walking out of Valley View to my car, I wonder why Cynthia forbids elders to talk about God. Is she afraid of religious arguments? Of losing her license if it looks like religion is being taught or religious groups are trying to proselytize? Of relatives who might object to spiritual dialogue, remove their elder from the home and thereby cause the facility to lose income?

Healing Companions have an opportunity to help reverse these fears and to become part of an elder's spiritual care. Being aware that there are differences between religion and spirituality, we can offer our elders a spiritual outlet without imposing any particular religious belief.

In his book *From Age-ing to Sage-ing*, Rabbi Zalman Schachter-Shalomi introduced the concept of spiritual eldering, which is respectful of the differences between believers who practice a specific religious approach and those who don't.

Spiritual eldering encourages an "inner search for God, a self-directed flowering of the spirit that unites all people in a common quest, no matter what their affiliation." [2]

When seen as a common quest, this inclusive perspective provides elders with an opportunity to enjoy sharing an inner search with each other. Listening to others talk about their enlightened spiritual experiences may inspire elders to seek peace, joy, a deeper relationship with God; or, for agnostics, a connection with the unknown or infinite. Even though some elders prefer keeping their spiritual life private and do not want to share it, others do and can, while still retaining a commitment to their own religious or nonreligious views. Coercion into a specific religion or religious organization that has a particular set of prayers, rituals, and doctrines is not the goal; spiritual transformation is.

What does spiritual transformation mean in an elder's life? It can mean coming to terms with life's changes; removing hindrances to peace, contentment, and joy; expanding their hearts to care about the destiny of the earth, our society, and each other.

While religion can provide a dependable framework, a serene and joyous atmosphere for expressing devotion, seeking comfort, and singing praise, spirituality includes an internal experience of God's presence, felt as an opening of the heart, a sudden outpouring of love and compassion for everyone, even for those who have caused us great suffering. God's presence may become a mantle of peace overshadowing turmoil in the body, mind, and emotions.

For Healing Companions, it is essential to enter into such an inner relationship with God by whatever pathway is appropriate to each of us. As seekers, we learn from sermons, yet we desire more. We need, as Rabbi Zalman Schachter-Shalomi writes, more than intellectual "secondhand descriptions of spiritual revelations"; we need our own "direct inner experience." [3]

Healing Companions can benefit from Rabbi Zalman's concept of spiritual eldering. He counsels that it is vital for elders to leave a legacy for future generations, to harvest the wisdom gained from years of living, to repair the past, and to come to terms with their mortality. These spiritual pathways also add meaning to the lives of confined elders for whom spiritual exploration has benefits: renewing spiritual roots, finding guidance to cope with unwanted changes in lifestyle and health, seeking peace on the journey toward death.

As we learn more about spirituality, Healing Companions can invite elders to experience a spiritual life within health care settings on a daily basis. The physical and emotional challenges elders face are far greater than in youth. Deepening a spiritual dimension is essential for meeting the rigors of living and dying in the last cycle of life.

Spiritual Dialogues

Deciding to ask elders how they perceive spirituality, I invite a few to a Seekers' Circle at Mountain Pines nursing home. "Is there more to us than a body, mind, and emotions?" I ask. In spite of mental impairment, disorientation, emotional instability, their answers are enlightening. Many health care professionals, as well as well-meaning relatives, might not expect such responses:

"We have an alter ego, an inner self, an intuition—an entity not visible but highly felt."

"It's the spirit within us, the amazing crown of life."

"It's an all-seeing eye who watches over us."

"It's the you in you." This last response from Veronica, whose ideas often trail away from the topic at hand, expresses a profound reality in spite of her moments of mental confusion.

Such spiritual dialogues pave the way for spiritual practices, which can go beyond words to an experience of supreme peace. One day I experience the benefits of these dialogues with my client, Lorena. Her daughter, Martha, a clinical psychologist, is unaware of her mother's need for spiritual nourishment. Although I haven't seen Lorena in over a year, and Martha has emphatically assured me that Lorena won't know me, as soon as I walk into Sea View Terrace nursing home, Lorena not only recognizes me, she remembers my having played a musical instrument and asks me if I have brought it. Her enthusiastic, lucid response dramatically contradicts her daughter's assessment. Martha had said that Lorena had been "sliding downhill, no longer knows her grandchildren, doesn't remember going out for dinner last week, is generally noncommunicative."

Near the end of life, Lorena's eyes are lively, her beauty radiant. A coral necklace frames her long neck. White lace sleeves taper at her wrists, which are resting on the edge of her wheelchair; her long, elegant fingers are placed quietly on her lap. Her features, rather than becoming diminished with age, are gently sculpted, regal; furrows on her forehead, like rolling hills, are as graceful as her life has been.

"I can't believe it's you!" she exclaims.

Even though she is quite frail, I decide to talk to her with the same depth we used to have when we went into the essence of things. I ask: "Are you afraid of the unknown?"

"Not at all; I've never tried to fight fate. I love life just as it is." She smiles.

Facing a large bay window overlooking a glimpse of the

sea, we gaze at an expanse of blue sky.

"This vast blue . . ." I pause. "The sky seems to have no beginning, no end."   Knowing Lorena is drawn to eastern spirituality, I add: "This vastness reminds me of the teachings of Sogyal Rinpoche who likens our mind to the sky. What does it mean if our mind has no beginning and no end, like the sky?" [4]

"When we die, we don't cease—our spirit lives on."

"Do you feel you can connect to infinite space . . . no beginning, no end?"

"Sometimes. By contemplating 'my spirit has no beginning, no end,' it makes me think . . . what is the answer to life?" Her eyes gaze intently inward, as if looking into a deep, clear pond.

"Lorena, can an older person actually contemplate?"

"I do. I meditate, sit still, think. It's like a prayer. I may not see or hear as well, but the essential spirit goes on. I'm happy."

More fragile than a year ago, Lorena's normal brain functioning has slowed down. Yet our dialogue is no different. I simply shorten my sentences so that she can absorb my questions with greater ease.

"Do you experience a kind of love which has no beginning, no end?" I ask.

"I can't make it happen. Meditation allows me to let love come in the quiet of spirit. To have peace and the fullness of love, you have to stop thinking and allow yourself to be."

Before entering Lorena's room, Lorena's daughter had informed me that her mother was now incapable of understanding or receiving anything and that there would be no further purpose for my visits.

Does Lorena know we will not see each other again? As we embrace, she looks deep into my eyes. "Seeing you today," she says, "is just like I saw you yesterday. There's no separation. Such relationships are rare. Throughout my life, I haven't had many like it."

Neither had I.

Close spiritual relationships, especially near death, are a treasure. Whether ill or well, old or young, Healing Companions may provide spiritual closeness for those who desire it. Because an elder experiences dramatic changes in memory, communication, or comprehension, families and health care professionals should not assume that elders no longer want or need a meaningful spiritual connection. Sometimes they need it even more.

The value of spirituality cannot be underestimated. In an interview with spiritual director Valerie Stevens, she speaks of it as "an inner conviction, a knowing there is more to life than what is visual and measurable, something beyond our physical and emotional nature. This knowing calls us to seek a Higher Power as the only thing that can bring joy and peace in the midst of trauma.

"St. Augustine called this the God-shaped vacuum within each of us that only God can fill. Though many of us thirst for more than what is here in physical life, we don't have to preach our own beliefs to others. What we need to do is address the hungering of the spirit."

Many may not know they hunger for spirit. For some, it may be easier to deny emptiness, live without passion, become addicted to television, stay asleep in a chair; in short, live a shallow life. Rabbi Shlomo Carlebach says of this chosen lifestyle that the greatest sin in the world today is to be shallow.

But although outwardly such elders may appear to be indifferent to spiritual concerns, not all of them are. Healing Companions need to be careful about judging elders who do not respond to spiritual dialogues. The use of medications, the slowing down of vital energy, organic brain syndrome—and in some facilities, limited provision of social and educational activities, and hours of sitting in front of TV—any of these dull an elder's zest for life.

Those elders who are not dulled and have lived, or now live, contented lives, sense there is something more than a day-to-day existence. An inspired Healing Companion can awaken a thirst, celebrate a hunger for becoming a seeker. But dare he or she try it?

I'm Still Seeking

I felt the need to discover the truth. Had I been asking elders to enter into spiritual discussions to appease my own hunger? Was I trying to influence them inappropriately, thinking I had discovered spiritual answers and practices through my own spiritual commitments without recognizing that many elders could teach me more than I could teach them?

With these questions in mind, I sheepishly enter the recreation room at Mountain Pines nursing home. Rosh Hashanah, the Jewish New Year, has just ended. Influenced by the experience I had with Rabbi Don Singer in Malibu, I ask these elders if they would think I was trying to convince or convert them into the Jewish religion if I shared the inspiration of Rosh Hashanah. Various members replied:

"You always give us the freedom to accept or reject; you never force anything on us."

"By no means do I think you are handing me a religion; I believe in your sincerity."

"Your religious feeling is flooded with life; it's never static. Yet you don't share it in hopes of making me join your way; you encourage me in mine."

"If I think I know my God, I stop searching. But I'm not this conceited. I'm still seeking, and our discussions help."

"When we have a Source of help, strength, and faith which gives us happiness, we don't need a religion, though it may be profoundly meaningful. Once, in a hospital, a nun told me to go for help to the chapel on the fourth floor. I thought to myself that I didn't have to go to a building or a floor to say 'God help me.' Every path leads to God; every hurt, every misunderstanding goes to his feet; all we have to do is leave it there. If we have the peace that passes understanding, we don't need a fourth floor."

The group's initial comments inspire me to continue our dialogue. Grateful to them for their encouragement, I begin the session.

Vera, in her usual posture of boredom, sits with elbow braced on the arm of her wheelchair, cheek pressed against her hand. Head slumped, her eyes stare at the floor. Heather gazes out of the window at nothing; her expression, glum. Rebecca, the only Jewish elder, fidgets with her skirt, twists the fabric with her fingers; meanwhile, Dorothy hums absentmindedly.

"What would it be like to fall in love every day?" I ask. All eyes are suddenly riveted on me. "How would you feel if every day you were bursting with joy and couldn't wait to see your Beloved?" My question is inspired from the Hebrew words *Ani Le-dodi Ve dodi Li* ("I am my Beloved's, and my Beloved is Mine").[5] Realizing this devotional outpouring depicts the spirit of Rosh Hashanah and that some spiritual elders are not devotional, I begin to feel sorry I asked.

But in a flash, Vera looks up, eyes suddenly eager, and leans forward in anticipation of what comes next. Rebecca's eyes dance with delight; a young child's enthusiasm lives in her. She can hardly wait for something miraculous to happen. Heather, gripped by the question, looks at me intensely; her eyes no longer stare at nothing.

"Could there come a time when you might fall in love with the One that created everything? Do you think your emotions can go beyond the personal love you have for a husband to that of a love for the One who causes the sun to shine and night to follow day?"

This is risky; it is not my intention to get them to believe in a deity, but to spark what they do believe and allow them to express it. The word "One" implies there is a God. Rebecca does not believe in God as an entity. Should I worry about offending her? Her smile tells me otherwise; I can trust her ability to accept, reject, or spontaneously find her own way to express love.

Disagreements may occur when speaking about spiritual life. A Healing Companion accepts disagreement as a natural part of being human. Differences between people are normal. Shielding elders from discussing their differences on the assumption that they are too fragile to handle conflict is a false premise. The value and challenge of dialoguing about spirituality is to inspire peace between people who express their differences. We do this by developing tolerance, hearing each other's views, cultivating the self-discipline to stay neutral and avoid the urge to convince someone that only we have the best approach.

Still, I am concerned that I may have overstepped my boundaries. Dorothy suddenly raises her hands to the sky. Glowing, she looks upward as if in prayer: "Why, isn't it wonderful to love God!" As usual, she is enraptured by spiritual themes. As a Christian, will Dorothy be able to relate to the Jewish New Year described by the Jews as the days of awe? Awe is a good theme and a universal experience. Can awe be re-ignited today in all of us?

"What if you spent every day in the arms of your Beloved, who called you, sang to you, carried you on his wings of love? What if this Beloved never left you day or night?" In a subtle way, I am unintentionally addressing Heather's unhealed grief over the loss of her husband eight years ago, a grief too often personified in a glum stare. Is it time for her to move on?

The atmosphere in the room is suddenly charged. Heather blurts out: "That might be all right for you, but it doesn't work for me. My love is in the grave. He's not coming back, that's all I know. I think of him every day; I'm so lonely."

Humbled, I realize I have done Heather a disservice. A Healing Companion cannot try to save or preach, become rescuer or Messiah. Unconsciously I have watched Heather's grief with a biased view based on books I have read which imply that healthy grieving should not last past a few years. Have I forgotten the ten-year grieving process I experienced over the death of my father?

To insist that Heather, a very practical, earthy woman, take on a relationship with a Beloved she can't see is to create a pseudo-spirituality, a path not her own. If I create a spiritual bypass by denying her feelings of grief over her husband, I will be disrespectful of her choice to grieve as long as she needs to. My view of spirituality is becoming too narrow. I forget the spiritual teachings I studied in India: wife is God, husband is God; we love and serve God in each other. It's a tough spiritual discipline, one that Heather has lived by devoting fifty years to her husband. Her remembrance of their love is a gift.

"Suppose you could look at your daughter," I go on, "your husband," I look over at Heather, "your best friend, as if you had never seen them before, as if you were seeing them for the first time. Can you imagine what it would be like?"

"Of course, pure joy, a miracle," Rebecca says, her eyes

wide, a playful light dancing in them. "We should do that every day about everything; a flower, a rainstorm, a rainbow."

"Well, that's nice for all of you, but I want my husband back," Heather says. With sudden mischief in her eyes, she tells us: "He never wanted me out of his sight." She smiles. "I had all that once . . ." her tone drops, "but no more." Realizing there is a difference between healthy remembrance of love and living in the gloom of depression, I wonder what would release Heather from despair.

"Stop thinking of him, it won't do you any good." Vera's tough tone shocks me but doesn't faze Heather, who remains tall and staunch in her chair. "I never think of the past," Vera goes on. "I make myself forget, never look back."

Watching this interaction between Heather and Vera, I realize their physical frailty does not make them weak in their convictions. Do caregivers sometimes assume that confined elders are delicate, need coddling, require distraction from the tough stuff of life?

Returning to focus on the Jewish New Year, I begin: "Rosh Hashanah is not only a time of awe, it's a time to do *Teshuvah*, to regret the mistakes of the past, to examine our actions, to mend our ways, and with a broken and contrite heart,[6] return to our Creator. Return and be healed. We do as it is written in Agnon's book, *Days of Awe*: "Return unto Me, and I will return unto you."[7] One of the ways we return, Agnon explains, is to station an officer at the gates of our senses.[8] What does it mean, the gates of our senses? Why is an officer stationed there?" I ask.

"I don't want any gate on my senses, particularly when I want to touch some nice young man!" Heather's face breaks out in a broad smile.

"I do. I want a gate over my mouth when I talk too much!"

Rebecca laughs.

I look over at Vera; it might do her good to have an officer at the gate of her mouth. She can be cruel; criticizing comes easy to her.

"Sometimes we're impulsive, say something before we think," I say, glancing at her. "We hurt people. Do you think we need to have control over the door of our lips?"

Vera vigorously agrees. Will Dorothy realize by listening to these words that her violent stories, often repeated and embellished in our meetings, do violence to herself and those around her?

"When we have control over what we hear, when we station an officer near our ears, we may hear what someone is really saying, beyond their words, even beyond the story they tell."

"Well, I'll tell you my story, and it's true. I want my husband and if I can't have him, I don't care about anything," Heather says.

"One time I knew a heavyweight champion who didn't have control over *his* lips!" Vera's cheeks flush as she recalls the young man. "He came up to me in the park and tried to kiss me. I swung hard and my fist knocked him out!" Vera laughs, and everyone laughs with her. Looking at Vera's powerful right arm, her leg braced with a steel support, I wouldn't want to be in her way then, or now.

Coming to the end of our discussion of Rosh Hashanah, I search for a common thread to bring these elders into the ending ritual. Since most of them are not Jewish, what will make this experience their own?

"When the Jewish women go outside to the lake or to the sea, they place bread crumbs in the folds of their skirts, and toss them into the wind and the waters. Why do you think they throw the crumbs into the sea?" I ask.

"They're throwing away their sadness," Rebecca says, joy spreading into her smiling eyes. Rebecca is the one Jew among them. I can see her dancing with twelve brothers and sisters the way her mother taught them to do; it was her mother's way of instilling joy as the foundation of life. In spite of their precarious situation as Jews in Poland, and the early death of her father, Rebecca carries her mother's joy-filled legacy into her ninetieth year, and transmits it to us, too.

"Those women are praising Jehovah," Vera says, a quiet joy radiating from her face.

"They're loving God with all their heart, all their soul, all their might, and he is protecting them from a mean father like mine," Dorothy says. Touched, Rebecca reaches over to pat Dorothy's hand.

Looking at each of them, I ask: "What do you think we need to cast into the sea?"

"We need to cast away gossip." Does Rebecca find joy in this discussion because, as a Jew, she relates to spiritual truths she heard as a child?

"Cast away fear, anger," Vera says.

"I'm not going to cast away the past," Heather says. "I'm always going to look back. I treasure every memory." Heather looks at Vera defiantly; Vera simply shakes her head in friendly disagreement.

Sharing my Rosh Hashanah experience unites us, opens a door to bonding between elders of different faiths. It no longer matters that only one of these women is Jewish.

"Last week I was on the beach for a ritual with the rabbi at the conclusion of Rosh Hashanah," I say. "He invited the entire congregation to walk to the ocean. As we stood facing the sea, white foam sprayed salty mist into the windy afternoon and bright sun stars danced on the waves. Splashing against the shore, the ocean sang the awesome symphony of creation. As each of us was given breadcrumbs, the rabbi began to speak. Awe, the predominant theme of Rosh Hashanah, came alive in that moment. In words like these, he said:

"Now we come to face the depths of the ocean, the vastness of the sky. Vast and deep, sky and sea—we face ourselves, for we too are vast and deep. Going off to be alone, each of us will cast these bread crumbs, these our sins, into the sea."

Pausing, I notice the group of elders is listening in rapt attention. I continue, "I went off alone, thought of what I needed to cast away, said a prayer, and watched the bread crumbs fly into the wind, into the lapping waters." Applause breaks out. Rebecca turns to Vera, joyfully grasps her hand. The dull, flat stares that greeted me when I arrived have now become animated faces. Everyone is smiling.

Creating a Spiritual Environment for Caregivers

At Sun Valley nursing home, the joy of spirituality is encouraged in the nursing staff. Administrative reticence about allowing spirituality is absent. Director of Nurses Carole Sale deeply honors spiritual life within herself, her staff, and the residents. Her spirituality is the core through which she directs fifty-two staff and sixty-six residents. When troubled by difficult situations, she retires to her office where she keeps a prayer candle, chimes, a stone, a praying angel. In this spiritual atmosphere, she sits quietly and lets God take over in ways she cannot.

When training her aides, Carole inspires them to realize that they have been chosen for a purpose. Their job is not simply to make beds, adjust a bedpan, and brush teeth, but to create an environment that helps elders to heal. This healing cannot take place, Carole tells me, unless "we center ourselves with love, compassion, and tolerance." In hiring an aide, Carole looks into each person's heart and asks, "Is it loving? I can teach them skills, but I can't teach them how to have a caring heart."

Carole instructs her aides: "Each of us is used by God, a higher source, or whatever spiritual tradition you believe in, and it is this source or energy which comes through us and heals." A loving touch is crucial, and Carole reminds her staff that nurses have been involved with laying on of hands for years. In fact, in earlier times, sleeping pills were rarely given. Residents received a nightly massage for up to fifteen minutes to aid relaxation and sleep. "Now," Carole says, "due to time constraints, we give pills."

At St. Andrew's, a Catholic nursing home, spirituality goes a step further. Prayer is offered three times a day and is the central foundation for eldercare. Nourishment of spirit is as important as nourishment of body. Fountains and flowers create small, private areas for solitude and contemplation. Residents who require less care are invited to attend daylong silent retreats held in the chapel.

Unfortunately, spiritual care does not exist at Valley View residential home. A few weeks after we had endured Cynthia's pacing and carried on with our spiritual dialogue, I arrive to learn that Dawn had died that night. Cynthia does not approve of spontaneous prayer among residents, with or without me. She is the administrator, so what am I to do? As soon as I sit down, Catherine begins talking about Dawn's death, the arrival of the paramedics, morning tears, missing Dawn's jokes, and her small acts of kindness.

The others speak about Dawn, too, reviewing over and over all that transpired last night. Forty minutes pass. Realizing it is time to add another dimension to this discussion, the challenge for me is how to invite God's presence into a group of Christian women without using the word "God." Simple prayer is what I want to do, but it is the one thing I can't do.

Quietly, I begin speaking to Dawn aloud: "Dawn, we miss you. It hurts that you are not with us. But you gave us so much, and now when we talk to you, we feel your presence. The memory of who you are will never leave us. We are richer because we have known you. We are richer by gathering courage to let you go. We ask you to help us do this. We bless you to be unafraid in your new place of being. And we rejoice with you that you have gone where you wanted to go—home."

Although I do not use the word "God," the women recognize my words are praying words. Everyone in the group believes in God; why can't we pray openly? Is prayer only legitimate when a priest or minister is present? Do we need a formal religious structure in order to express what is in our hearts, our sorrow and our joy?

Elders are not vulnerable children whose minds are permeable, who need protection from religious influences. Years of living give elders the capacity to accept, reject, or seek God. At the end of life, wholeness depends upon inclusion of whatever source of comfort and consolation elders seek.

A group of elders from different backgrounds has an opportunity to discover that wholeness together. They can join hands in a unity of love, a desire for peace, a spontaneous joy in expressing their inner feelings toward God. United in spirit, they can transcend differences and experience a common bond greater than the individual beliefs they profess.

When those entrusted with providing eldercare come to realize that spirituality is the light that animates our joy, our sense of wonder, and the love we feel for others, there will be no reason to fear it. The unseen life that balances the rhythms of the tides, sun, moon, and stars is the same divine spark given to each of us uniquely. This spark ignites into a bright flame whenever we see a waterfall and feel joy; when we have a flash of illumination while studying science or composing music; when we experience moments of unbounded love. This spiritual essence is our wholeness, our birthright. Why should we fear it?

⚘ Steps for Healing ⚘

Insights that can help heal

◆   A spiritual dimension exists in every person.

◆   Spiritual care is the encouraging of an interior life
     that awakens peace, joy, and inner healing.

◆   When we connect to the awesome mystery of creation,
     we touch the infinite.

◆   Cultivating awe rekindles life-giving energy in spite
     of physical decline.

◆   Focusing on spiritual moments, past or present, redirects
     painful emotions and enhances healing as well as
     the acceptance of life as it is.

Helping yourself heal

1. Take some time to experience the wonder and mystery of creation. Become open to feelings of awe and wonderment when you see, touch, taste, or hear something beautiful.

2. It is important to develop your own spiritual life, to find a spiritual framework in which to appreciate your elder's spiritual journey. Find a quiet time to expand your awareness beyond your physical reality. Reflect on humanity's magnificent ability to create. Take a walk in nature. Are you able to dwell on, or feel part of, a larger reality? Do you sense there is more to you than a body, mind, and emotions?

3. As your elder moves toward a nonphysical reality, you can relate to his or her journey by understanding yourself. Reflect on this question: What is your relationship to a nonphysical reality?

Helping your elder heal

1. Give elders permission to speak about their spirituality and encourage them in their spiritual search. Many elders will help you in yours. They are eager to talk about spiritual issues. Allow their questions and feelings to surface. Although it is fine to share your own beliefs, be careful not to proselytize.

2. Help elders share in a spiritual dialogue by initiating discussions and giving them a focus. Read aloud from the world's scriptures, spiritual stories, and poetry. Guide elders into talking about their spiritual background and their beliefs in an afterlife.

3. You can mediate spiritual discussions with elders of diverse beliefs by setting guidelines. Let elders know that their spiritual differences will be honored and that by sharing them, everyone benefits. While each person stays rooted in his or her own beliefs, everyone learns from and respects the beliefs of others. This process becomes a mirror for creating a peaceful world. In this way, elders can become peacemakers.

For your inspiration

I am part of all creation——the infinite sky, the womb of the earth, the rays of the sun. The elders whom I care for may seem diminished by age; lost in pain, sorrow, or forgetfulness. Yet, they too contain this infinite dimension. In this, we are one.

FIFTEEN

Exercising Our Spirit

And God is always there, if you feel wounded.
He kneels over this earth like a divine medic,
and His love thaws the holy in us.
—St. Teresa of Avila

Our internal flame keeps us
from falling, keeps us from
going "bump" in the night.
—Catherine, age ninety

SOME ELDERS NEVER stop worrying about money. As a result, their internal flame may be so dim that going "bump in the night"—feeling anxious and fearful—is a regular occurrence. Catherine's Irish humor sums up the folly of financial bondage: "One night on his way home, an old Irishman was held up. The robber said: 'Your money or your life.' The Irishman replied: 'Take me life. I'm saving me money for me old age!' "

Rabbi Zalman Schachter-Shalomi writes about our culture's attachment to wealth, success, and productivity, and about psychologist Carl Jung's view that middle-aged people experience depression and emptiness because they have not developed an inner life.[1]

Gerald is an example of this. "Have I got any Allied stock

left?" For years he asks this question while living in a nursing home. His anxiety may be a symptom of dementia; it may also be a lifetime anxiety over money. His need to save and own, his emphasis on financial gain at the end of life, is a cry of suffering.

Fear of loss is another familiar refrain in health care settings. "Someone stole my shoes!" "Who took my blanket?" "You can't keep anything around here without it being taken!" Whether these losses are real or imagined, the desperate need to cling to possessions is prevalent in some elders who depend on what they own to fuel their happiness. Acquiring, achieving, and identifying with their material possessions may have been a way of life in former years. Or clinging to what they own may now be a reaction to the fear of death. The frustration over attachment to money and possessions—and the frantic fear of losing them, of losing life itself—becomes a spiritual crisis.

Sharing Spiritual Wisdom

When Healing Companions make the effort to share wisdom teachings from various cultures, it can bring meaning and inspiration into elders' lives, and help them accept their losses. For example, Jon Kabat-Zinn, who writes from a Buddhist perspective, shares this wisdom teaching: "When we can be centered in ourselves . . . not having to look elsewhere for something to fill us up or make us happy, we can be at home wherever we find ourselves, at peace with things as they are."[2]

The ideas of Father John Powell, a former Catholic monk, remind us that as human beings our natural tendency is to seek permanence: "A great deal of suffering is the awareness that everything is passing. Even my own life is not mine; I can't hold it. It's like trying to hold water cupped in your hands; the water leaks out all over the place." ³ He concludes that life, death, and suffering are not problems to be solved. Life is a mystery; all religions, philosophies, and cultures have struggled in vain to understand what cannot be grasped.

The Jewish tradition also offers wisdom regarding how to ease the agony of loss and the accompanying lack of self-esteem that elders face. It teaches that in each pocket the Jew has a saying: in one, "I am dust"; in the other, "the world was created for me." Compared to the immensity of the cosmos and the splendor of the Master of the Universe, I am nothing. My belongings, my demands, my complaints are not important. On the other hand, I am so important that the world was created expressly for me, a human being, precious in the sight of God. God created me to enjoy life and to be a blessing of joy in this world—and, because I am alive, I celebrate this privilege.

Francina was in no mood for celebrating the day I found her waiting for me. She did not experience herself or her life as a special gift of creation. What could be special about giving up her house and spending her remaining years in a nursing home? She never tires of telling us about her "boredom," a central theme which she repeats daily. I am reminded of Rabbi Samuel Seicol's view of boredom. "Boredom is a spiritual crisis, the loss of the ability to create value, purpose, and meaning," he said at a conference of the American Society on Aging.⁴ Reflecting on this, I wonder how boredom and loss can be healed.

Boredom comes from doing nothing and is one of the major killers of the human spirit. Our culture prizes achievement. What purpose will Francina's life have now that she is no longer able to do anything? In the last years of life, instead of *doing* something, it is time to *be* something. But how do we find joy in simply *being*? Nature is one spiritual pathway that can bring beauty back into the soul when all seems lost.

As I begin my group today, only Francina and Veronica are present. I have no idea how to address Francina's boredom and underlying depression. Looking away from her drawn face, her gray-blue eyes dulled with inertia, I gaze out the window where blue jays perch on the tulip trees. Noticing small green leaves beginning to grow, I allow nature to speak to me and muse aloud: "Sometimes our lives are like the seasons; we feel dry and dead like dying autumn leaves. But if we look out this window, green leaves are awakening to the sunshine, the wind, and the air pungent after the last rains." Francina turns her gaze to the window, her eyes suddenly alive. Seeing beyond herself, she peers with clear absorption at the garden, as if delving into nature's mystery.

"Like the seasons, part of ourselves dies when our old way of life dies," I continue, "and we have to wait until new life buds *within* us. We need to know there is something new ahead, something to look forward to. Like the stark, bare tree that waits for the season to turn, we too must wait until a new spring arrives."

Francina smiles, her eyes now reflecting an inner peace. Outside, a breeze stirs the budding leaves. I go on. "The wind blows away the curtain from our eyes, and our eyes become new. Life teems out the window—butterflies and daffodils. We ask ourselves: 'Where is life teeming inside of me?' I need to open the door on the inside for life to come in." Francina reaches over, rubs my hand affectionately.

"If I keep repeating: 'I'm bored, nothing is good, I want to die,' I live inside a closed door. But if I open the door, sunlight enters. I hear the symphony of birds; I receive the beauty of Creation."

Francina's face shines, her depression lifts. It seems as if our discussion has made her feel more in tune with the rhythms of nature.

But sometimes nature's lessons are not enough to overcome life's sufferings. I tell the elders gathered in my group that nature can sometimes be the cause of unbearable pain. I relate to them the experience of Joe Portale, who was on a mission to the outback in West Africa. Driving a group of young people and nurses across the Sahara, his VW van bounced over rugged roads, and the group struggled to endure the hot, thick dust.

"Nature is not always benevolent," I say. "The smothering dust forced Joe and the group to wear thick bandannas around their mouths.

"They stopped for lunch under a baobab tree. It was too hot, and very still. Suddenly a shrill scream came from behind the tree. Joe went to investigate. Killer bees angrily swarmed around everyone. All of Joe's exposed skin was attacked. Afraid to open his eyes, the wild buzzing made it impossible to see. Kids screamed, ran, retched. One pretty young girl lay on the ground, stung by hordes of ferocious bees.

"Joe dropped to his knees, tried to pray. At first, no words came. Suddenly he found himself thanking God for his creation, even for the bees. When he opened his eyes, the swarm had thinned. A nurse dashed to the van for medicine, braved the wild bees, ran back to the girl on the ground, who it seemed might not make it.

"Joe continued thanking God for life, for all of his creatures. When he finished praying, the helpless girl was lifted into the van. They took off to a missionary infirmary two hours away. Within an hour, the girl awakened. She recalled Joe praying in the midst of the swarm and said: 'a cool breeze swept over me and I was able to breathe again.' [5]

"Those killer bees challenged the highest human potential:

to tap into an inner strength which rises above disaster," I conclude. "Joe could have focused his prayer solely on his panic, begged God for help. But he went a step further. He loved God so much he thanked him in the midst of dire calamity. How was he able to do this?"

Veronica looks at me expectantly. "He trusted God," she answers.

"Do you think your trust in God is firm enough to immediately praise him if you toppled out of your wheelchair right now and landed on the floor?"

Francina laughs. "I don't think I'd immediately praise him. I'd thank him when I got healed, but I'd be too miserable while I was laying there."

"Most of us are like that. I bet Joe had formed a long habit of prayer, had spent a lot of time keeping his mind and heart on God. When an emergency came, he automatically returned to this habit, which miraculously released the intensity of the horror he faced."

Francina beams. "My mother thought about God all the time. She made a deal with my brother. She only phoned him in an emergency. One day she called his office. 'Hurry home, there's a miracle in the backyard.' My brother arrived. 'Look, it's hardly raining over there in the neighbor's yard.' My mother was excited. 'See, the Lord is only raining in my backyard. It's not raining anywhere else!' Water was pouring down. My brother looked up at the sky. The cooler on top of the house was spraying water all over the yard."

Veronica laughs. "That's what happens when you think of God all the time—your mother was so charmed by life that she saw miracles when there weren't any."

"How do we think about God all the time?" I ask.

"We have to train our minds," Veronica says.

"How do we do this?" I ask.

"Get yourself off your mind," Francina exclaims. "Think of someone else, someone you love." Francina certainly wasn't thinking of love when she threw water in Clela's face in the middle of the night, which I'm sure she's forgotten.

"We can find ways to free our minds from self-centered, negative thoughts by deciding not to allow negativity to run our lives," I say. "We can deliberately focus on what's good in the present moment. If we activate our will, we can move our thoughts away from fear and celebrate the wonderful moment we have right now. Then we aren't so overwhelmed. If we did this for even five minutes a day, we would benefit."

"I'm definitely going to try," says Francina. I am surprised by Francina's sudden resolve, even if it proves to be only momentary. Francina has been inspired to exercise her will over bouts of crying and depression. If she shifts her attention, for even five minutes, away from her daughter's continual rejection of her, Francina will definitely benefit.

"Once we tell ourselves about something good in the here and now, we banish fear in that moment," I say. "A Hasidic rabbi, who was also a composer, focused his mind and liberated himself from fear and pain when he needed an operation and was unable to receive anesthesia. During the operation he composed a song and sang it. By focusing on singing, the rabbi's joyous song bypassed his pain entirely."

"Wow, that's something. I can't liberate myself from impatience, let alone pain," Francina says. "I think I'll find that rabbi and nudge him for a few singing lessons!"

"Singing spiritual songs is one way to train our minds," I say. "Spiritual music can turn our thoughts into joy, which lifts us beyond ourselves, surpasses our physical weakness.

"Another way to train our minds is to know with complete

serenity and certainty that God's love can heal. Virginia Harris, a Christian Science practitioner, told of that certainty at a conference sponsored by Harvard Medical School. A vibrant, truly inspired woman, Virginia shared her story of healing without medicine to a medical community open to exploring spirituality in health care."[6]

Although none of the elders are Christian Scientists, I have a feeling Virginia's story will inspire them as much as it did the Harvard researchers, doctors, and medical personnel who were at the conference.

"Twenty years ago, Virginia was in an accident on a freeway in Detroit, trapped alone in her car for almost forty-five minutes. Her first thought was 'Oh God help.' Immediately she sensed God's love and assurance. Instead of panic, she felt calm, and began praying for the other people in the accident.

"In the emergency room of the hospital, her internal injuries were so severe that there was little hope she would survive. Intuitively, however, she felt a 'deep sense of God's care.' She accepted God's love and decided to trust him to heal her. Instead of remaining in the hospital for medical treatment, she went home."

"I'd never do that, I'd be terrified," Francina says.

"So would I," I say. "Virginia made it clear that many people are better off staying in a hospital to receive medical care, and to pray there. But she had an intuition, a conviction of God's commitment, and a deep sense of peace. She was inspired to go home and rely totally on God for healing."

"What happened?" Francina asks, her boredom now gone.

"At home, she thought she was dying but felt God's loving presence. She expected to be healed. And within two weeks, she was—completely."

"I don't see how she took that chance." Francina says.

"The strength of her spiritual life helped. Would you like to know more?"

"Definitely." Francina is now fully present in a way I haven't seen for months.

"Every day she prayed to know that 'God was all powerful, and to feel God's love.' She experienced God's care for her as a loving Father and Mother. She prayed to understand who she was as a child of God, and what that told her about her 'spiritual nature.' And she reflected that her relationship as a child to a Mother/Father God must mean that this relationship is 'indestructible, invulnerable, unbreakable.' Even when she thought she was dying, she realized this relationship would uphold her."

Francina and Veronica listen avidly. Concerned that these elders might think I want to influence them to abandon medicine and rely totally on God for healing, I assure them this is not so. What I do hope to impress upon them is that Virginia's story inspired a particular medical community to acknowledge all forms of healing. We might learn from their open-mindedness.

"Are you inspired?" I ask them.

"Hurry up, we want more," Veronica laughs, gives my shoulder a playful nudge.

"Virginia talked about Mary Baker Eddy, the founder of Christian Science, who discovered that 'thought is the patient, thought needs to be healed, thought is the arena where change needs to occur in order for healing to take place.' "

"I agree. Our thoughts need to be positive. We are our thoughts," Francina says.

"Christian Science believes that fear impedes healing," I say.

"Fear impedes everything," Francina responds.

"They believe that fear is lessened or overcome when we become more spiritual. Virginia said that when God's love shines in our thoughts, we are filled with peace and wholeness. She feels that as God's presence fills our thoughts, there isn't room for thoughts of fear, disease, or despair. She concludes that it's the patient's thoughts that need to be changed.

"We don't have to be Christian Scientists to be open to the possibility that this view of spiritual life may be applied in many situations. Do you think it applies to boredom?" I ask Francina.

"I suppose so. If I thought more of God, less of me, maybe I wouldn't be bored so much."

"Maybe spiritual life helps loneliness," Veronica says. Veronica's intense and frequent bouts of loneliness worry me. "Sometimes I get so lonely, I feel I could die. It's like all of life has left me. Nobody knows how bad it is—and I'm not sure if they care."

"We care," Francina says, reaching over to hold Veronica's hand.

"When I'm lonely I feel unloved," Veronica says, then smiles at Francina, "but right now I feel better."

"Suppose you dwelt on God as Virginia did, only in your own way. Or you followed her guidelines, thought about who God is, who you are in relation to him.

"One day I felt so lonely I couldn't stand it," I say. "I grabbed my Bible, found a Psalm. The Psalm turned into a melody: 'I keep the Lord always before me, I shall not be moved / therefore my heart rejoices / and my soul is glad.'[7] I didn't feel glad, emotionally I felt terrible. But I trusted in these healing words. After an hour of singing the words, my suffering was released. Loneliness might remain or return, but I was no longer overcome. I had the loneliness, the loneliness didn't have me."

"I'd like to arouse myself to do something like that, but it's hard to get the energy to do it," says Veronica.

"That's why we need each other," I say.

Clint, sitting behind our group, suddenly wheels his chair closer.

"All this talk about God and healing, God is not here," he says. "I can't see him, I've never seen him—he hasn't helped *me* walk. Why should I believe in him?" At age fifty, Clint lives in a nursing home. His social life consists of elders three decades his senior. Emotional isolation is his lifestyle.

"Yes, he's here, he's everywhere, and within us," Francina says.

"Well, I don't see him, so why should I say I believe?" Clint asks.

"I've never been to the other side of the world," Veronica says, "but I believe it's there. I may not see the sun for days, but I know the sun is there. I believe in lots of things I don't see."

"Lucky for you," Clint says. I note a hint of a smile and a playful light flickering within large brown eyes. Clint is naturally mild-mannered. His outspoken disbelief is not born of anger. He simply says what he thinks.

"You don't have to believe in God," I say. "Jesus said: 'Ask and it shall be given to you; seek, and you shall find; knock, and it shall be opened to you.' He also gave this teaching: If a man goes to a friend's house at midnight and asks him to lend three loaves, even though his friend is in bed with his three children and doesn't want to get up, if the man persists, his friend will get out of bed and give him as much as he needs.[8]

"So if you persist in asking," I conclude, "Who is God, where is God, what is Truth, where will I find it . . . eventually, you will receive. You might be surprised at what you get. Asking is a gift, even if you believe nothing. The blessing is your honesty, stating your truth moment to moment. Your willingness to share your feelings in front of us when you know others have different views takes a lot of guts."

"Really?" Clint's smile overshadows his grotesque body, maimed by a spinal injury.

Being Present for Spiritual Questions

Our discussion reminds me of one I had last week when I went to see Linnea. Depressed for the past few years, she no longer believes in God. As a minister's daughter, she was exposed to spiritual teachings every day. But after the loss of her husband and home, Linnea spends her elder years asking: "Why me? What's the use of believing any more?"

This question faces many elders. But when they suffer, do we enquire about the status of their faith? Do we recognize that loneliness, depression, and fear may be manifestations of separation from God, or the Source of life, the spring of wellness from which happiness flows? Do we consider the loss of church life for those elders who may have gone to church every Sunday for over eighty years?

Healing Companions have the opportunity to be present for such questions, to believe for the elder that God, healing, and joy can return, perhaps in a new way. The way an elder learned to pray, worship, or meditate in the past may not work in the present. The feeling of emptiness may feel like God is absent. Loss of faith may require openness to a new approach to being with God, to believing that our spiritual self can reawaken. In this situation, a Healing Companion can help elders to ask: What new gift will God reveal?

The following week, before I begin my group, I go into Linnea's room. Smiling, she says: "Today I've been lying here and, outside the window, high above the clouds, I see the sky people. I see children playing, a beautiful rainbow over their heads. I see it so clearly. It helps me to believe again."

Squelching any thought I have of possible hallucination, I assume Linnea means the "sky people" have given her the gift of believing in God again. Instead of assuming what she means, I decide to ask. Her response humbles me.

"I told my daughter-in-law, Ginny: 'I don't believe in God anymore. I think I have cancer; they're just not telling me.' Ginny said, 'Mom, if you can't cope, turn your problems over to the Lord.' I told her, 'I can't, I don't have faith.' She said, 'Talk it over with the Lord, ask him for forgiveness, ask where you've gone wrong, ask how to regain your faith.' "

Linnea gazes out the window, her eyes looking into the vast blue above the lemon tree. "Ginny helped me. My faith is coming back. I can see him so plain out there with the sky people, walking along a fence covered with morning glories, wearing his long white robe. He stoops to pick up a flower . . ." Tears of awe moisten her cheeks. "Oh well, it's just my imagination," she says.

Although this may be her imagination, Linnea's images and conversations with God help her heal.

The Spirituality of Wellness

After seeing Linnea, I walk down the hall to my group that's gathered in the recreation room. I realize that the Christian Science story of last week needs to be balanced with other views on spirituality and healing. I begin where we left off:

"Last week I spoke of Virginia's faith in God's love, how

her commitment to prayer healed her. But other healings may not be as dramatic. Healing can be emotional and spiritual, rather than physical. Love, life, and God are so mysterious that we don't know exactly how healing takes place in body, mind, or spirit. But we can develop the trust that healing occurs."

Healing Companions need to cultivate a humble attitude and learn from differing views expressed in the healing profession. I continue: "Dr. Larry Dossey, a faculty member at Harvard, believes in the healing power of prayer and love. He writes that 'love occupies a majestic place in healing' and is a 'bond that unites us all.' But he also cautions not to expect love to always create physical healing. Some people are not healed by love alone, and people who have various diseases can be made to feel guilty, an added burden for people who are ill. He concludes that love is mysterious, paradoxical, and does not guarantee good health." [9]

"The doctor's right," Clint says, "my physical therapist loves me, and I still can't walk."

"Well, I know I'm receiving healings through this group," Veronica says. "Lately, I feel I'm always with God. I used to think it took imploring with prayer to have God's attention. Now, I feel it's a hand in my hand, one I can't see, but I know it's there."

An intellectual, Veronica usually turns most discussions into mental gymnastics. Now she smiles broadly, places her hand on my shoulder, and looks straight at me. "You're a walking brain with a tiny ribbon in the back," she says. Her reference to the bow I wear on the back of my head makes me laugh. "You've shown me I can look inside myself, and I don't have to worry about what others think," Veronica says. "You know, you can tell this group is important if the mood is lasting, if it carries over into our lives. It does in mine; I mull over what goes on in our group for days afterward."

Surprised, I am grateful that Veronica is having this experience. She often cannot recall what happened yesterday. Something must be touching her profoundly.

"Some people don't want to heal," I say. "I've read of a young woman, a paraplegic, who never asked God to heal her legs. She felt whole because she was doing God's work. Her talks on radio and television inspired thousands of crippled patients to find hope. Hundreds of people saw her joy and marveled. Radiant, she never prayed for healing. Her faith in God gave her the confidence to live a meaningful life. Although she couldn't walk, she felt fulfilled."[10]

"She's nuts," Francina says. "I'd be praying to get my legs healed. This conversation is exciting. Go on."

"Dr. Dossey writes of radical spontaneous healings researched at the Institute of Noetic Sciences.[11] Their research shows that in spite of their disease, their patients did nothing to receive healing, did not even demand it. They accepted life as good, were grateful, and healing just occurred by itself.

"Dossey's own approach to healing offers hope. He believes that our 'authentic, higher self is. . . utterly beyond the ravages of disease and death.'[12] So illness can't mar who we really are."

"That's good, because I have a lot of complaints!" Francina says.

I continue with my readings on health and spirituality: "At a Harvard Medical School conference, Reverend Kevin Tripp, a Catholic priest, told of his ideas about integrating spirituality into health care. He believes that today many people live deeply spiritual lives without following a religious dogma. He feels it's important to include them in spiritual health care research."

"I'm one of them; he can include me." Veronica says.

"Me too," Francina says.

"Reverend Tripp's vision is to integrate spiritual care in medical settings. He feels that we need to learn about the 'spirituality of wellness.' "

The spirituality of wellness—thinking about this as the session ends, I carry the inspiration with me into my group at St. Andrew's nursing home. Expected to sing old favorites today, I begin. Suddenly I notice Sophia grimacing with pain. Her whole being contorts as the raw, excruciating pain increases. How can life be so cruel? Unable to go on singing while agony greets my song, I quickly leave the room to find a nurse.

When I return, Sophia is moaning. A devout Catholic, Sophia, a gentle woman with a sweet disposition, would never impose on anyone, would never ask for anything.

Fifteen minutes pass, and the nurse has not arrived. Placing my hand on Sophia's arm, I pray as I sing: "I can endure this pain; my Lord died and rose again." Over and over like a chant, I repeat this phrase, knowing Sophia's deeply religious spirit will be receptive.

Suddenly I see the pain disintegrate. Sophia's entire body melts into her chair, her eyes now soft. She smiles. Before my eyes I witness something I can hardly believe. Sophia whispers in German; she is saying the Lord's Prayer.

I begin singing again. I glance over at Sophia. Once more her face is strained; she clutches her stomach. Walking over to her, I speak firmly. "No. I won't give in to this pain; I can go through it. I have the power to endure; I will sing my hallelujahs."

Sophia looks up at me, suddenly on a threshold between pain and its release. "I am not abandoned," I go on, "my God is with me. He will see me through. I shall know joy even through this suffering. I shall sing my praises: Hallelujah,

Christ has died, Christ has risen, I too shall rise and praise shall be my song."

Where is the nurse? What's taking so long? But maybe a nurse isn't needed after all. Incredulous, I watch Sophia's face and body, now calm. Sophia smiles. There are moments of wellness in spite of pain. Prayer is the song that heals. Sophia's body is still ill, but her spirit is released.

In the midst of calamity, with mind and heart on God, our spirit can soar beyond our trials—and we shall sing.

☞ Steps for Healing ☜

Insights that can help heal

✦ When we seek permanence in life, we suffer.

✦ When we are aware that we are more than just a body, illness cannot diminish our essence.

✦ Life is a miracle every day when we see ordinary events as extraordinary.

✦ Nature is a spiritual pathway that brings beauty into the soul.

Helping yourself heal

1. To relate to your elders' spirituality, examine your own relationship to faith, prayer, religion, and spiritual enquiry.

2. Have there been times in your life when faith, spiritual or otherwise, has influenced your actions? Look for manifestations of faith in yourself, in nature, or in others.

3. What is your relationship to prayer? Discover your beliefs about prayer. You may not be connected to praying, but to be effective with elders who are, honor the places in your life for which you feel reverence.

4. Have you or a friend ever witnessed or been the recipient of a miracle or an unexpected healing? Have you been moved by a faith story? How has this influenced your life?

5. Focus on something in nature, such as the ocean, a tree, or a mountain. Reflect on the rhythms of nature and seek a deeper understanding of your life.

Helping your elder heal

1. Utilize your elders' beliefs to ease their pathway during times of illness or distress. Learn about your elders' relationship to faith, prayer, and healing. You can start by asking them about their childhood experiences.

2. Encourage elders to look for a blessing every day.

For your inspiration

I am a prayer in the arms of the universe, enfolded by love that has no end. My spirit transports me; my intellect clarifies me; my emotions and body move me to tears and to joy. Sometimes I sense my spirit could merge with limitless space, and I could fly across the heavens, alight in the singing breast of a bird whose song thrills me beyond all my earthly concerns. My elder also has a spirit that can fly where birds and angels sing. In this, we are one.

SIXTEEN

Ritual: A Window into Reverence

*It is when people are entrusted
with creating their own rituals, or
evolving variants from existing
rituals, that such rituals become
like lanterns, lit from within.*
—James Roose-Evans

*To create ritual
is to make art of life.*
—J. E.

"OLD PADDY MALONE forgot he was dead, lifted himself up, and shouted from his bed!" Catherine's Irish humor begins to warm up as she looks around at the seven elders seated in the living room at Valley View. "Paddy Malone was a robber. Everyone thought he was such a great guy. They gave him a proper Irish wake. Laid him out in his casket on the living room floor so everyone could wish him luck. Then the police came looking for him—so much for Paddy pretending he was dead! It was the end of the death ritual for good old Paddy Malone."

That day I decide to see if elders are interested in rituals other than Paddy Malone's. Recalling an evening I spent with my friend Gienne, I tell the group how twenty adults honored the birthday of Gienne's twelve-year-old son Aaron. By creating a ritual that signified Aaron's journey into manhood, the boy experienced a rite of passage he would never forget.

"Everyone sat in a circle, the women on one side, the men on the other, while a large woven hoop, designed by Gienne, began to circulate. Each adult was asked to bring a feather, stone, photo, good-luck card—any special object from nature or from home. As the hoop came around the circle, we each were invited to say something of wisdom as we fastened our object to the yarns of the hoop. My stone had a hole in it; I wound jute into the hole, tied the stone onto the yarn, and said:

" 'With this stone, Aaron, I bless you to find strength for the difficulties you are bound to meet along the way. Remember—you will gain strength in times of fear. And with that strength, add gentleness. If you have an open mind and heart, you will learn how to do this through teachers, friends, and your vision of God. If ever you need me, I will be there for you.'

"Later, in two separate circles, the men and women passed a ribbon around as each spoke of their relationship to Aaron and what he meant in their lives. When Gienne's turn came, she threw the ribbon over the table to Aaron and cut it. This symbolic act indicated cutting him free from his mother's domain."

Concluding Aaron's story, I say: "By the time three hours had passed, the entire group had initiated Aaron into manhood.

"We don't have many rituals in our culture for the transition from childhood to adulthood, and even fewer—if any—for the transition from retirement to dependency in the last phase of life. When we lose the ability to cook, bathe, remember our medications, a rite of passage might ease our feelings of loss of self-esteem, confusion, and fear of the future. Creative rituals could offer strength, encouragement, and hope for our journey into an unknown future."

I look around at the eager faces before me. Milka's eyes brim with tears as she says: "We'll never forget Aaron's wonderful story."

Surprised at the intensity of her response, I wonder if these elders yearn for a deeper sense of meaning in their lives. I decide to see if their connections with each other, and to this phase of their life, might deepen if they were to experience ritual.

Weaving a Circle of Friendship

Inspired by Gienne's ritual, I purchase a small wooden hoop, yarns, and scissors. Filling a basket with driftwood, shells, pebbles, old bones found at the beach, I hope to stimulate a discussion that will turn craft-making into something more meaningful.

One by one I take out the objects from my basket and listen as Milka holds a piece of driftwood:

"This puts me back into the woods. Very sad. I have a rifle, a .30-06, but I'm not a killer. I'm a hunter. Where is my gun anyway? As usual, my son takes off with my things. I have to make sure my gun is properly cared for, no telling what he's doing with it," she says, possessed with anxiety. Milka's fingers nervously rub the driftwood, anger rubbed into the smooth curve as she keeps ruminating about her son.

"Yeah, I had a gun, too," says Cambria, enjoying this sudden memory. Milka looks up, interested. "My husband hid me behind a bunch of dead logs. Four deer came, but I wouldn't shoot because one was a buck. The men all laughed at me. Why didn't I shoot, they wanted to know. The next day I killed a deer; it was our evening meal."

I had no idea these two women were capable of shooting guns.

"What about this bone, what does it remind you of?" I ask, passing it around.

Janeen laughs. "How should I know, I'm not a bone specialist!"

"How about this branch?"

"My father made whistles out of branches," says Janeen, fingering the smooth curve of the wood.

Changing the focus, I begin to weave strands of teal yarn around the hoop while reciting a poetic phrase written at home. Would this phrase deepen our conversation?

"The sky of my mind is filled with the vast blue of eternity," I say. "What does this phrase suggest to you?"

"The colors of your dress," Milka says, smiling. "Very pleasant, the tenderness I feel for you. It's something deep within me. I'd like to put you under my arm and take you home."

Avena: "It reminds me I have many things to look forward to. The circle goes on and on, there's no limit." I'm surprised. Avena usually expresses the feeling that her life isn't worth much.

"A quality that goes on and on . . . that's a good way to look at life," I say, continuing to weave green strands around the hoop. "Milka, take this strand from me and go on weaving." I hand the hoop to Milka and watch as her gnarled fingers wind the yarn across the hoop, her hands demonstrating the skill she has acquired through years of practice.

"Look, the hoop is warped," Milka lifts the hoop to show us.

"That's okay," Cambria says. "It challenges us to be creative."

"The crooked hoop is like our lives," Catherine says. "All of a sudden, there's an uprising, a jolt like an earthquake. And that's what makes people come together."

"Sometimes our lives are bent, not smooth," Cambria says.

"What about this yarn?" I ask. "It's really in a tangle."

"Our lives, too, knots we have to patiently untie." Catherine begins unraveling the knotted yarn while I reach into the basket for an emerald ball.

"All those yarns," says Janeen, "they're a bundle of joy."

Milka passes the hoop to Avena who weaves emerald strands around it.

"Here's a starfish," I say, lifting it carefully out of the basket, one of its delicate tips already chipped. I ask if they want to fasten the starfish in the center of our woven shades of green.

"Definitely, it's our star of hope," says Milka, "star of unity, guidance, and promise."

"We're all stars." Janeen smiles.

Catherine hands me her ball of yarn, the strands now smoothly wound.

"What's special about this women's circle?" I ask.

"I lost my whole family," Janeen says. "This group means a lot to me. You're going to have to be the family I no longer have."

Janeen's comment startles me. Not one for emotion, she rarely shows affection. I didn't realize the group was that important to her. Although I have seen residents sometimes holding hands, I have never heard elders express their need for one another.

"What should we name our circle?" I ask.

Janeen says: "We could call it Our Eternal Friendship Circle."

"What makes us an eternal friendship circle?" I ask. By this time I begin to recognize how important it is to learn the art of asking a living question, one that draws out the inner person. When Healing Companions ask such questions, the answers are not important; the awakening of an enthusiastic, creative response to life is the aim.

The living room at Valley View suddenly feels like home; I can almost hear a crackling fire in a fireplace as we weave by the hearth on a cold afternoon.

"This is an eternal circle because we're a group of lonely, forlorn women," says Milka, laughing, as she throws a ball of yarn across the circle to Catherine.

"We're not at all forlorn," says Janeen, miffed.

"Yes, we are; we're shut-ins; if it weren't for this group, we'd be losing our minds." Catherine turns to Janeen: "Give me the hoop, will you?"

Threading a needle for Catherine, I watch as she sews the starfish onto the yarns. These elders usually resist getting involved with crafts. But by weaving their view of life into the creation of making this decorative hoop, they have become dynamically engaged. The starfish seems to unite us all, as if each of us were a point on the star, in the center of which our hearts shine as one.

"Why not write a statement about our friendship circle?" I ask.

"We're a group of lonely, forlorn women . . ." I write. Janeen frowns, then smiles and adds: "with a lot of enthusiasm!" Quickly I write that down, and then include:

"Drawn together from the four corners of the earth. We are older and wiser." Milka bursts in, "We are thinkers."

"And sometimes we disagree." I go on, "We laugh, we cry, we . . ."

"Reason well!" Milka laughs.

"Of different faiths and nationalities . . ." I continue.

"We are born from enough varieties to be labeled Heinz 57!" Catherine says with a giggle.

"We're a patchwork quilt; one from England, one from Ireland, that one's from Yugoslavia, she's from Italy, I'm from Wisconsin," Cambria says.

"We have a common bond . . ." I wait.

"Minor as it may be, each of us has some kind of affliction," Catherine says.

Cambria adds: "And when we're together, we're not really lonely . . . because we have each other. Our families may indeed have their own busy lives, but we are busy rediscovering ours."

"Maybe we should end our declaration like this," I say. "How many women, like Milka and Cambria, are known to be hunters of deer and rabbit?"

Around the circle, applause breaks out. Suddenly I realize our eldercare facilities would do well to foster a sense of extended family, where personnel could be trained to envision an intimate family atmosphere for elders. Wouldn't this help to heal our elders, most of whom suffer loss and loneliness?

Rituals Create a Spirit of Meaningfulness

Our hoop event occurred during the Lenten season, after which a deep level of bonding evolved. Now Holy Week was beginning, and I wondered if there was a way to share the spirit of Easter without sparking religious discussions, which the owner of Valley View forbade.

Our group met on Maundy Thursday, the commemoration of the Last Supper, when Jesus blessed and washed the feet of his disciples, knowing that one of them would betray him. Entering the living room, I place my bowl of water filled with floating rose petals on the table. Dipping my towel into the water, I ask Milka to hold out her hands. Gently, I massage her fingers with the warm, wet cloth, and then dry them. Gazing directly into her eyes, I say: "Milka, I wish for you a peaceful life, free of fear, joyful in new discoveries."

"I wish the same for you, honey," she replies, her face flushed with pleasure.

Since these elders aren't agile enough to stand up and walk around the circle, why not have them bless each other aloud while seated in their chairs? Encouraging them one by one to bless Milka, at first they seem embarrassed. But soon a momentum takes hold. A warmth of love floods the circle as I proceed to wash and massage the hands of each elder. After the massage, each elder receives a verbal blessing from each member of our circle.

I think to myself how seldom we humans bless each other unreservedly. Friends and family come and go; do we bless them, not simply in a silent way, but aloud so they can feel our love? How many elders are given a communal opportunity to bless each other and their caregivers? Would elder rituals such as this one open a door for more meaningful days?

Momentarily allowing them to get beyond their petty likes and dislikes, this ritual helped my group of elders share genuine love. When I spoke to them of the hoop ritual several years later, they remembered it vividly even though they were unable to remember what was said an hour earlier. Remembering the joy, awe, and love that are inspired during such rituals, elders are left with an imprint on the heart, a sense that life is full and spiritually rewarding.

Reflecting later on the elders' involvement in the hoop weaving and Holy Thursday rituals, I realized the importance of taking a day, or even a few hours, out of ordinary time to create special moments, to express love in action. Instead of allowing the days to flow into one another soon to be forgotten, if we open ourselves to ritual, our lives are placed in the context of something greater than the unwanted changes we suffer—illness, aging, and death. Chaplain Rabbi Samuel Seicol once said that "we need rituals to build a spiritual moment."

As Christmas approached, I wondered what kind of spiritual moments could be created inwardly, to balance the exterior activities of Santa, sweets, and Christmas carols. I began by asking elders if any unusual Christmas rituals took place in their families. Milka told of hers:

"Ours was a Serbian Christmas. We always had suckling pig, killed especially for Christmas on our farm. My mother worked much to give much—raisin bread and strudels. Father made beeswax candles. Before we ate we stood up to pray, then all of us walked around the table and kissed each other. When we were young, we were respectful to Mom and Dad. As we got older, we thought this was old-fashioned. We kids got Americanized; we pushed the good things out of our house."

Aware that some elders view ritual as mere sentimentality and others dislike rituals because they have become meaningless, and still others are attached to traditional rituals, I proceed cautiously. The elders at Valley View are open-minded, and I decide to try a new Christmas ritual that I created just for them.

In the center of our circle I place a decorative wooden dish with wooden candleholders around the rim, and I begin to read aloud a ceremony I wrote before arriving:

"In this Christmas season, as we prepare for the celebration of new birth in our lives, we must first empty ourselves of selfishness, unkindness, stubbornness, prejudice, fear, jealousy, self-righteousness, anger, lack of forgiveness, and false pride. Opening ourselves to receive the birth of Love within us, we commit ourselves to sharing that Love with each other, our families, and friends."

Placing small pieces of paper on which I have written one simple word into a basket, I instruct each elder to take a piece of paper and pass the paper as a gift of love to the elder on her right. Each paper has one of these words: compassion, tolerance, peace, thankfulness, joyfulness, quiet, patience. Each elder shares a memory or thought related to the word found on the paper. Then a new phase in the ritual begins.

"We now will celebrate those who have showed us the pathway of love," I say. "We honor our roots by beginning with our mothers."

Handing Milka a candle, which is lit by a small battery, she places the candle in one of the holders on the dish and says: "I wouldn't exchange the philosophy of my mom for any money in the world. I'm glad we weren't rich. I couldn't gain her wisdom from money. I would love to tell Mama how much she meant to me; if only she knew what was going on inside me now—it's both beautiful and sad."

"My mother never complained, was always giving. Her sewing machine was never empty," Janeen says as she places her lit candle in the candleholder.

"Mine was so compassionate; even when I was stubborn, she made excuses for me, consoled me," Avena says, holding her candle.

"Mine . . . my mom's been gone all these years," Catherine says, "but she still comes when I need her. When I don't know which way to go, I ask her. She's always in my thoughts; she lives on inside of me."

Touched by Catherine's declaration of love, I am reminded of the respect elders are shown in Orissa, east India. In Puri, grandparents living at home with their grown children have the final say in family matters. Grandmother is the heart of the home, the guiding light, and is consulted whenever problems arise. When parent or grandparent enters the house, it is not uncommon for children to bow and touch the elder's feet.

Native Americans also teach children to follow the wisdom of their grandparents. Tom Porter, Mohawk chief of the Bear Clan at Akwesasne, New York, acted upon the guidance of his grandmother, who, when reading the tea leaves, correctly foretold the events that would shape his life. True to her vision, Tom Porter waited many years until he met his beloved bride, and lived out an ideal, twenty-year marriage.[1] How many children of today would follow the guidance of their grandparents?

As we conclude the honoring of mothers, I am aware of the festive glow of our candles. I go on with my ceremony: "We welcome the light of love coming from our roots. Now we honor our caretakers. Love has many blossoms, and we offer ours to them." I give each elder a silk rose, and they place them in a bowl; they will later give them to their caregivers.

"Some people in this house don't know who they are, don't even know their own names," Catherine says. "They stay in their rooms or wander off. We need to see in them what we see in children—beautiful, loving people. These old ones belong with us even if they aren't sitting in our circle."

Catherine doesn't have many outlets in which to express her caring nature. Her compassion, framed through the creation of this ceremony, now blossoms.

To end our ritual, I say: "We invite the birth of Love into our hearts, and say yes to rising up out of darkness into a marvelous light; yes to Love, which overshadows us with wings of healing; yes to a new song in our hearts."

Our Christmas ritual is over. The ritual not only deepened our feeling for Christmas, it opened us to a deeper connection with our inner self, shed light on who we are and what we can become.

Rituals Allow the Release of Deep Feelings

I made an important inner discovery one day during a hospice ritual. About three hundred people gathered in a church to honor family and friends who had died throughout the year. At each pew, unlit candles were given to the participants. After the speeches by hospice personnel, a gospel choir sang.

Then we as guests walked from the pews to the front of the church with our unlit candles, and each of us received a rose. Photographs of the departed were displayed on an easel. Walking past these photos, we formed a line going toward two hospice workers stationed at the center isle. Each held a lit candle from which we lit ours and then returned to our pews.

Counselor Michael Pugh suggested that as we looked into our candle, the flame could help us remember the faces of the ones we love. He affirmed the hospice belief that love is greater than the devastation of loss; hope is stronger than despair; light is more abiding than darkness; grief work is love work, and the power of love helps us to heal, to grow, and to go on. He then asked us to affirm a commitment of compassion and sensitivity to others who grieve, to reflect on what a playwright once said: death ends a life, but not a relationship.

As I gazed into the glow of candlelight my tears overflowed. A flash of intense thoughts poured through me. I saw the face of my rabbi and realized it was time to stop being angry at God for allowing him to die when he had so much joy still left to give; I saw my departed friend of forty years and knew I needed to be broken with tears to soften my heart, which had judged her for not being the way I wanted her to be; and I saw the face of Elisabeth, my friend living in India, and suddenly understood I needed to ask forgiveness for clinging to her spirituality instead of taking responsibility for my own.

The gospel choir sang joyously. As my thoughts rode on their song, my suffering was released. I knew in the deepest way that although there would never be another rabbi like mine, I could now accept his death with grace. In spite of the loss of my longtime friend, I believed a new friend would come to fill my days. And I gave back to Elisabeth her spirituality, with a willingness to cherish my own.

This hospice ritual awakened a voice of wisdom, hope, and healing, making very real losses into gains. The awakening of such insights is valuable for any Healing Companion. The ritual heightened my feelings of love and revealed a depth of emotion not always experienced in daily living when schedules are busy, distractions occur, and the heart loses contact with itself.

How often do caregivers give themselves fully to the life they live, to the care they give to elders, to the nurturing they give to themselves? By experiencing suffering and its transformation, a Companion's interior journey is excellent training for understanding elders in depth.

One evening that depth touched me in a Hanukkah ritual and made me ponder the problem our society has with expressing a spiritual dimension in health care. Sixty elders, mostly non-Jewish, gathered for a Hanukkah celebration that I was leading. Difficulties in obtaining permission to hold this event had surfaced the week before. After many phone calls to administrators, it was decided the event could proceed as long as it was not religious. With elders coming from varied backgrounds, the concern was understandable; it was not appropriate to teach religion.

Preparing for the event, I wonder how to bridge the gulf between religion and spirituality. Hanukkah has a deeper aspect than simply eating potato *latkas*, playing the *dreidl* game, and receiving gifts. The essence of Hanukkah is lighting the *Menorah*, an eight-branched candelabra that signifies the rekindling of spiritual light within every Jew.

I begin by lighting the Menorah and explaining the historical event of Hanukkah. In about 165 BC, the Syrian kings, under Greek influence, forbade the Jews to observe their sacred traditions, massacred innocent people, and desecrated the Holy Temple.

In the small village of Modiin, the Maccabees, a family of five sons, formed a small army, much smaller than the powerful Greek-Syrian army, and for three years waged war. The Jews were finally victorious. Although this was a victory of the weak over the strong, the significance of Hanukkah is not about winning a war. It is about the struggle for religious freedom. The ancient rabbis taught that real power is not in fighting but in increasing devotion and commitment to the Jewish culture.

When the Jews prepared to rededicate the temple by lighting the Menorah, they discovered amid the rubble a flask with only enough oil to last for one day. But a miracle occurred—the flame lasted eight full days. Thus, Hanukkah became a celebration of light.

Since lighting candles is a universal experience, I ask the group: "What does lighting candles mean to you?" Many spoke of birthdays, weddings, or memorials.

"What do you cherish most in life?" I ask. "What beliefs do you hold most dear? Reflect on something you do which is sacred; it could be a simple act of going out every spring to pick flowers in a meadow." Pausing a few moments to let this idea sink in, I then continue:

"Hanukkah is about the threat of losing what the Jews loved most—their spiritual culture. They would rather die than give up practicing the rituals of their tradition, lighting their lights, and singing their songs. How would you feel if someone tried to take away your right to light these candles or to sing songs that give you joy? That's what Hanukkah is about, reclaiming the light of joy."

I know there is more, but can I bring in Rabbi Shlomo Carlebach's spiritual teachings without overstepping the religious boundaries made by the administrators? I decide to chance it.

"Rabbi Carlebach said that on Hanukkah the deepest question is 'When the whole story is over, what remains inside of me? Am I in touch with the inside of my soul? Is there any light left in my heart? If . . . I discover that there is still light left inside of me, then I owe it to the world . . . If after all these holidays, the world around me is still in the dark, then I must ask myself, "What good was it all?' "

Sudden applause breaks out from the Jewish elders in the back of the hall, giving me confidence to risk sharing more of Shlomo's teachings: " 'When does God take all the hatred and pain from our hearts? When are we healed? When do we recognize the Light in ourselves and in all of those beautiful people around us? The answer my beautiful friends, is on Hanukkah.' "[2]

Amid much singing, joy abounds in the faces before me. After the ceremony, while sampling *latkas*, sour cream, and applesauce, a Japanese man bent with age approaches me. Leaning on his cane, he looks at me with tears in his eyes, and says: "I never thought I would be involved in anything as beautiful as this."

❧ Steps for Healing ❧

Insights that can help heal

◆ Every day we live ritual; we create order, dependability, and rhythm to our days.

◆ Creating new rituals offers new ways to encounter wisdom, hope, and healing within ourselves.

◆ Personalized ritual leaves an imprint on the heart, creating unforgettable moments.

◆ Communal elder rituals can create a new source of meaningful connection.

Helping yourself heal

1. Setting time apart is the essence of ritual. It is a time to choose a special place to specifically contemplate something important in your life. Select a theme taken from your life, or ritualize a time for replenishing your spirit.

2. Rituals need balance. Organize this event with a beginning, middle, and end. The beginning and end signify the special quality of the time apart, and should include a special action. Light a candle, partake of bread and wine, say a prayer, or listen to music. The ritual may be fifteen minutes to a full day. Plan the middle of the ritual to include activities related to your theme.

3. To develop your skills for creating meaningful rituals for elders, find an opportunity to conduct a ritual for a friend. Create one that is relevant to your friend's life.

Helping your elder heal

1. When time is set apart and ritual objects are used, an event is created that has the potential to make an imprint on your elder's memory long after the event has passed. Use what you have learned for yourself to pattern personalized rituals for them. Utilize holidays, seasons, anniversaries, and birthdays.

2. Within the ritual, remember to include your elder's memories, blessings, relationships, and celebrations. Rituals can create moments of healing.

For your inspiration

I am a creator of holiness when I express joy over the smallest details in my daily life. Doing this, I create blessing, and blessing creates harmony. I create harmony by making others feel special. I do this by creating moments people will always remember. I am a joy to my world. My elder is also a creator of joy and blessings, of moments people will never forget. In this, we are one.

SEVENTEEN

Serenity in Motion

*Come to the inner dance
and your whole being will
glow with the essence of
who you are.*
—J. E.

HIDEO'S FINGER JABS the air. Pointing straight at me, he says: "I'd refuse to put up with a man who drinks and divorces his wife. I'd throw him out. And if he came around again I'd call the police!"

His response doesn't surprise me. Hideo's lack of empathy and tolerance, his need to punish those who do wrong, are familiar themes threading their way through his life. But Hideo's need to threaten others is an empty roar. At age seventy-nine, Hideo has Alzheimer's disease.

One of a group of elders at a local day care center, Hideo's face is taut, his almond eyes dart to and fro. If I don't change the focus of our discussion quickly, he is apt to wander out of the room, anxiously open the door to the parking lot, feel lost and afraid he won't be able to get home.

I place a cassette in the tape recorder, instruct the elders to glide their arms from side to side. Lyrical Irish music inspires simple swaying motions. Glancing at Hideo, I see a smiling face, graceful movements.

Hideo's pleasure is obvious. But there is more than just pleasure. Immersed in the music and movement, Hideo is lost to himself, his old attitudes, his circumstances. Gazing beyond the confines of the room, his face is rapturous. The pleasure of doing a simple dance has unmasked a depth of joy so intimate, so united with the rhythm, the motion, the sway of life itself that suddenly I feel like an intruder in a private moment between Hideo and his Creator.

Getting beyond his self-righteous protests and need to control others, Hideo has danced his way into his soul.

When I return the following week, I lead the group in slow, spontaneous movements. Hideo glides his hands gently along his thighs, back and forth, breathing in and out to the rhythm. I ask him to teach the group his breathing and motion exercise.

"I saw them doing this in Tokyo in the park," Hideo says, smiling. "A wonderful feeling, the silence, the balance, the rhythm." Becoming the group's leader, he guides us in the movements, saying, "Now we will all breathe as one."

Movement and dance often unite elders in feelings of goodwill. But sometimes, it takes a miracle for this to happen.

Can Physical Exercise Inspire Love?

One day, fifteen residents at the Glen Oak Alzheimer's residence sit in front of me as I demonstrate gentle exercises. No one is smiling. Vacant stares, drooling mouths, slumped bodies. Not one person is present. On a sudden impulse, I begin to sing. A smile, then another; hands start clapping. Inside these cloaks of skin, muscle, and bone, elders are singing and light is flickering.

My heart bursts seeing their eager faces. I blurt out, "I'm so grateful for being part of your lives. Thank you for allowing me to be here. I love you."

"That's a lot of crap. You don't love us; you're lying." This vehement response from the woman sitting next to me jolts my enthusiasm. Her watery eyes, disheveled hair, snot dripping onto her dress, repelled me when I first began. But now I feel love.

"Lying? Why should I lie?" Scanning the faces in front of me, there is no response. "I'm not lying. I love you."

"It's not true."

Remaining firm in my belief, I reply, "Would you be willing to tell me why you don't believe me?"

"Yes, I would. You don't love us because nobody could love *Us*."

The word "us" reverberates in the air, smacks against the living room walls. Ashamed of the times I have felt repulsed by smelly, slovenly bodies, I am now touched by them, by the pulsating heart of people hungering for love.

Physical exercise may inspire love when it includes body, mind, and spirit. But sometimes elders first need to express the shadow side of themselves before love can bloom. Milka taught me this at Valley View.

Connecting Movement to the Spirit of Nature: Qigong

"I'm not speaking to my daughter, I'm finished." Milka scratches her scalp furiously until blood dots her fingers. "I wipe my hands of her, that's all."

"We're going to do a simple exercise," I say to the group, ignoring Milka's outburst and thus diffusing any further agitation. Our exercises are done with elders seated, so they don't lose their balance and can freely move their arms and legs. "Gently press both palms forward as you breathe out. As your palms come in toward your chest, breathe in. Repeating this exercise several times, as we breathe out we push away resentment, anger, fear. Breathing in, we gather into ourselves a new attitude of peace, forgiveness, love."

Hearing this instruction, Milka joins us. Within a few minutes, her gaze is deeply focused inward. When the exercise ends, Milka is calm. She says, "You know, I need to think differently about my daughter. It's not good to hold a grudge against her. I'm going to change my attitude."

"I am, too," says Cambria. "Even though I was at peace when I made the decision to sell my house, I get depressed when I think about the commitment to live here for the rest of my life. But as we did the exercise, I said, 'Dear God, remove all impurities and unhappy thoughts. Throw them away, and bring in baskets of joy, peace, happiness.'"

Avena says: "All I could see was my husband in front of me. I haven't seen him for such a long time. It was so peaceful. I realized we aren't separate. It made me feel important."

Realizing Avena's response is a gift that bolsters her poor self-esteem, I repeat the same exercise again, adding: "I push away the attitude that I have nothing to offer. I bring in the attitude that I have gifts to share. I push out the thought that I'm not good enough. I bring in the feeling that I'm a special person."

After reinforcing Avena's self-esteem, I go on: "Now we're going to start with the same exercise and turn it into spontaneous movement. Reaching out and gathering in, do this motion in front of you. Then reach out to the side, and come back in to your heart. Then do the same above and below." Realizing these elders cannot easily initiate movements without first seeing a demonstration of them, I briefly move my arms. Wanting them to find their own movements, I soon have them close their eyes so they will not be influenced by mine.

Soft music encourages flowing responses. "Now as you continue moving, find an image—ocean, bird, air, water, flower, whatever comes to mind. Allow the image to change if it wants to." Their spontaneous movements rise and fall with the music as I again shift the focus. "Now imagine someone you care about in front of you. Reaching out with your arms and gathering in, communicate from your deeper self to that person."

"Dawn died last week but I saw a dove flying to her, bringing her peace. It was beautiful," Cambria says.

"I felt love, contentment, happiness flowing through me," Milka adds.

These responses remind me of Dr. Thomas Moore, who wrote: "Body exercise is incomplete if it focuses exclusively on muscle and is motivated by the ideal of a physique unspoiled by fat. What good is a lean body that can't hear Thoreau's owls or return a wave to Emerson's wheat?"[2]

These elders experienced not only physical exercise but their inner feelings and the beauty in nature through Qigong. Qigong is the inner experience of Tai Chi, an ancient Chinese movement exercise. In Chinese, the word "qi" means "life force"; the word "gong" means "to cultivate." Cultivating the life force within the body, absorbing the life force in nature, awakens the potential for healing. Qigong's slow-motion exercises are excellent for elders. By including nature images, elders have access to nature's healing resources. When connected to deep breathing, the exercises may awaken feelings of unity. The flow of movement from sky to earth and earth to sky, and the process of maintaining balance between them even in a wheelchair, creates a sense of continuity, security, stability, rootedness. Gradually, these qualities may become internalized, creating peace of mind, self-confidence, quiet joy.

Qigong energizes the major organs of the body, extends the range of motion, and relaxes the muscle fibers. Along with the exercises, deep breathing increases the flow of oxygen to the brain. Conscious breathing enhances circulation, releases toxins, and aids the body's immune system. The movements increase vitality and mental alertness. Qigong calms the nervous system and inspires mental serenity and emotional well-being, which may reduce anxiety and sleeplessness. These latter benefits may occur even in elders who cannot, or will not, move. Simply watching the movements and hearing soothing music aids in the healing process.

"As we exercise today," I say to the circle of elders at Valley View, "we want to remain serene in the circle of infinity." Slowly and gently I breathe in, allowing my arms to rise above my head in a Qigong exercise. Breathing out, my arms float down to my sides. Up and down in a continuous flow, I encourage these elders to join me. Drawing upon images in nature to help integrate peace, beauty, and harmony within our movements and our lives, I decide to find out how elders relate to nature images. Stopping the exercise, I ask: "If you were climbing a mountain, what would you see?" I expect to hear "birds, rocks, trees." Instead, they say: "We would have freedom, joy, peace."

Not convinced they prefer an inner connection to the mountain image, I again ask: "If you had a camera, what would you take pictures of?"

"Joy, happiness, serenity."

I hadn't expected such answers. Clearly, these elders hunger for depth, for an inner life. Encouraged by their response, I begin to focus on the process of filling up and letting go, a process inherent in breathing, a process vital for both living and preparation for dying.

Returning to the exercise of arms rising up and floating downward, I say, "I am like a sapling in autumn. I release the leaves of judging others, criticizing, blaming. I watch the leaves of disappointment drift down to the earth. I let go of trying to make someone I love be perfect." Continuing the movements as I say these words, the elders do the exercise with me.

"Releasing resentment, I am willing to forgive myself and others. As I watch the leaves of anger and hurt drop off, even if I don't feel ready to forgive, I desire peace."

Forgiveness cannot be forced; it comes with grace. Relating the need for forgiveness to meditative movements is one avenue in the process of preparing to forgive.

Simple movements leave the mind uncluttered, free to explore feelings, images, even prayer. When appropriate, scripture images flow easily into movement exercises. "Put off the ashes of mourning; put on the garment of praise. Put off the spirit of heaviness; receive the oil of gladness."[1] These adapted phrases help to avoid the tendency to become mechanical when exercising. Scripture brings meaning into movement, inspires the body to deeply express the challenges of life.

Guiding elders in movement meditation is more meaningful than simply having fun through aerobic exercise. Although I sometimes teach rhythmic chair dancing, which diverts them from depression and boredom, the gift of serenity flowing through Qigong exercises has an eternal quality. I continue with my group. As they slowly raise and lower their arms, I say:

"As you sit under a cherry tree, soft pink blossoms fall over you like rain. A gentle breeze sends blossoms cascading over your shoulders into the river below. One by one, the blossoms float downstream; each petal represents a problem in your life. Now you let go of each one.

"You experience the joy of life anew through this simple exercise. Deeply breathe in as your arms gently reach forward and up, palms facing the sky. Gathering the cherry blossoms over the top of your head, you breathe out as your arms continue moving downward, palms facing your head, shoulders, chest. Once again without pause, the rising motion begins until the exercise becomes one continuous circular motion.

"As this motion continues and your arms rise and fall, a white dove alights on your shoulder. Feel its softness, its gentleness; it is the dove of peace. Now the motion changes. After your arms rise, you breathe out, bend at the waist, reach down to your feet, dip your hands into the river. Breathing in, bring up the cherry blossoms, place them in your lap.

"Once more your arms rise, fall, reach down. This time gather up the white dove and place it, too, in your lap. The movement shifts again. Breathing in, both arms rise and become wings as they circle into a wide arc stretching out to the side, then down. Gently your breath falls with them.

"This circle of grace is created by the wings of the dove lifting you up and over the world where you glance down at what your life has been. Elements of conflict, confusion, turmoil, strife are now far beneath you.

"Now your wings glide down and come to rest in your lap. Resting for awhile, your right arm and bent knee slowly begin to rise and, feeling suspended like a bird, you become balanced, poised, calm. You will not fall apart when sorrows come, you will not be thrust off balance when emergencies arise. You are held by the peace of the dove, the joy of the cherry blossoms, the song of the river that carries all of life down its stream.

"Breathing out, your knee and arm now descend back to earth and you begin the exercise again, lifting your left arm and knee. Holding the pose, you remain firm, anchored, strong, for you have the life of the river, the sweetness of the blossoms, and the peace of the dove living in your heart."

❦ Steps for Healing ❦

Insights that can help heal

◆ The expression of emotions through body movement aids healing.

◆ Releasing negative feelings allows healing to occur.

◆ Nature images heal the mind, body, and emotions.

Helping yourself heal

1. To learn about therapeutic movements, enroll in a Tai Chi, Qigong, yoga, creative movement, or dance therapy class.

2. Pick one exercise from this chapter. Breathe deeply. When you are comfortable with the movement you have chosen, voice your feelings aloud as you move. Add healing images from nature, a biblical phrase, a prayer, a phrase from the chapter, or your own affirmation of love, hope, or triumph.

Helping your elder heal

1. Notice any physical limitations your elders might have. Adapt your chair exercises accordingly. Give them movements you make up, or defined movements you have learned through other disciplines, with or without music. Always include an awareness of breathing.

2. Many elders hold rigidity in their bodies. Assure them there is no need to do the movements exactly right. Encourage them to find their own way of moving. Help them discover smooth, free-flowing movements.

3. Try this exercise with your elder: push away negative feelings with your arms. Then gather in with your arms healing words and images. Take a few moments to invite elders to share what they pushed away and the healing words that they received.

For your inspiration

Moving my body slowly, I sweeten my days with serenity.
I breathe in the peaceful light of dawn; I breathe out calm morning
light bathing me in joy. My internal rhythms sway and sing with
the rising and setting of the sun, with the ocean tides, with the
moon shining over the waters. The pulse of life's ebb and flow moves
through my mind and body, bringing quietness, gentleness, balance,
and peace. When I guide my elders in gentle flowing movements,
they too feel at peace. In this, we are one.

EIGHTEEN

Guidelines for a Spiritual Journey

*Let thy Love's sunshine kiss
the peaks of my thoughts and
linger in my life's valley
where the harvest ripens.*
—Rabindranath Tagore

"As DAWN BEGINS to awaken another day of life, imagine that you are gazing at a mountain. The sun begins to rise over majestic peaks, sending a chorus of joyous sunrays across the earth."

This is New Year's Day, an auspicious time to embark on a spiritual journey with my client Kari, who rarely leaves her small room at Valley View. Since Kari is spiritually inclined, I decide to introduce her to a simple meditative practice. Will Kari and other elders enjoy such practices?

Kari smiles as we begin this spontaneous meditation. I am not certain that Kari, a Christian by birth, is inspired by the faith with which she was raised. But I do know she is open to spirituality; therefore I choose a neutral, nonthreatening meditation. Although I use a practice other than Christian, as her Healing Companion my intention is to enhance Kari's cherished beliefs and to refrain from diluting them.

"These sunrays of love pour into the dawn's stillness," I

continue. "Breathe in the crisp mountain air, listen to the awakening of dawn. Bathe in the silent waiting for the earth's first morning birdsong; bask in the sun's radiance as it bursts into golden rays over the mountain, pouring a golden pulse of healing light into every cell in your body."

Kari sighs, lifts her face heavenward. "Allow the dawning rays of the sun to shine love into your mind," I say. "Allow the sun, clothed in glory, to descend from the crown of your head and rest on your throat, bringing wisdom and compassion into your speech. As the sun descends into your heart, its rays reflect a quiet glow of love. Descending still further, the sun warms your abdomen, bringing strength and calm. Descending to your feet, the sun enlightens them with balance and joy. As you sit in your chair, feel your feet, steady and strong as they touch the earth.

"Now return to your heart, where the sun shines radiant love out into the world. Silently pray: All over this planet may upheaval come into quietude; may all peoples help each other to live in peace."

Kari sits quietly. Five minutes pass. Slowly she opens her eyes, and says: "I've wanted to do this all of my life. It's wonderful."

The following week I return for our second session. Years ago in New Zealand, a medical doctor told me of Geoffrey Hodson's healing meditation. Instructing his patients to do the meditation by an open window, the doctor said it did them more good than the medications he prescribed. Again I choose a meditation apart from Kari's Christian tradition. Using meditation as an entrance to discerning her spiritual pathway, I begin with an adapted version of Hodson's meditation:

"Visualize the Divine Life everywhere around you. Above your head, a radiant glow. Reach upward with the power of thought and will. Aspire to become one with the Divine Life, and let it flow freely through you." Closing my eyes, I sit quietly. When I open them, I find Kari's right arm stretched high above her head, her hand open as if to receive. Usually meditation practices are motionless. Even though I have not instructed her to move her body, I do not interrupt Kari's spontaneous gesture. Surprised by it, I wait to see what she will do. Slowly she lowers her hand, places it in her lap.

Five minutes pass. Kari opens her eyes and says, "I could do this for hours."

So I continue. "Dwell upon the Divine Life as the source of all power. Seek to lose yourself in it." Since Kari is an intellectual, she may resonate well with this abstract meditation. Although visualizing "Divine Life" is difficult, intellectuals such as Kari may prefer it. For those who have an emotional or intuitive nature, meditations using the senses, as we did in the sunrise meditation, may be more compatible.

Kari again closes her eyes.

"You are a chalice into which the Divine Life is poured," I say. Another five minute pass. Kari murmurs: "A feeling of peace overcomes me."

"This Divine Life is a glowing, golden splendor pouring down upon you. It fills your cup to overflowing, it heals you completely. As you breathe into this splendor, it flows through your heart to help heal the sufferings of the world."[1]

After a prolonged silence, Kari says: "This golden splendor brings me closer to God. Also to my parents, my husband, and boy; they've all died. As you said these words, I was remembering my family, how they used to make me feel restful and happy. I felt their presence."

Through meditation we may feel a sense of continuity when we experience love from family and friends who are no longer living. At a later time, when Kari is in the process of dying, her caregivers can remind her of joyful memories, which may avert her fear and aid in a peaceful death. Also, the spiritual practices that bring her happiness now may help her to surrender with serenity when her death is near.

I leave Kari at peace.

Divine Listening

The following week I return for our third session. When entering into our inner selves, we become vulnerable. Before beginning, I pray for Kari's protection from harm. It is wise for a Healing Companion to pray or visualize being surrounded by light before entering into spiritual practices. This time I honor Kari's Christian roots with an exploration of *Lectio Divina*, divine listening.

This ancient way of seeking God was practiced in Egypt, Syria, and Palestine by Christian desert monks during the first three centuries of Christianity. The roots of Lectio come from the people of Israel, whose oral tradition gave inner meanings to the Torah by hearing the scriptures read aloud. In the monastic tradition of the early Christians, Lectio is experienced as a meditative reading of scripture.

While rooted in the Judeo-Christian tradition, Lectio can be used in any spiritual tradition. While slowly reading and/or listening to scripture, poetry, or an inspired text, the reader and listener reverently listen for a word, phrase, image, or symbol that touches his or her heart.

In his retreat at the New Camaldoli Hermitage, Father John Powell spoke of Lectio leading the seeker into an intimate encounter with God, with Love—a meeting that causes profound transformation. He said that Lectio is a way of "recognizing God's Word hidden in the world, in other people, in our hearts—hidden in the least likely places and people, in all of creation." To listen on the level Father John is describing is to listen at the deepest level. For Healing Companions who desire to deepen their experience of Lectio, they may seek guidance from a spiritual director or go on a retreat.[2]

As Kari's Healing Companion, I am careful not to overwhelm her with a religious context she might not be open to. I refrain from beginning with devotional prayer or scripture. Without mentioning the potential for divine intimacy, I begin instead with one of several poems I wrote while reflecting on various challenges elders face. This one focuses on the need for surrender.

> *"A lone leaf falls*
> *without protest*
> *into green rushing rapids*
> *where I surrender*
> *all my evenings into*
> *the murmuring waters."*

Slowly I read this verse aloud several times, and ask Kari to listen for a word or phrase that touches her. I instruct her to silently repeat the word or words that come alive in her heart. After three or four readings, I ask if she has found a word.

"Surrender," she replies. "With feelings of love and peace, I am to surrender memories of my loved ones. God will help me to be alone."

A theme emerges, reminiscent of our first session: Kari's remembrance of family. Many elders live in the past. By now Kari has told me that family and church were the most important things in her life, and that she studied scripture for an hour every evening over dinner with her husband.

Knowing that scripture is important to Kari, I return the

following week to begin our fourth meeting, this time including scripture as the sacred reading. A five-day retreat with Norvene Vest some years ago inspires me to read scripture aloud from her book on Lectio: "A new heart I will give you and a new spirit I will put within you; and I will remove from your body the heart of stone and give you a heart of flesh. I will put my spirit within you."[3]

After reading, I ask Kari if she hears a word or two that touches her. "Heart and spirit" are her first words. Another reading of the same text brings the words "flesh and stone." Reading the text again, I ask how the words make her feel.

"They inspire me to have a heart of goodness," she says. Following Norvene's instructions, I read the same passage again, asking if any images come to mind. She has none. Again I read as Kari remains attentive to the words. I ask her to listen for what God wants her to do or to be in her life this week.

"I prayed the Lord would give me the power to know people heart to heart, to reach the people around me," Kari replies. "Most people build walls around themselves. You can know them a long time and not know them. I feel that way about the people here. Every day I see them but I don't know them."

"How do you feel about that?" I ask.

"My feeling is: 'How can knowing them heart to heart best be done, oh God?' "

After praying together for God's response, I get up to leave. Kari says: "I'm not close to anyone. My daughter visits occasionally, but I don't want to burden her with my thoughts. I feel closer to you than anyone I know." After these four visits, Kari feels intimacy. If spiritual practices are included in health care, perhaps elders will feel less alone.

As I drive home after the session, I reflect on the practice of Lectio, listening in the inner silence. Healing Companions who carve out quiet time in their lives to listen within will be able to share Lectio with their elders. As in any discipline, the deeper the Healing Companion listens, the better he or she can facilitate spiritual experiences with elders.

Not all elders and Healing Companions are spiritual seekers. But for those on an ardent spiritual quest, Father John's description of those who seek union with the Beloved through Lectio may be an inspiration: "When you're in love with someone . . . you can't get enough of that person, you long for a word . . . a deeper intimacy."

This longing to be with the Beloved is expressed in a line from a monk's prayer: "So give me, Lord . . . at least one drop of heavenly rain with which to refresh my thirst, for I am on fire with love."[4]

Whether such words from the soul are meant for God or for a human lover, family member, or friend, they express adoration and devotion. If words of longing like these resonate with an elder, Healing Companions know that the elder has a devotional nature and that it is appropriate to share devotional poetry or scripture.

John Cassian, a monk who lived in Bethlehem and Egypt 365-435 AD, interprets the biblical story of Mary and Martha, giving a glimpse of the blessing of spiritual longing. Mary chose to stay by the feet of Jesus and listen to his teachings, while Martha looked after his physical needs. Martha's actions, although virtuous, did not inspire a response from Jesus, who praised Mary for her spiritual devotion. Cassian indicates that the highest spiritual intention is one of contemplating beauty and the knowledge of God. Martha did praiseworthy acts, yet tending the body gives only temporary benefits, while tending to spiritual life has eternal merits. That is why Jesus said of Mary: "It will not be taken away from her."[5]

For Healing Companions and elders who do not long for a
Beloved or believe in a personal God, the desire to become a
more loving person paves the way for peace in the last years.
Relating to an elder as a beloved one for whom love is poured
out will be a tender offering from the hands and hearts of
Healing Companions.

The Practice of Chanting the Name of God

Returning to Kari the following week for our fifth session, I
realize the value in becoming acquainted with a variety of
spiritual practices. I decide to focus this session on an ancient
Christian and Hindu prayer practice: repeating the name of
God day and night, as a means of keeping the heart and mind
always aware of God's presence.

Namasmarana, the Hindu practice of saying a *mantra*, was an
essential part of the life of Mahatma Gandhi, who daily read
the *Bhagavad Gita*, the Hindu scriptures, and said his mantra,
"*Rama.*" As a youth, Gandhi was terrified of other boys, even
ones smaller than himself. A family servant told him never to
run away when afraid, but to repeat his mantra over and over.
At the moment of his assassination, Gandhi said, 'Rama, Rama,
Rama," which means: "I forgive you, I love you, I bless you." The
mantra made Gandhi's love of God triumphant at his death.[6]

When repeating God's name over and over as a mantra, the
mind is automatically drawn toward Gods presence. To have
God's presence, or the presence of a great being of peace, alive
in the mind and heart at the end of life is a deep blessing.
Within each spiritual tradition, a variety of sacred names may
be uttered.

In the Buddhist tradition, the sacred name may be *Avalokita*, calling upon the Great Being of Compassion. For the Muslim, the name may be *Allah Mahabha*, calling upon the God of love. For the Jew, the name may be *HaRachaman*, the Merciful One. A deep bond, a sense of oneness, and the touching of souls grows between an elder and Healing Companion when a sacred name that an elder loves is chanted or sung. Reciting this name may help bring about a peaceful end.

This once happened when I visited a woman who converted from Christianity to Islam while living in Iran as a nurse. Her family could not understand her, and a split had occurred between them. Confined to bed in a nursing home, she could barely speak due to a severe stroke. Her nurses encountered much anger and lack of cooperation, and asked me to visit her.

During the visit, I began to sing a few religious Arabic words. Her eyes lit up, she smiled broadly, and in wonderment she began to mouth the words and eventually was able to sing some of them. Her disposition improved and she greeted me warmly in every visit. I began to sing in English the meaning of the Arabic words, bringing the words into a singing prayer. Our bond deepened, and she felt less alone before she died.

While I sit with Kari in this session, I begin saying the name of Jesus, the Christian version of a mantra. "I knew a professor whose prayer was simple," I tell her. "He prayed 'Jesus, Jesus, Jesus' a thousand times a day. One day he became so ecstatic he forgot where he was. Oblivious to everything, he blissfully walked into the ladies' room to use the bathroom!"

"So if I pray like this, I'll walk into the men's room!" Kari laughs.

"When you think of saying the name of God, what name comes into your mind?" I ask.

"Jesus, precious," she replies.

Since the prayer has a rhythmic quality, I suggest Kari use

her beads while silently saying her prayer, moving one bead for each phrase. Together, we pray. A Healing Companion does this prayer with an elder without expecting any visible signs of an elder's response. He or she trusts the interior process of being strengthened through God's presence within.

Our fifth session is over. I accompany Kari to the dining room, where she joins five elders at a festive table for the evening meal. Greek dance music is playing on the tape recorder. Food is served. Clinking forks and bouncy dance music mask human silence. No one talks.

Valley View offers excellent health care and is run with a view toward privacy, respect, warmth, and friendliness on the part of the staff. Yet Cynthia, the facility administrator, will not permit these elders to hold hands before the meal as a form of silent prayer, even if they want to do so. She is afraid of being sued by one of the families, who might accuse her of bringing religion into her assisted living facility.

Kari misses prayer before the meal; she misses going to church every Sunday and receiving Communion. Clearly, Kari's spiritual needs are not being met. Unfortunately, Valley View's policies reflect a poverty of spiritual care, which could easily be changed by educating staff and families about the importance of providing spiritual nourishment to elders.

Leaving spiritual care in the hands of an elder's family and expecting them to be a provider for their elder sometimes does not work. Some families may feel awkward and misunderstand the spiritual needs of an elder. Relatives may not be spiritually inclined, or they may have differing spiritual views and feel threatened by an elder's spiritual preferences. Sadly, an elder's spiritual yearning can be undermined by well-meaning family members.

Unlike families and caregivers, whose lives are a bustle of

activity, elders live an essentially passive life. Busy caregivers and relatives may not be able to tune in to their elders' needs or to their own inner life. Reaching out to God or responding to the light from within requires a quiet inner listening, a slower pace. An elder lives in that slower pace and has an opportunity to use spiritual disciplines to complement a passive lifestyle. This time of life can be an opportunity for spiritual enlightenment.

After the five sessions with Kari are over, I review them. Healing Companions may simplify the sharing of spiritual practices by choosing one or two best suited to an elder's temperament. Too many practices may be confusing. The chosen practice may be repeated at each visit to root the prayer deep within, establishing it as an ongoing anchor in which an elder can find security. Security is not in the prayer; it is in God or a Higher Power. But reinforcing repetition develops the habit of prayer. An inspired reading before the prayer begins may awaken the heart and help keep the prayer from becoming cold and lifeless.

When Healing Companions share spiritual practices from any tradition, they need to be cautious not to play the role of missionary and assume every spiritual elder wants to engage in these practices. Some are content without them. One of the most important qualities that a Healing Companion can cultivate is humility, which, at its very core, allows them to be with an elder without having to teach or guide a meditation but to simply just wait, listen, and be. Being together may be enough.

Care also must be taken not to trivialize spiritual practices, making them into a technique instead of a way of life. Spiritual disciplines, handed down through generations, contain a history of wisdom, the heart of which is communing with the Divine Source of creation.

A Refuge in Melody and Silence

One day I find another way of communing. As I enter the elegant home of my ninety-six-year-old client Anita, I find her sitting in her living room. A highly cultured, attractive artist, Anita is wearing a royal blue gown, jade earrings, and a beatific smile. She is no longer able to talk. Sitting in her chair, she hums a childlike melody. She hums day and night without pause. To control her excessive bouts of crying and screaming, of feeling lost and alone, Anita has been given a small dose of an antipsychotic drug, which allows her many long hours of happiness.

Healing Companions view Anita's singing as her attempt to initiate a spiritual practice, even if she does so unconsciously. Instead of relating to Anita's repetitious melody as a form of dementia, compulsion, or drug-induced activity, a Healing Companion chooses to identify the repetitive singing as a spiritual process, a way of self-comforting and accessing loving memories.

From singing to silence: Healing Companions who keep company with silence, whether in nature or when praying, sitting silently, or listening for God's love speaking to them through scripture, learn the art of solitude. Solitude and silence may help heal.

At St. Andrew's nursing home one day, a healing opportunity came unexpectedly through "silence therapy." Silence became a clue to dissolving panic attacks. Brigette and I sat quietly in front of a crystal cross for up to twenty minutes after a bout of shouting. Brigette calmed down as I closed my eyes without saying a word. Occasionally my eyes opened to glance at Brigette. When I found her furtively looking at me, I quickly closed my eyes again and continued my silent communion in attentive concentration.

Brigette realized I was serious. She saw I was immovable. She too became still. Together we found a silent refuge amid passersby and people conversing in the hall. My ability to be still enabled her to remain enclosed in a friendly silence, oblivious to the activity around her. For those few moments, her bizarre, angry shouts and frantic fight for survival settled down. Brigette loved the silence. Together we found peace.

For those elders who are drawn to spiritual life, the communion built up through years of seeking God or an inner light may embrace an elder's heart and soul in his or her final moments. The last cycle of life is ripe for contemplation. It is a time when waiting is already built in to the day's rhythm—waiting for the next meal, the next friendly visitor, the next entertainment. Waiting for death.

As Brigitte and I sat waiting in the silence, were we both building up a communion of peace that might embrace us in our last moments on earth?

⊰ Steps for Healing ⊱

Insights that can help heal

◆ Spiritual practices can help us surrender to the flow of life, thereby bringing peace to our soul.

◆ In the silence, we discover our deepest self.

◆ By continually building communion with our inner divinity, we strengthen our capacity to live in harmony.

◆ For those who are drawn to it, the last cycle of life is ripe for living in a contemplative mode.

◆ As we cultivate humility, we find it is the key to gentleness, tenderness, and love.

Helping yourself heal

1. To increase your ability to befriend the silence, take time to sit and be still. Begin by observing your breathing. When thoughts arise, see them as clouds passing by without trying to stop them. This may lead you to quietude of mind.

2. If you feel comfortable trying to lead a meditation, practice on yourself by reading one aloud several times.

Helping your elder heal

1. When you become comfortable befriending the silence, you can then help your elder become calm through the use of *silence therapy.* If some elders have trouble being still, remind them to become aware of their breathing.

2. Offer the practice of repeating a sacred word or sound. Choose one that is meaningful to your elders.

3. You may choose to lead your elders in the practice of *Lectio Divina.* After reading a sacred passage aloud, encourage your elders' participation by asking them what words have touched them, and what feelings have been evoked.

For your inspiration

When I open myself to receive the rising light of dawn, every cell in my body shines, sparkles, and trembles with light. I am rising on this new day with the vast breath of the universe breathing into me health and wholeness. A sea of splendor opens to the sunrise within me. Out of this glorious expansion, I know my birthright—joy and peace. In this, my elder and I are one.

NINETEEN

Pathways to Peace

*The special privilege of
being human is the
ability to be a window into
the infinite.*
—Michael Shapiro, Jewish mystic

"A ROSE HAS a scent as deep as God's passion," Alesandra tells
me. "When you smell it, the scent enters your whole being and
you know he's resting in you." Her smile is rapturous after a
guided meditation I have just given her. Without realizing it, I
awakened an experience which began years ago when her husband divorced her, left her with three children, and went off
with another woman. To offer solace, her neighbor brought her
a rose and placed it on a table next to a candle. It was then that
Alesandra began meditating on the rose. She sensed the small
bud would help her heal. It did.

Our meditation begins as Alesandra lies in bed at Mountain
Pines nursing home. I place a battery-operated candle on the
table by her bed. Its glow helps to create an atmosphere of
comfort and peace. Alesandra closes her eyes. To prepare for
the meditation, I say: "Place your hand on your heart, imagine
you are breathing in God's love. As your breath goes out, you
are breathing out God's love." Alesandra easily goes into a

deep silence. "Now imagine a rose in the center of your heart. Wait and watch the rose slowly unfold. To keep your mind centered, silently say the word 'beauty' over and over." Elders often fall asleep during long periods of silence. Instead, Alesandra is deeply concentrating. After twenty minutes, I say: "Inwardly, silently, say the word 'peace.' In this way come out of the meditation. Slowly open your eyes."

"I could have stayed with the rose for an hour," Alesandra says. "But it's really too exhausting when I don't feel well. Look, my hands and my feet are sweating." Struggling with diabetes and arthritis, Alesandra teaches me her limits. Next time I will shorten this meditation. But even in her physical discomfort, she has received spiritual comfort and peace.

"God's love first came as a tightly closed bud," Alesandra goes on. "Gradually the petals opened, the scent increased. Resting in this wonderful scent, it encompassed me. I've been meditating on the rose for years. At night when the pain is intense, I take this dark bud into my heart, let its petals open. A deep scent invades my being, gives me God's calm. The rose helps me bear pain. Strange, when you first walked in, I thought I smelled a rose, but I know there aren't any here."

Flower meditations are practiced in several spiritual traditions. Rabbi Aryeh Kaplan writes that total concentration is required to experience the full beauty of a rose or any other object in nature. Inwardly saying the word "beauty" keeps the mind focused and enhances the experience of appreciating the flower. "This serves to amplify one's sensitivity. . . . so that the flower will actually appear to radiate beauty. . . . If one then realizes that the source of beauty is the Divine in the flower, then this beauty can also become a link with the Divine."[1] To do this, practice is needed.

Unlike beginning meditators, Alesandra's capacity to focus

for long periods is already developed, so she doesn't need to inwardly say the word "beauty." Elders who are new to meditation may find that saying the word "beauty" helps to keep the mind centered.

In our next session, I further explore the Jewish tradition. Although she is a Mormon, as a child Alesandra went to the synagogue, as some of her ancestors were Jewish.

"Would you feel comfortable with Hebrew words? *Ruach, Nefesh, Neshama?*" I ask.

"Oh, they bring such joy! What do they mean? They sound familiar."

"Rabbi Arthur Gross-Schaefer interprets these words this way: *Ruach* is breath or wind. *Nefesh* is your soul resting within you. *Neshama* is your soul expressing itself in the world."

"Ah, very good," Alesandra says, smiling.

"Let's meditate." Alesandra closes her eyes. "Don't change your breathing pattern, let it be. As I speak, allow the words to enter your breath. *Ruach.* I breathe in the breath God gives me. *Nefesh.* My resting soul breathes out peace into the world. *Neshama.* I breathe in my thanks that God has given me life to help make a happier world."

Alesandra's eyes remain closed; she smiles broadly. "*Ruach, Nefesh, Neshama.*" Slowly I repeat the words while carefully watching Alesandra's normal breathing. I remind her to simply allow her breathing to be natural, without worrying about it. Continuing to say the words, they flow into the rhythm of her breathing.

"*Ruach,*" I say, coordinating the word with the rise of her chest as she breathes in. "*Nefesh,*" I say, in rhythm to the fall of her chest as she breathes out. "*Neshama,*" she breathes in and the word seems to become one with her breathing. "*Ruach,*" we begin the cycle again as she breathes out. Alesandra's lips move. She repeats the words quietly, then louder until together we are chanting.

Twenty minutes pass. Alesandra opens her eyes. I am concerned the meditation has been too long, but Alesandra tells me otherwise. "Before you walked in, I was so hyped up I couldn't relax. But when the meditation started, I began to feel that I am God's breath coming into me, and the exhaustion is going out." Alesandra's joy shines in her brilliant smile. "I'm excited, I tingle all over, prickles are going through me. I've been given energy I didn't have."

Healing Companions who are not familiar with Hebrew may use English words to coordinate with the breath, such as "my spirit" on the inhalation; "rests" on the exhalation; "in peace" on the inhalation. With the help of an elder, Healing Companions will discover the words the elder prefers.

Inspired by Alesandra's response, I sing a Jewish chant, *Modani Lefanecha*. This morning prayer as interpreted by Rabbi Judith HaLevy, says, "I thank you God for giving my soul back to me for one more day. I may not have had a perfect yesterday or even a perfect today. You must have great faith in me to give me one more day of life."

"*Elohi Nishama Shenatata Bee T' Hora Hee . . .*" I continue chanting this rhythmic morning prayer, spontaneously expressing its meaning as Alesandra's feet tap out the rhythm; she seems to dance in her bed.

"My God, you have breathed my soul into me. You have made it pure. You have formed it, and made it yours. One day you will take my soul from me. Through your infinite goodness, in the time to come you will bring my soul back to me again. As long as I have breath in my body, in joy I will give thanks for this great gift."

Alesandra's face glows. I did not expect her to be so affected by Jewish prayers. Healing Companions may want to explore the possibility that some elders may enjoy and find beauty in prayers from other faiths.

The following week, knowing that Alesandra longs for more Hebrew, I share with her the holiest of the Jewish prayers, the *Shma*. This prayer is said morning and night, at every holiday, and at death.

"Shma Israel Adonoi Elohanu Adonoi Echad."

"I remember this well," she says. "Tell me what it means."

"Rabbi Arthur Gross-Schaefer explained it to me like this: *Shma*: Hear, obey, awaken. Listen, you who struggle with God. *Adonoi*: The God whom you can never fully understand. *Elohanu*: Your personal God, your unique path to God. *Echad*: God is one. All of life, its mystery, belongs to God.

"The rabbi adds more," I continue. " 'The Lord is one. You and I are part of that one. God is one, has always been one, will always be one. Since you and I are part of that one, we too always were, are, and will be. As God is eternal, so are we.' "

As I leave, Alesandra seems ecstatic.

One Sacred Word

The next week I return to share a simple meditation, focusing on one holy word. Asking Alesandra if a sacred word comes to mind, she says: *"Shalom*, peace! I've meditated on the word 'peace' for years. When I say 'peace,' a warm feeling goes through me, takes my whole body into the Lord. It's like a cloak wrapped around me, bringing me close to utter serenity. I'm resting in his hands. When I feel abandoned, I turn to him and know he is thinking of me."

Elders often have a word or phrase they frequently say or

even sing when needing solace or help. I discovered this in one of my Seekers' Circles when elders told me phrases they had been saying for years: "Be still and know that I am God." "I am with you always." "God is my help in times of trouble." "Adorn my heart with Your love." "Jesus, free my heart for joy."

Retreat director and former Roman Catholic Byzantine nun Linda Sabbath advises carefully choosing a special word. If an elder is Mexican and her father, Jesús, was a drunk who beat up her mother, the word "*Jesús*" (Spanish for "Jesus") will bring ugly memories. Instead, these words can be used: "*luz*" ("light" in Spanish) "*sí*" ("yes" in Spanish), "hope," "love," "faith," "spirit," "God."

The words Linda Sabbath refers to are suggested by retreat leaders who teach centering prayer, a type of prayer developed by Thomas Keating. A Cistercian priest, monk, and abbot, Keating writes that the essence of centering prayer is an effortless resting in God's presence, an ". . . opening of mind and heart, body and emotions—our whole being—to God, the Ultimate Mystery . . ."[2]

When Healing Companions help elders to engage in centering prayer, it simply consists of a gentle, silent repetition of one word chosen by the elder. When thoughts arise to distract the mind, the sacred word is repeated, bringing the mind back home to the word. Eventually, in its deepest form, centering prayer is a silent communion with God in which thoughts, even the sacred word, cease.

Whether an elder is religious or nonreligious, silently repeating an inspired word helps to quiet the mind. Since the prayer does not require seeking or reflecting, thinking about God or looking for God, its effortless quality lends itself to practicing the prayer even when one is ill.

Keating views centering prayer as consenting to God's presence within. His vision of the prayer offers inspiration: "Let love alone speak . . . We cannot know Him with our mind; we can only know Him with our love . . . The experience of being loved by the Ultimate Mystery banishes every fear."

When practicing centering prayer, one may experience a timeless dimension, which allows us to sense the body separating from the spirit. This separation is "delightful" and thus our anticipation of dying, Keating writes, "is not so threatening." We may intuit that "no great change is going to take place."

Prayer practices are offered to elders to root the prayer deep within, to establish an ongoing anchor in which they can find security. Security is not in the prayer itself but in God. Over time, a prayer practice may lose its attraction in the heart, and a new practice may be introduced.

Meditating on Loving-Kindness

Returning to Alesandra the following week, I reflect on who she is. As a young woman, she lived in Europe, Egypt, and Iran. Perhaps that is why she is comfortable with Hebrew words and a variety of spiritual practices. Perhaps that is why, some months back, she exclaimed to me, "How dare they try to wipe out my intelligence! I refuse to be made into a mush brain!" On that particular day, an aide had wheeled her in to the recreation room to be entertained by performers whose program was geared to the level of young children.

As I enter her room, I decide to try another spiritual practice, *Metta*, a Buddhist meditation on loving-kindness. In the Pali language, Metta means unconditional love, the love that pervades the entire universe.

"Often when Buddhists meditate, they smile," I say.

"Ah, that feels right," Alesandra says. "When you're smiling inside, you manifest joy. Even when you breathe, you can breathe in joy."

"Smile, imagine looking in a mirror," I say as we begin the Buddhist meditation practice. "Silently say as you breathe in: 'May I be happy.' As you breathe out: 'May I be healthy.' In, 'May I be peaceful.' Out, 'May I be free from harm.' " During this meditation, some elders may fear keeping their eyes closed. If so, a Healing Companion encourages them to keep their eyes open. But Alesandra has no problem. She immediately closes her eyes and begins the practice.

After I leave, Alesandra continues to do *Metta* every day. Within a week, she reports that "things don't go right when I don't do it. Even though I didn't feel like it yesterday when I had no peace, I made myself say 'may I be peaceful.' Life went better after that."

A week later Alesandra finds Veronica screaming in the dining room. Silently, Alesandra says: "May you be happy, may you be healthy, may you be peaceful, may you be free from harm." Veronica calms down. So does Alesandra, whose usual response to Veronica's outbursts is irritation or anger.

A month later, Alesandra falls and fractures her coccyx. Lying on the floor, the first thing she says is "may I be happy, may I be well, may I be strong of spirit." When her son arrives to see her, he comments, "Mom, you seem to have no pain."

"For some strange reason," Alesandra tells me, "it was true, I didn't."

Surprised at the remarkably positive effect this particular meditation is having on Alesandra, I recall a conversation with a hospital chaplain. He told me that for some people *Metta* brings up unresolved hurts, grief, and longing. Fortunately some elders are resigned to the way life goes and have healthy defense mechanisms to avoid traumatic emotions. But if such emotions surface, a Healing Companion supports an elder through his or her suffering.

Alesandra breaks through my thoughts. "Since we've been thinking about spiritual practices, I'm not in as much pain now as I was a half hour ago. But when you're not here and I lie down, pain comes. Then I have to start thinking right again."

Alesandra cannot move her body. When her three aides lift her into her wheelchair, she says, "May I be happy, may I please move my leg!" Coughing endlessly in the night, with a harsh croak, she says, "May I be happy, may I be in God's good care. This cough shows me I'm getting rid of it! I'm going to say my 'may I's' whenever I can!"

One day I give Alesandra prayer beads. Overjoyed, she tells me she hasn't had beads since she was young. Now she will use them for this Buddhist practice.

Three months pass. Alesandra falls again, fractures her hip in three places, as well as her shoulder and arm. Rushed to the hospital, her first request is for her prayer beads. "I'll come out of this," she says. "I'm saying my 'may I's.' 'May I be faithful, may I be free from pain.' "

But the shock is too much. Alesandra admits she is despondent and stops the *Metta* practice. Within a month, however, she tells me, "I don't know what happened, but suddenly I'm saying my 'may I's' again. When the aides come in and see my lips moving, they know I'm doing something important even though they can't hear anything. They tell me that when my lips move, I'm doing something good for myself, and for them. So I feel I'm still here for a purpose."

Feeling a Holy Presence

Months after Alesandra's fractures heal I decided to try Sogyal Rinpoche's Tibetan Buddhist meditation.[3] Practicing at home first, I sat on a cushion in my prayer corner. Now Alesandra practices the same meditation while lying in bed in the nursing home as I sit by her side.

Preparing her for the introduction, I begin by saying "Now we will both relax." The day is so hot that even a sheet seems superfluous. Tugging the sheet over her toes, Alesandra sighs with the effort, and her head plops back onto the pillow.

"Take a few deep breaths," I say, "let go of all the cares of the day. Sink into peace."

Adapting Sogyal's instructions so that she can more easily understand and absorb the words, I repeat some of the phrases several times during the meditation.

"Now we will begin to '. . . invoke the embodiment of whatever truth you believe in, in the form of radiant light. Choose whichever divine being or saint you feel close to.' " Alesandra smiles. I assume she will choose Jesus; for another resident, it might be Buddha, Mohammed, or Yahweh.

"Alesandra, '. . . feel with all your heart the vivid, immediate presence of God, the Holy Spirit, Jesus, or the Virgin Mary.' " Sogyal's instruction is excellent for Alesandra, a Christian. For nonreligious residents, Sogyal's further guidance is helpful: " 'If you don't feel linked with any particular spiritual figure, simply imagine a form of pure golden light in the sky before you.' "

Alesandra frowns. Did I offend her by suggesting an image of Jesus or Mary? Because of her Jewish ancestry, is she opposed to images, as are some Jews who believe images represent idol worship? Setting aside my concern, I continue: " 'Don't worry if you cannot visualize them very clearly, just fill your heart with their presence and trust that they are there.'

"Now pray: 'Through your blessing, grace, and guidance, through the power of the light that streams from you: May all my . . . destructive emotions . . . be purified and removed, May I know myself forgiven for all the harm I may have thought and done, May I . . . die a good and peaceful death, And through the triumph of my death, may I be able to benefit all other beings, living or dead.' "

Alesandra remains very still. Outside her room, the aides talk. Their voices sound like shouts blasting out of the deep, calm silence created by the meditation.

Just then, one of them walks into the room. She opens Alesandra's cabinet, rummages in the drawers, closes the cabinet, and walks out, oblivious to anything special going on. I am irritated by this insensitive intrusion, but Alesandra remains unperturbed. Humbled, I realize a Healing Companion's training must never cease. Diligent practice of meditative silence is essential for gaining some measure of peace and equanimity, the ability to remain calm in spite of all outer disturbances. I go on:

" 'Now imagine that the presence of light . . . is so moved by your sincere and heartfelt prayer that he or she responds with a loving smile and sends out love and compassion in a stream of rays of light from his or her heart. As these touch and penetrate you, they cleanse and purify . . . destructive emotions. You see and feel that you are totally immersed in light.' "

Alesandra sighs deeply, smiles, and murmurs, "Such peace, this is peace divine." Not wanting to break her concentration, I pause and then continue:

" 'You are now completely purified and completely healed

by the light streaming from the presence. Consider that your very body . . . now dissolves completely into light. The body of light you are now soars up into the sky and merges, inseparably, with the blissful presence of light. Remain in that state of oneness with the presence for as long as possible.' "

It is very quiet in the room. The usual chatter in the hall of the nursing home, the announcements from the loudspeaker, the food cart rolling along the corridor cease, as if in silent concert with this peaceful silence.

For some time Alesandra hasn't moved. Should I say something? Deciding to trust the silence, I close my eyes and open myself as I did at the beginning of the meditation to the presence of light, and wait until Alesandra breaks the silence. Ten minutes pass. Then, a rustle of sheets, a quiet voice: "Oh yes, Lord, thank you," Alesandra says.

I open my eyes and gaze at Alesandra's beatific smile. Asking what the experience felt like, Alesandra replies: "I feel pressed close to something; it takes my breath away, makes my whole body quiver and shake, a peace all encompassing. I have been released from some very ill feelings I had toward someone today." Through spiritual practice, Alesandra is cleansed from negative emotions, released into a loving attitude.

Wanting to learn why she frowned at the beginning of the meditation, I ask whether she was uncomfortable with choosing a divine being. She was not. She chose Jesus, she said, which was just right for her. Her response taught me that Healing Companions need not always view body language in psychological terms. Alesandra's frown might have been a moment of intense concentration, a momentary physical discomfort, a passing negative emotion. The lesson for a Healing Companion is "do not assume, ask."

Alesandra's spiritual nature guided her in a recent

conversation with her daughter. She tells me: "We spoke like deep, close friends for two hours yesterday. I knew she felt she hadn't done enough for me. I told her: 'If there are any deeply rooted feelings you feel guilty about, please tell me.' She expressed fears of hurting me. I reassured her she was doing fine. When it's my time to go, we'll be at peace." Alesandra's spiritual practices have allowed her to accept her eventual death, embrace her daughter lovingly, and create peace between them.

Receiving Grace Unexpectedly

For those who do not engage in spiritual practice or even believe in any sort of spiritual dimension, an unexpected experience can forever change them. And their experiences can in turn influence another elder's response to dying. I tell the following story to a group of elders:

"My agnostic veterinarian friend Jack Vincent was on a plane coming home from a vacation when he had a medical emergency. His blood pressure had reached severe levels, he was coughing up blood, and he was in intense pain. He thought he might be dying and wondered: 'Do the lights go out and that's it? Is it painful?' He said a prayer: 'I don't know whether you're there, God, but if you are, I'm sorry for the wrongs I've caused, and like the criminal on the cross, please find a place for me.'

"Then Jack waited to die. To his astonishment, he saw a loving, ethereal golden Being sitting next to him. The Being transmitted ideas into his mind. He wondered how he got these ideas when he didn't hear anything. He knew the ideas weren't his. He asked the Being, 'How did you do this?' The Being smiled.

"The essential message to Jack was this: 'It doesn't really matter whether I live or die, all that matters is love. Love is essential in everything.'

"The Being stayed with him, comforted him for a long time. Because he was aware of sounds, and of everything going on around him, Jack felt he was not hallucinating. The Being was real, an authentic spiritual intervention. Much later, Jack looked out of the window, and when he turned back, the Being was gone. He wished he had been carried off with this Being into the loving place he experienced. Instead he made it to a hospital, his symptoms were treated, and later he survived a tumor operation.

"This event profoundly influenced his life. Jack became a more loving person, lost his fear of death, came to believe there is a loving God, and that all people have access to a higher power. He knew he was cared for."

Elders benefit from hearing such stories. They offer the hope that something loving, kind, and spiritually healing awaits them when they are dying. Hearing that others have experienced an overpowering love and peace while at the edge of death lessens an elder's fear.

Unlike Jack, Linda Sabbath dedicated herself for years to spiritual practices. Raised as an atheist Communist, she was not permitted to talk to Christians as a child; instead, she ridiculed them. It was only later, when she became a mother, that she began to meditate. She saw visions of Jesus, who "filled me with a love I had never dreamt existed and could not be described. After a valiant resistance, I was brought into the world of spirit where Jesus dwells, drawn by an overpowering love. I have been shown eternal life."

Linda says it is not necessary to believe in anything to experience bliss, unconditional love, the link between this life and the next. When I read aloud to my elders the poem that Linda wrote about her near-death experience, "Dual Citizenship,"[4] they are inspired to be open for grace to touch their lives. An excerpt of grace is spoken through her poetry:

Caged in the kingdom
                                    of the cracking whip
contiguous to a car seat,
lashed with the sinews
                                    of a safety belt
soon shattered,
I watched from my penitentiary
the jaws of death
                                    in hot pursuit.
The driver was a bullet,
his car was a gun.

*   *   *

From inaccessible infinity,
down the precipice of my rage,
into the chasm of my fear,
strident gold embraced me
in a strenuous and Divine grasp,
retracting
            the stinging sharpness
                        of my horror,
overcoming time, space, and substance,
stilling my frenzied blood,
injecting love beyond love,
cremating my consciousness into glory,
unhinging the doors to paradise,
catapulting me into

an illuminated crater of bliss,
conferring upon me
citizenship in Heaven.

*   *   *

Threads from eternity
have woven for me
a vestment of wonder.

*   *   *

I saw myself being born
in the core of my substance,
swaddled in Divine splendor
shrouded by holy dust,
fragrant with the essences of destiny . . .
embraced and caressed
by the hands that molded
the untangled garden of the constellations.

❧ Steps for Healing ☙

Insights that can help heal

✦   We have within us a reservoir of spiritual beliefs that can be
strengthened through meditation and contemplation.

✦   The purpose of meditation and contemplation is to awaken
to the spirit of love within.

✦   Sharing spiritual practices with elders allows them to
express their own spirituality and to activate their
inner resources.

Helping yourself heal

1. Be open to allowing an inner spiritual practice to come to you, bringing peace, compassion, understanding, and self-love.

2. Continually engage in a spiritual practice that helps you establish regular attention to your spiritual life.

Helping your elder heal

1. When you are a companion in your elder's spiritual life, your role is to help them strengthen what is already within them. You do not have to be a meditation teacher to do this.

2. To relate to your elder's spirituality, find out about various spiritual practices throughout the world. Ask permission from your elder to share the wisdom traditions of other faiths and cultures. Exploring world faith traditions with your elder can help illuminate and clarify their own inner beliefs.

For your inspiration

When I meditate, I enter into an inner world to discover that I am a living soul longing for the flame of love to capture my heart, longing for this love to hold me in an eternal embrace. There I rest in bliss and safety and find the joy I have been seeking. I seek to know love beyond all description before I die, that in my leave taking I may receive the kiss of death in peace. My elder also longs for love, comfort, and peace. In this, we are one.

TWENTY

Coma: Mending the Heart, Minding the Spirit

*No one can go back and make a
brand new start, my Friend,
But anyone can start from here
and make a brand new end.*
—Heartland Sampler

THAT'S WHAT HE needed, a brand new end.

Ronald had been an alcoholic for forty years; he was now sixty-five years old. The last time he was hospitalized, he threw milk at the doctors and ripped down the curtains. Later, in the recreation room of a nursing home, he pounded and kicked the furniture. Everyone knew him, and most facilities wanted nothing to do with him. When at last an assisted living facility accepted him, his desperate family hired me to bring some measure of peace and well-being into Ronald's life.

Standing in the doorway, I am not certain I want to enter Ronald's room. As I approach, he appears to tower over me even though he sits in his chair. I can't help it; I fear an attack.

I know therapeutic music will be too gentle for him. Deciding to stay neutral, I gear our visit to talking about the weather, food, and bicycles. He used to have a bicycle, he says, but even though I try to draw him out, his face remains impassive, not a hint of pleasure. Nothing seems to interest him.

A few months pass. One day a massive stroke brings Ronald to the hospital. As a Healing Companion, I am often part of an elder's journey from wellness to illness, from private home to assisted living facility to hospital. Now as I enter the hospital, I realize I am embarking on the next phase of Ronald's journey.

Receiving a Message of Hope

A totally different man awaits me. Lying immobilized in his bed, eyes unseeing, a lifetime of physical prowess is reduced to utter helplessness. Ronald drifts in and out of a coma. Is this the end of our communication?

A conversation some months ago with hospice nurse Susan Storch comes to mind. She told me coma patients can hear, and that when a person is dying hearing is often the last function to go. She advised me to speak to Ronald aloud, telling him: "You are a great soul and I am asking you to rise above anger, forgive all who have hurt you, and go into the light." Aware I don't have the courage to do as she suggested, instead I find myself singing:

> "There is a very great Love
> There is a very great Love
> It can bring us home to peace."

As the spontaneous song continues, the music obliterates the disturbing chatter of the aides in the bathroom near the bed. The odor of sickness, the sight of a plastic cover on the bed sheet symbolizing a cold, sterile atmosphere, is transcended by singing. A Healing Companion may transform a claustrophobic, unhealthy atmosphere into an ambiance of spring fragrance, filling the room with joy. Hopefully this joy is imparted to Ronald inwardly. Outwardly he remains totally unresponsive.

Forty minutes pass. I stop singing and reproach myself. How dare I sing a spiritual song to a man who is not spiritually inclined? I decide to ask him:

"Ronald, I know it's hard for you to talk, but will you please nod if the song was alright for you?"

"Yes," his weak voice replies, "oh, yes." I didn't expect speech. Shocked, I see a hint of a smile. Somehow I know I am on the right track.

But later, Ronald slips back into a coma. His doctor informs me he will never come out. I recall my client, Mary, whose doctor had said the same thing. Yet Mary not only came out of the coma, she went home and lived another two years. Since patients are able to hear while they are in a coma, isn't it best to bring words of encouragement? While not denying the dying process, we need to be sensitive to the slightest possibility of recovery. Imparting a death sentence may be detrimental to recovery, hope, and peace of mind.

The next day I reflect on Ronald's condition, the importance of releasing negativity before death, and of dying with our thoughts turned toward love. It occurs to me that Ronald's situation is an opportunity. No longer the aggressor, he is now in a position to receive.

But what will he receive in a coma? Ronald's life story suddenly comes to me in music, and I sing it out loud while I am at home:

> "What did I do with my song?
> It's been hidden in the dark for so long.
> Now is the time to sing free
> of all the past insanities.
> I was wild, belligerent, bold

acted crazy, angry, defiant.
I see I was wrong
I'm ready to move on
to begin my life anew.
I tried to prove I was strong
Maybe there's a wiser power
Beyond what I used
Beyond what I abused
I'm ready to change for the better.
What shall I do with this song?
It shall sing its way through me.
Make me a new man
The one I now become
The one whose battle is won."

The song guides me in how to be with Ronald on this stage of his journey; it tells me what might happen if Ronald chose to have a change of heart. The music gives me a direction to aim for, a message of hope. Could Ronald accept this message on some unknown level, even though he is in a coma?

I am undecided as to whether I will sing the song to Ronald. It will depend on his condition as well as his family's response to my visits. Will his family accept the song as a way to guide Ronald at this juncture in his life? Even if Ronald never comes out of the coma, as a Healing Companion I am convinced that, through our work together, he has begun an inward journey—and the song might help him along his way.

My telephone rings, interrupting my reflections. Ronald's son, Larry, a psychotherapist, is on the phone: "My father is taking too many pain-killing drugs, dulling his alertness. His state of mind is too intermittent now for any more visits. They wouldn't be useful."

I never had the chance to sing to Ronald his song.

The Healing Power of Music

Jenessa was not in a coma, yet I went through a process with her that was similar to what I'd experienced with Ronald. Jenessa was in the advanced stages of Alzheimer's disease. In her eighties, she was still gorgeous; sea blue eyes, high cheekbones with abundant curls framing a wide, smooth forehead.

Her son asked me to see her several months before her death. I watched Jenessa's body shake violently, heard her constant monologues filled with fearful images: "They're coming, something terrible is about to happen! It's happening, oh my God, the fall, the break, beal, break, beal, oh where is he?" Her fingers would claw the air, the skin taut around her lips, "the night is turning, burning . . ."

Jenessa was incapable of making coherent sentences and was continually in extreme states of anxiety. A few weeks before her death, I brought my tamboura to her bedside. Jenessa began to speak about a teacher who blamed her. Knowing she would soon die, I guided this discussion toward a peaceful resolution. Would Jenessa be willing to forgive the teacher?

"Deep, deep in my heart, yes, yes," she replied. Jenessa loved music and had been a musician. Music is often the easiest, calmest way to communicate with an Alzheimer's patient. I began singing her words: "Deep in my heart I will bless the one who hurt me, I will let her go." Jenessa sang with me.

In an article in *Reader's Digest* on the healing power of music, Dr. Oliver Sacks discovered that patients who cannot talk or move are often able to sing. Dr. Raymond Bahr at

Baltimore's St. Agnes Hospital is quoted as saying that "half an hour of music produced the same effect as ten milligrams of Valium" for patients in the critical unit. Some of these patients hadn't slept for days and easily fell into a deep sleep.[1]

Although the music relaxed Jenessa and perhaps eased the strain of trying to talk coherently, my purpose was to use the music to help us enter a new dimension of communication.

"The garden, it's in the garden," Jenessa said.

"What about the garden?" I asked.

"Who does the running, who does the trampling?" Her fingers began to twist the bed sheets.

"In the garden we don't have to run," I said softly, "we just plant flowers and watch them grow."

"Yes, sir, that does it alright, as long as nothing goes wrong."

"Nothing goes wrong in a garden," I said, "because whatever grows up fades back into the ground at the end of its lifetime and is soil for new life. There's no such thing as not having new life."

"What a lovely way to live," Jenessa's fingers relaxed. "The garden is now finished; it's all lovely and clean."

"It's like our life. When we get our mind and heart lovely and clean it just becomes a beautiful garden to grow into God's love," I say.

"Yes, yes, that's it alright."

I was aware then, as I had been with Ronald, that I had stretched my boundaries. There is no way to know for certain if the thoughts I expressed related appropriately to either Jenessa's or Ronald's beliefs. I knew Jenessa was religious; I knew Ronald had no place to go but up. As a Healing Companion, I took a risk. Since both elders were open, relaxed, and at peace at the end of our visits, I trusted that the visits were effective, that these elders had the ability to inwardly reject my suggestions if they disapproved. Since Healing Companions do not assume a role of authority but establish a relationship of mutual mentoring, I felt these elders would know I respected their right to freedom.

By filling in the sentences Jenessa could not complete by herself, order was made out of chaos. We achieved a sense of mental and emotional wellness. Jenessa was at peace when she died.

Silently Listening

Juanita's family was not at peace. Juanita had been in a coma for three years. The family was keeping fifty-five-year old Juanita alive on life supports, but they were too upset to see her in this condition, so they rarely visited. Even if Juanita had no awareness of what was going on, perhaps if the family had read Mary Kay Blakely's story of her nine days in a coma, they would have come more often and given Juanita joy, comfort, humor, and hope as did Mary Kay's family and friends.

Mary Kay heard everything that went on around her. Her sister, Gina, stroked her head, neck, and shoulders, and talked to her as if she were awake. She brought music, books, stories, and jokes to share. One day Gina came in with a new pair of yellow boots, told Mary Kay all about them and paraded up and down the room. Mary Kay heard the clatter of footsteps. Internally, she witnessed everything.

Gina encouraged the staff to say Mary Kay's name when speaking about her in her room. Instead of saying "she," Gina wanted to reinforce the attitude that Mary Kay was an alive, pulsating person with the potential to understand what was being said. Her boyfriend, Larry, stayed by her side for hours. Mary Kay felt his overwhelming love.

While she went in and out of hallucinations, Mary Kay experienced intense loneliness whenever a family member or friend left the room without saying why. She felt they had deserted her in those instances and felt unloved. If one of them burst into tears without speaking about it, her yearning to know why only increased her feelings of isolation.

Mary Kay realized that, although she had lost bodily sensations, she could still think. "If you didn't have a brain . . . how would you know you existed? How would you know you are loved?" While in a coma, Mary Kay came to the conclusion that to know the truth, to know who you are and why you are here, is all that remains when the body dies. She confirmed her belief that "thought . . . seemed to be the only immortal thread of human existence."

In addition to these realizations, Mary Kay had mystical experiences. "The brilliant light that filled my head had enveloped me in such powerful love, such magnificent peace . . . the blinding white light blurred all distinction between where I left off and the benevolent presence began. It felt as though my body had been lifted from a damaged delivery package . . . and then held up to a warm, welcoming light."

Before Mary Kay recovered she experienced a "spectacular peace." After she recovered this sense of peace continued. She was transformed from a frenetic woman overloaded with causes, deadlines, parties, kids, and relationships into a woman of unshakable calm.[2]

Caregivers and families can be inspired by Mary Kay's experience to honor the life that still exists within a coma patient.

Living for years in a coma, Juanita may not have experienced anything like Mary Kay's insights and sense of calm, but she may have experienced more than anyone knew. Although Juanita's family may not have visited her often—perhaps fearing they wouldn't know what to do if they did—they still were not ready to let her go.

When death finally approached, Juanita's young son and daughter came to be with her. I was holding Juanita's hand and began to sing softly: I thanked Juanita for the good she had given; acknowledged the sadness of her children and how hard it is to bear separation; assured the children they could be a gift to Juanita now by showing their love, courage, and strength to go on with life, knowing all would be well for Juanita as she journeyed onward with our blessings of peace. Singing these words seemed to calm the family and hopefully gave them the courage to release her.

Sogyal Rinpoche once told the story of a grieving woman whose husband was in a coma. The wife had never told him of her love, had never said good-bye. A hospice worker encouraged her to tell him everything. The woman told her husband she loved him, would miss him, but didn't want him to suffer any longer. It was all right for him to go. Immediately, as if waiting for his wife's permission, her husband died.[3]

Albert Einstein found a loving way to relate to his sister, Maja, who was in a coma after suffering a stroke. Einstein read Plato aloud to her for two hours every day. He believed part of Maja's mind was alive and that his love would be communicated.[4]

Communications with people who drift in and out of a coma can be inspiring. Leonard Bernstein had such an experience with Nadia Boulanger, one of the world's greatest composers, conductors, and music teachers, who died at age ninety-three.

Nadia had been in a coma for several months. When Bernstein, who had been a student of Nadia's, came to see her, he was restricted to a ten-minute visit by her caregivers. He ended up staying an hour. As Bernstein knelt on the floor by her bed, Nadia suddenly began speaking. A few words conveyed everything. Commanding him to stay, she insisted she was not tired at all.

Bernstein questioned her about whether she heard music within her. She replied, "All the time." Naming her favorite composers, he asked if she heard music now. Her answer: "A music . . . without beginning or end."[5]

Music without beginning or end—such an inspired journey can take place inside the confines of a coma, inside the mystery of human life.

❧ Steps for Healing ❧

Insights that can help heal

♦ Tending a person in a coma can become an inspirational experience.

♦ People in a coma may experience a vivid inner reality even though they are unable to communicate.

Helping yourself heal

1. In order to understand your responses to someone who is unresponsive, first acknowledge your reaction. Disappointment, anger, fear, or self-doubt? Accept these feelings without judging them.

2. A person in a coma has nothing to give. You are the giver. When you give with your presence, your wisdom, and your joy—without expectations of anything in return—you practice the true act of selfless love.

Helping your elder heal

1. When visiting an elder who is in a coma, act as if your elder is perfectly able to receive you, hear you, and respond to you.

2. To help yourself face an elder's physical deterioration, imagine a wonderful light shining in your elder's heart. Talk; read a poem, story, or sacred phrase; sing or chant. Sometimes singing can help you feel more connected to your elder and inspire you to know what to say. Visualize the words or music going into your elder's heart.

3. If you feel the need to be more active with your elder, you can create a healing practice with your hands. With an attitude of faith, accept the possibility that hands can heal even when they do not touch the body. As you pass your hands several inches over your elder's body, imagine you are giving him or her a peace blessing. While doing this, you may sing, pray or be silent.

4. When your elder is in a coma or is dying, you cannot know whether your elder is aware of what is going on. Therefore, you may want to refrain from speaking about a hopeless diagnosis or about funeral arrangements. Instead, focus on soothing words. You will contribute to the presence of peace and be at ease in yourself that you have given blessings to make your elder's transition easier.

For your inspiration

In the deepest recesses of my soul, I am alive.
Though I may barely breathe, speak, move, or respond, I live in an
unseen world, in a timeless universe. From within this world
beyond words, a shining silver thread connects me to the people I
know and love, connects me to a touch, a sound, a blessing.
Do not discard me because I live in realms you cannot go,
for I am still here and all my life history still sings.
Elders in a coma cannot say these things.
As an act of honoring them, it is I who can speak for them.
Some day I may be ill, unable to say what lives in me.
With this understanding, my elder and I are one.

TWENTY-ONE

When Death Is Near

Whatever God gives,
O heart of mine,
Take what God gives
O heart of mine,
And build your house
of happiness.
—Author unknown

"I'M GOING TO call you my 'jewel of the morning.' " Camilla's eyes dance with joy as she gazes at me. "My twin sister is amazed that you want to be with me at my glorious departure!"

I wonder to myself, how many elders think of their impending death as a "glorious departure"?

"I can't wait to die," Camilla says. "I don't really need anyone. The Lord will be very close. Nothing is more thrilling than to be in his Presence. Whatever he wants, I want."

Dying Sweetly

Although feeling needed in a meaningful way is one of the primary benefits of being a Healing Companion, I know that Camilla is particularly pleased that I want to be with her during this final period in her life. Because her spiritual life is the center of her being, she is radiant even during the months when she is dying. By thinking of God continually, she is an example of spiritual wellness, of the beneficial effects of spiritual life. The blossoming of her spirit becomes an excellent lesson for Healing Companions.

"Real joy was mine only after I came to live in the nursing home," she tells me, smiling. "You have that joy, my jewel of the morning, and you've been giving it away. Now I have it, too. It's pure joy, and it comes from God. My father wanted me to be courageous. Now I am—through the joy you bring me."

Courage through joy, which awakens and grows in the least likely places—even in a nursing home. As I recount stories about monks living in the monastery, Camilla's happiness increases. Daily, joy abounds.

"When I go to sleep at night, I'm not worrying, wishing, or thinking. I smile," she says. "Every night I look at myself smiling. If I were on a mountaintop, I don't think I could hold any more joy. I'm completely relaxed. Sometimes I get a strong impression from Heaven. It wouldn't be this way if I were rushing around, cooking, washing, and cleaning. Lying in bed, life gets more wonderful all the time."

Camilla doesn't see obstacles; she sees opportunities. One day she tells me one of her arthritic hands hurts more than usual. This morning the aide has been insensitive, roughly examining and moving her fingers, shoving her fingers against the guardrail. Camilla asks me to get a nurse. It is not typical for Camilla to ask for a nurse; she must be in pain. The next day she tells this same aide: "You're not to blame for my suffering, you're so kind." Later she confides to me: "I won't report her; I'll pray for her."

Silence is Camilla's deepest form of prayer. Often I honor

this by praying silently with her. Her prayers do not ask for anything; she simply rests in God's presence. The minister who teaches Bible studies for the nursing home tells Camilla: "I wish I had what you have." Although she doesn't belong to a church, she has an inner spirituality that shines through. She tells me that, as a small child drawn to God, she recited Bible verses she had not memorized but simply "knew."

Camilla sees holiness in the mundane activities of life. "When the aides wash the floor, I feel clean all over," she says, "and I tell them so." Finding joy wherever she looks, she also finds it in her dreams.

"I had a dream I was in Heaven. It was blissful. I woke up thinking I had to make a plate of food for each family member. Cuckoo! But isn't the Lord wonderful? He creates people, and then follows up with food that turns into lips, eyes, ears, expression."

Her expression is beauty. Even though she is too weak to hold a fork, she glows. This wasn't always so. Suffering entered Camilla's life more than once. One daughter is in a mental institution; the other died. Her husband was a Communist and divorced Camilla when she became a Christian. As a Healing Companion, I become witness to a painful confession: asked as a young teacher to travel across the country initiating a nationwide reading program for mentally challenged children, Camilla refused.

"How could I refuse God's work? I failed Him." This is the only time I have heard Camilla express real sorrow. She tells me that instead of committing herself to the welfare of the children, she committed herself to an intimate relationship that didn't last. Normally, Camilla knows how to love rather than punish herself when discovering mistakes she's made. Once she told me: "I have deeply selfish traits but I don't blame myself. We are born with a certain makeup; the Lord is patient."

Yet as she nears death, Camilla still needs to heal particular emotional wounds. Since forgiveness is essential for spiritual wholeness, I encourage Camilla to pray for forgiveness. As we talk out her feelings and pray together, our prayers awaken acceptance of God's forgiveness, and Camilla is able to forgive herself. Her guilt is released and her joy restored. Camilla goes forward toward her death with peace.

As she is dying, Camilla looks like a Madonna. Her hair is wrapped in a softly woven pastel pink and blue shawl, with fringes fanning her serene face like the wings of angels wrapping her in an embrace of love. Everyone in the nursing home is sending her their love as well. Janitors, aides, and nurses come and go in her room day and night, just to glimpse her radiant peace. I have lost count of how many while sitting for hours reciting Psalms by her bed.

Even her deaf roommate Leona, unable to talk or walk, knows Camilla is dying. A physical therapist wraps a belt around Leona's waist, holds her upright, and helps her walk to Camilla's bed. Leaning over, Leona lovingly pats Camilla's cheeks, caresses her face, and soothes her brow.

Camilla does not talk but nods and smiles. At one point she loudly says "Isaiah!" when asked what she wants me to read. Throughout the long night and into the early morning, I know Camilla hears the Psalms. She often smiles. Without fear or resistance, she is dying so sweetly. She lives her dying, participates consciously even though she no longer talks. Occasional discomfort arises. The right Psalm appears and gives strength to endure.

At sunrise, silent prayer replaces Psalms. Suddenly, Camilla says: "I am perfectly at rest in the Lord. Beautiful, beautiful." What is beautiful? She is too weak to say. But it is a perfect end.

Yet not quite. As I walk out of her room, a nurse walks in.

"Your lungs are filled with fluid. You have an infection. Do you want us to suction your lungs and give you antibiotics?"

Camilla nods her consent. A few questions and a nod reverse life's natural flow into the downstream current of death at age ninety-six. Instead, Camilla is suddenly taken on an arduous, upstream struggle. Through drugs she must try to live while her spirit and body want to die. Why is her life being saved? Was she capable of making a rational, responsible decision to choose life as she lay in the twilight zone between life and death? Was it purely the survival instinct, an automatic reflex, which motivated her choice for recovery?

Within twenty-four hours, Camilla glows. Grace has given a purpose to an extended life: "I saw a vision of Heaven." Wonderment lights up her eyes. "It is bright, wonderful. Everyone is radiant. The faces are young and peaceful. This was the most extraordinary experience of my life." Camilla lived for another six weeks. She endured a tube in her nose and labored breathing, yet she continued to radiate spiritual wholeness. Although it took an hour of listening to hear only a few joyous sentences, it was worth the effort. The joyousness she expressed in her final days were messages of wisdom and love—and an inspiration to all of us.

Enhancing the Journey toward Death

Camilla's lifelong spiritual journey helped make her death a "glorious departure." However, spirituality does not always guarantee a peaceful death. What about those elders who have not lived an exultant spiritual life? What will their experience of dying be like? Grace comes in mysterious ways. Death may be beautiful for an atheist, while for others with a more spiritual outlook it may not be as joyous an experience as Camilla's. Regardless of the spiritual background of our elders, as Healing Companions we can help them to create a more peaceful and joyous pathway to death.

Our culture honors the birthing process but, with the exception of Hospice care, it doesn't know how to honor the process of dying. Instead of embracing wholeness, inspiring inner wellness, and providing solace, in-depth counsel, and spiritual enhancement for the dying, many caretakers and family members feel inadequate, indifferent, frightened, or confused about the dying process. Sometimes our elders are not given the option to die as they have lived, to complete their cycle in surroundings that make them feel nurtured in their last moments. Too often they die accompanied only by the sound of a television.

Therese Schroeder-Sheker's inspirational Chalice of Repose Project attempts to change this through music for the dying. Her project recognizes dying as a "spiritual process . . . an opportunity for growth," with the "possibility of interior deathbed healing without curing . . . Here, healing occurs in the realm of soul or inner life, not necessarily in the physical body."[1]

Inner healing is possible even as an elder is dying. An elder may need to share pent-up emotions, feelings of isolation, and unhealed wounds of the past.

Irene desperately needed such healing. Terminally ill, she refused to talk for over a month. Asked by the staff at the nursing home to visit her, I gently place my hand on hers. Within a few minutes Irene pours out her rage, and then begs me to stay.

Later when I meet with her social worker, I ask if he would visit Irene on a regular basis to help support her through her newly exposed vulnerability.

"We don't offer psychotherapy here." His reply stuns me. Will anything be offered to ease Irene's state of mind? I didn't have a chance to find out. Two days later, Irene died.

One of the ways that Healing Companions can help pave the pathway to death with more peace and acceptance is to offer elders the chance to heal their wounds. Simply listening and holding a hand may be all that's needed. What's important is that elders have the chance to express their deepest feelings and move forward toward death with a clear heart and mind. Healing Companions aid elders in acknowledging unresolved anger, guilt, and fear; they help to inspire in them the desire to repair negative attitudes through forgiveness and letting go of the past. Through this process, elders may be awakened to spiritual joy and peace and some may receive the gift of becoming fully present in the experience of their dying moments.

Sabrina was fully present during her journey toward death. A former singer, songwriter, and journalist, she lived in a nursing home where few of the residents were capable of conversing with her. Without a trace of self-pity, she told me: "I never thought I would end up in a place like this." She confessed that she hated her husband and would have killed him if it weren't for her family and God. Seeking spiritual solace after finding him with another woman, she found that through prayer her heart softened toward him.

One day I raced to Sabrina's room. A brainstorm had hit me. Aware that her songwriting expertise had been lying dormant, I asked if she would help me find the right note for a song I was writing. Thrilled with my request, she consented. "You're not singing the right notes," she advised me. "Try it like this." Sabrina sang in perfect pitch, clear and strong.

A month after our lessons began, Sabrina became weak.

Although she was confined to her bed, we continued our musical bond. I spontaneously began singing biblical phrases that seemed to penetrate Sabrina's unresolved hatred for her husband. "I am ready to give him up," she said. "He couldn't help what he did. He was weak, restless, and didn't believe in himself. Poor man."

A week before her death, barely able to talk or move, Sabrina is "dancing" in her bed, her arms waving above her head in joyous celebration while I sing. Sabrina went out with what she knew best—with music and the joy of its expression in her soul.

❧ Steps for Healing ❧

Insights that can help heal

◆ Even when the body is dying, spiritual wellness is still possible.

◆ A truly joyful spirit accepts all that happens without resistance.

◆ When a person embraces death as a glorious departure, he or she shows others the way.

Helping yourself heal

1. To embrace your elder's journey, become aware of your own feelings about the potential for an afterlife.

2. When you become aware of a resistance to letting go of people and things you cling to, find a ritual or wisdom teaching that represents the ebb and flow of life.

3. Look for areas in yourself and in your life that require forgiveness.

4. If you become aware that your elder reminds you of some grief from your past, acknowledge this to yourself. Try to stay in the present moment.

5. Explore your vision of how you would like to leave this earth. By doing this, you may be better able to help your elders. You may want to include fabric, color, scents, sacred words, or music that resonates with your spirit. Write your preferences and leave them with your family and caregivers. You can also engage in writing notes of thanksgiving to people you love.

6. After your elder dies, set aside the time you need to grieve.

Helping your elder heal

1. Remove loud noises (such as rock music, loud speech, or scraping chairs) in and near you elder's room.

2. If you are not certain that your elder has the capacity to hear, reassure your elder that you are in the room. Make your presence known by a gentle touch.

3. At the bedside of an elder who is dying, make a silent intention to be a peaceful presence in the room. If you get lost in feelings of helplessness or grief, take an inward action: silently repeat the word "peace" as you breathe in and out.

4. You may want to reassure your elder by repeating aloud something like this: "Do not be afraid. You are going toward the light. The light is your true home."

5. When you know that your elder is dying, you can create a vigil. It may be a few hours or a few days. Encourage others to alternate the hours with you. When reciting readings, diligent repetition may be helpful, as well as shortening sentences if needed. Add music if it is appropriate.

For your inspiration

Participating in my elder's journey, I offer these words: in this my last destination on earth, I embrace with courage the toil I face in the arduous process of dying, physically and emotionally. I prepare for my leave-taking with the faith of looking into an unseen future, knowing I have done the best I could on earth, hoping I may become a beacon of light in the world to come.

My elders are ahead of me on this journey. They are my teachers as they wait at the gate of the Unknown. As we prepare to leave our bodies, our spirits awaken to a new and mysterious joy, to an attentiveness to vistas beyond our physical reality.

In this, my elder and I are one.

TWENTY-TWO

Prayer Therapy

I want on my tombstone:
'She died from joy.'
—Author unknown

THE NURSE RUNS down the hall to stop me as I head out of the hospital. "What have you done to my patient?" she asks.

Startled, I wonder: Did Johanna die as soon as I left her room?

"You should see her. She's sitting up in bed, her cheeks are rosy. She's no longer hyperventilating, and she's eating! But what's so amazing, she's been moaning day and night, and now she's completely calm. What were you doing?"

What I was doing began two years earlier when Johanna's family, too far away to spend time with her, included my services as part of her treatment. "I want you to help me sing my way into heaven through the scriptures, and to help me with my fear of dying," Johanna told me. Although I was not adept in Bible studies, I was willing to go on a scripture journey with her and together we would learn. We spent the next two years preparing for death by praying our way through the scriptures. This preparation was now paying off.

That morning I had found Johanna gasping for breath, her

skin pale. She seemed on the edge of death. Her doctor claimed this was one of the worst cases of congestive heart failure he had ever seen. It was unlikely she could survive much longer.

For months, Johanna had repeatedly requested that I pray from the book of Isaiah. I took Johanna's hand and prayed: "Fear not, for I have called you by your name. You are mine." Johanna nodded her head slightly. "When you pass through the waters, I will be with you." A brief smile.

I sang the next words: "And the rivers shall not overflow you. When you walk through the fire, you shall not be burned."[1] Johanna begins to tap the rhythm. Her doctor has predicted she soon might die. Is she now gathering strength? I continue in prayer:

"When I take refuge in these promises, I have all the peace I need."

"Uh huh!" Johanna exclaimed.

"He will set me high upon a rock."[2]

"Uh huh!"

Then combining scripture with prayer I sang: "Longing to be clothed upon with our dwelling place from heaven,[3] we are eager to put on a body of light, to be freed from this old flesh which keeps us imprisoned!"

"How beautiful!" Johanna exclaimed, her voice much louder now.

After leaving the hospital, I phoned to see how she was. Johanna had dramatically improved. She no longer needed intravenous feeding and remained calm throughout the night.

Three days later I found her sitting up in bed. She looked beautiful. I knew she believed in miracles and the promises recorded in the Bible. Was it her belief that caused her healing? She and I had spent hours immersed in her scriptures. We knew intellect could not bring us to an actual experience of the words. We didn't want to simply read the Bible as we would any other book.

We wanted something more, something that would transform us. Each time we approached her scriptures, we opened ourselves to contact the Presence *within* the words; to experience a living reality; to find awe, hope, exaltation, and peace. For an elder of a different faith, other sacred texts could be used. But for Johanna, we prepared for death by celebrating Life as it is described in the Bible. Was it the memory of those joyful moments that returned to Johanna in her deepest hour of need?

Later, she told me: "When I was in the hospital, I couldn't breathe. I knew I was dying. The experience wasn't pleasant. But it wasn't that bad, either. Suddenly I was unafraid. I guess I'll never be afraid again."

Johanna has now returned to Garden Terrace residential home. As I enter the living room, a gentle glow descends from the skylight, tinting the room with gold. Greeting Johanna, I am grateful for the friends I met in New Zealand some years ago, who taught me an ancient approach to prayer: *pray reading*. I did not know then that this seed of pray reading would one day bear fruit in an elder's spiritual recovery.

The prayer consists of dwelling on each word of scripture as if it were a jewel, taking delight in one word at a time, speaking with a playful spirit until each word begins to shine. Would pray reading help Johanna now as she slumps in her wheelchair, her head hanging on her chest? Desperately she says: "Please tell the nurse to take me to my room. I need to lie down." For Johanna, it is torture to sit. But the nurse insists she must sit; her recovery depends on it.

Holding her hand, I look quietly into Johanna's eyes. "'They that wait upon the Lord shall renew their strength.'"[4] My voice takes on a tone of joyous anticipation, one we often experience when praying together.

Johanna gazes at me with keen interest.

"We have a power within us, a strength that rises above exhaustion and waits patiently. Our inheritance is far greater than this physical body!"

Johanna's eyes brighten. "Yes," she exclaims with excitement, "we are clothed in light!"

"Clothed in light." I repeat her phrase, touched by her response. "We rise above physical discomfort. We dwell in eternity now!"

Johanna, wide awake, remains receptive.

"Rising up now on wings as the eagle, we soar."

A burst of joy seems to lay hold of us. Johanna sits spellbound, not a trace of agitation in her body. By now I expect her to be slumped in her chair, unable to hold up her spine. Most elders would be screaming to be put to bed, but not Johanna. She is totally immersed in this moment as if nothing was bothering her.

"We are clothed in light!" she says again, presses my hand with enthusiasm.

"And new life." My response to her enthusiasm seems to energize us. Although I forgot my Bible today, an outpouring of verses along with spontaneous prayer surprises us both:

"We are partakers of the divine nature,[5] dwelling in divine life now. We run with endurance the race set before us . . . [6] we run with our inner spirit to the one who gives us joy!"

Swept along in this current of Love, Johanna has become oblivious to her physical discomfort. She gazes at me in total alertness. I am amazed. It is difficult to detect that she is ill. Johanna looks at me with eager anticipation. A half hour has elapsed. She has come through this with grace.

A few weeks later, another heart failure, another hospital

visit, and now Johanna is back at the home again. Faint, weak, unable to eat, she lies in bed, her translucent blue eyes absolutely clear. Looking far off into the distance as if she is seeing heaven's door, she listens as I begin to pray her scriptures again:

" 'My grace is sufficient for you, for my power is made perfect in weakness.'[7] Through weakness we have access to a perfect power beyond any we might hope to achieve on our own."

Serenely, Johanna listens.

"I can boast of my weaknesses, for the power of God rests upon me."[8] I place my hand in Johanna's hand; our eyes meet.

Johanna responds with a delighted smile; her spirit, too, seems vibrant. She is fully present. Softly, like waves lapping upon a shore, I repeat the phrase over and over. Her lips move; she whispers the phrases with me.

Before I entered her room, Johanna's nurse informed me Johanna was unable to respond to anything. I find her in bed, motionless. My intention is to elevate her spirit so that she is not overcome by weakness and exhaustion. I sense Johanna's spirit awakening as my words call her away from physical trials into a meditative prayer:

"I take my rest in him. I lie in the grasses of his meadows, green, fresh, ever scented with spring flowers. I am a sweet smelling scent in God's heart and he loves me. I am lying in his grasses, growing ever new; newness of life breathes over me as God rests upon me."

Johanna's eyes close. She is not asleep; she is drinking in the words, sinking into a deep resting in her spirit.

"He covers me with his love, his protection. He is like a gentle wing, his breath a wind of spirit now softly settling over my heart."

Johanna's eyes remain closed. Totally relaxed, she breathes easily.

"I lie in the meadows of his love, am embraced in the meadows of his peace."

She nods in agreement, opens her eyes.

"I am content with weaknesses . . . for when I am weak, then I am strong."[9]

Johanna smiles.

"How can I be strong when I am weak?" I continue. "When I am weak, I learn more about this one whom my heart loves. He is the strength within my weakness. When he rests upon me, he creates a heavenly meadow in my mind, a glorious sunshine in my heart."

The warmth of Johanna's hand in mine, the clear openness of her eyes, indicate she is willing to be healed, whether in body, mind, or spirit.

"Well, honey," Johanna says, "how are things going?"

"Very well. I write often now."

"Honey, be sure you put radiance in your writing."

"Radiance?"

"Yes, your radiance."

"It isn't *my* radiance, you know."

"Well," she takes my hand, holds it tenderly, "I am putting some of *my* radiance into you."

I am touched. Johanna's heart muscle has been severely damaged. The doctor didn't expect her to live as long as she has. Yet she still gives of herself.

She squeezes my hand, makes the sign of the cross over me.

"My radiance is a bit low—but here's what I've got. Now you go out and spread peace and joy."

As I leave the residential home, I reflect on our sessions. Johanna once told me that until we began praying together, she had never, in all of her church experience, found anything spiritual relating to her personal life. In our sessions, we focus on what matters to her.

Johanna and I affirm health and joy. By turning away from sickness without denying its existence, we imbue ourselves with exalted thoughts. During a life-threatening illness, this is almost impossible to do without a partner.

When ill, the mind is infected with every nuance of the body's struggle. It is a rare person who can turn away from the sickness they're experiencing, to find another dimension of reality. An elder with a life-threatening illness usually cannot initiate or sustain this type of focusing on his or her own. A Healing Companion is needed.

Two days later, Johanna is much weaker. As the body weakens, so does the will. As Healing Companion, I need to be that will for her, to be an impetus for building up spiritual energy. Johanna's mind easily wanders away in distress. My function is to help her mind shift from sickness to thoughts of love and healing. In the past, whenever her thoughts have veered off into the discomfort of illness, I have stoked the fire by prodding the coals within her spirit. A blaze builds, and the fire becomes a warm, bright, dancing joy where only smoldering ash had been.

Can this happen again today? Johanna is in bed, ill and discouraged. Once again as I have consistently done, I follow Johanna's lead. Instead of turning to myself for guidance, I turn to her source of healing: her love of scriptures.

"I am putting off the old self, behold all things have become new; I am a new creation."[10]

Johanna rests both palms on her heart. She continues to listen as if she were still lying deep in the grasses of those peaceful meadows. She is perfectly calm. Suddenly her eyes flash open. "I am putting on a seamless garment of light," she declares, as her weak and faltering voice gathers strength.

I begin a spontaneous chant. Johanna's lips move, repeating

silently after me:

"I am being healed in that garment of light!"

"I am being released in that garment of light!"

"I am refreshed and renewed in that garment of light!"

"I am in bliss in that garment of light!"

The image of light is one that Johanna spontaneously found in our past sessions. Johanna's mind is not wandering as I guide her in a meditation: "As I lie here in this seamless garment of light, the angels ascend and descend along my body." This angel image, inspired by the gospel of John,[11] expands.

"The light of the angels moves up my feet, legs, abdomen, ribs, heart, neck, face, head; then descends down my back, buttocks, legs, and into my feet again, making a glorious dance of light up and down my body . . . soon I will hear the angels sing."

I pause. There's a sweet silence. Johanna opens her eyes, looks at me the way she does when she feels well. "God will work things out for you, honey," she says. The session has taken a turn. Johanna now blesses me.

Moved to tears by her tender caring, I reply, "Johanna, I love you."

Johanna, strong and unsentimental, looks directly at me. For the first time in three years, she says, "I love you, too."

The days progress. One day I arrive to find the nurse insisting Johanna will sleep her way through our session; she suggests I come another day. But I know better. Often while sleeping, Johanna is awake in some part of her being. She once affirmed that while she slept, she indeed heard me.

Standing by her bed, a song is singing within me, and I sing it to Johanna. It is a lullaby. Though Johanna looks as if she hasn't the strength to do anything, she quietly repeats every phrase I sing. She squeezes my hand over and over.

Suddenly her hand begins to tremble violently. She is so frail and has struggled so much. Now this. I feel helpless. Then a strange thing happens. The lullaby emerges again, simple, soothing. Suddenly my mind becomes like a pond, very clear and quiet. Something lets go within me. Within the melody, stillness grows. I have the sensation of drifting off to sleep.

How can I slip into sleep while singing? The lullaby seems to float through me. Johanna looks into my eyes. She too seems to be sensing this quiet stillness, this touch of spirit making the song sing itself.

When I get up to leave, Johanna's hand is at rest, not a trace of trembling.

An important event has taken place, a challenge many caregivers may face. Watching Johanna's weakness increase, unknowingly I have been *trying* to get through to her, *trying* to help her change, *trying* to save her from being moved to a nursing home. Through singing this lullaby I realize Johanna will receive healing through God's way, not mine. "Neither is He served by human hands as though He needs anything, since He Himself gives to all life and breath and all things."[12]

Momentarily, I had forgotten that I am not the helper. "He is able to help those who are being tried."[13] This biblical guidance releases me to realize that when I try to help on my own, inner tension is the result. If I am overcome by my desire to release Johanna's suffering, I am in anguish. But when I can let go of my expectations of myself and leave the healing in God's hands, there is peace. For Healing Companions and elders who are not drawn to the Bible or are not religious, other resources can be used to find a way to give without so much effort, a way to let go of trying so hard.

What we do is not so important; it is what God does in and through us. Mother Teresa clearly showed this. Brother

Andrew writes that when Mother Teresa talked about her life and work, she said, "It is God using nothingness to reveal his splendor."

"She is so convinced of her own nothingness," says Brother Andrew, that Mother Teresa requests, "Please pray for me that I don't spoil God's work."[14]

As the days pass, Johanna rings the call bell continually to summon the nurse. The staff is agitated, and Johanna is distraught. Our session begins:

"We call upon the one who casts out this need to call upon caregivers to solve what only he can solve. We have faith that the demons of fear, restlessness, and lack of self-control can be cast out!"

Johanna listens with rapt attention. I speak the words I know she wants to say.

"When the nurse says I might be moved to a nursing home, my response is fear. But I turn to God dwelling within me. I am rooted and grounded in his love.[15] I am being healed of anxiety. Love is my sword and shield!"

Johanna nods her approval.

"What is my real problem? I have forgotten joy. I don't feel joy. Why? Because I've been trying to live out my situation *on my own*. Now I see I'm not alone: 'In thy presence there is fullness of joy.' "[16]

Soon after this session, her ringing of the call bell stops. Except for emergencies, Johanna rarely uses it again.

Johanna is now in a new phase. She only speaks a few words. Listening to long sentences overloads her mind. Prayer has to be simplified. She appears to be having a crisis of faith when she tells me, "I want tangible proof of God's love." Johanna's request startles me. I never expected her to doubt God's love.

I share with Johanna the words of Mechtild of Magdeburg, written in her old age: "Lord! I thank Thee that since Thou hast taken from me the power of my hands . . . and the power of my heart, Thou now servest me with the hands and hearts of others."[17] Would Johanna begin to realize that God is present for her in the hands and hearts of her caregivers?

The day is hot. Moistening a washcloth, I gently massage her feet with the cool cloth. Never before have I ministered to her physical needs. Softly, I begin to hum. The hum soon becomes a song, telling Johanna she has proof of God's love through all of us who love her. Our relationship has reached a beautiful crescendo. From this simple act of love I feel closer to Johanna than ever—closer to Love itself.

From this day onward, Johanna never again requests proof of God's love.

Johanna's condition worsens. She must be moved to a nursing home. She becomes despondent, and I realize that she needs to know that spirituality does not exclude despondency. Spirituality does not mean constant joy. To overcome her despair, she requests hymns of praise. Joyous melody replaces anxiety; the more praise, the more power; the more power, the more a fortress of inner strength is being built.

Within the next two weeks, Johanna is rushed to the hospital twice with congestive heart failure. Back at the nursing home, she is content. At sundown when the home is quiet, we enjoy a nightly songfest. Before she drops off to sleep, I sing: "The spirit of God is a living stream / I sing of the peace that he always brings." Johanna indicates that talking, even listening to talking, drains her. But singing gives her life and peace before she falls asleep.

Now that talking ceases, Johanna's silent responses grow. As I sing, she claps her hands, taps to the rhythm on the gourd of my instrument. Some nights she is conductor, waving her hand from side to side. Participating as if she were well, Johanna, on the verge of death, astounds me. With each passing evening, we create stepping stones of joy.

One night I arrive exhausted. Suddenly I hear a song being created just for her:

"The Lord will spread his tabernacle of peace over you

And you will sleep the sleep of peace;

And you will dream the dream of angels;

And you will look into the Light of Life;

And in the dawn you will become

A new creation."

The song creates a sacred space as we get ready for the fulfillment of the promise that we "shall go out with joy and be led forth in peace."[18] How sweet it would be if Johanna completes her journey now as our song dies into dusk. Will she?

Not yet. Six weeks later I find her nurse, Gabriella, leaning close to Johanna's ear. She speaks softly, assures Johanna she need not fear when she feels something press tightly on her arm. Gabriella is taking Johanna's blood pressure. Surprised, I have never seen a nurse go to the trouble of reassuring a resident during this simple procedure.

Ever so gently, Gabriella lifts Johanna's arm, tenderly wraps the strap around it. At that moment, Gabriella becomes more than nurse; she is all warmth, all comfort, similar to the symbiotic rapport of mother and child, an intimate, embracing kindness now reflected in the beautiful, round face of Gabriella. Gabriella has been a nurse for twenty-five years. Rarely have I seen such devotion.

Standing outside of Johanna's room, I start to cry. Gabriella has finished her task and now enters the hallway. Seeing my tears, she embraces me, tells me she too cries whenever she loses one of her elders.

But my tears are more than grief. They are tears of thanksgiving. Yesterday, one of the nurse's aides insisted that Johanna eat, even though Johanna had stopped eating days ago. Standing in the doorway of Johanna's room, I watched as the aide tried to feed Johanna with a tone that implied: "I know what's good for you. Do as I say." I suggested to the aide that perhaps Johanna could not eat, and the woman glared back at me: "Are you telling *me* what to do?" After fourteen years on the job, the aide would not tolerate a challenge to her authority. She was doing her job.

But Gabriella was going far beyond her job description; she was serving a dying woman with love, an act that touched me to tears. I recalled the advice of a priest: "When you enter Johanna's room, leave your grief behind. Enter with thoughts of illumination."

I take this inspiration with me at 2 a.m. Johanna's last hours are sweet. Since I want to be attuned to Joanna's spiritual life, I slowly move her rosary beads as I call upon the one Johanna is most drawn to, her comforter, Jesus:

"Your name is peace to my mind / joy to my heart / comfort to my emotions / bliss to my soul."

It is now 3 a.m. All is quiet. Johanna looks at me. She can no longer talk. But that doesn't stop our joy.

"In his splendor, I am going home," I say quietly.

Ten or fifteen minutes pass in silence.

"I am shining with joy in my spirit." A timeless pause again, as I synchronize my rhythms with the slowing down of hers.

"I am coming home to the Kingdom of Light."

Johanna smiles faintly. The priest enters to say the last rites. Afterward, he turns to me: "It's hard, isn't it?" *Hard?* Yes, in her body she suffers, but in her spirit?

After he leaves, I continue to pray for Johanna: "I am leaving this body of troubles / Oh joy in my heart, oh joy!"

Johanna raises her hand in the air as if in agreement. Suddenly her eyes are wide open. She gazes upward as if in awe and amazement. Does she see or inwardly hear something magnificent? Her breathing is no longer labored; it is calm and slow. The space between one breath and the next becomes longer. In that space comes peace. In that pause, no movement. Between two breaths, the Peace Giver sounds a silent blessing: stillness. An immense rapture of suspension. No more struggle, no pain. Breath that is now no-breath. Within that silent space a song hidden in the silence:

"I am flying on the wings of a dove / Going Home to the Lord of Love."

❧ Steps for Healing ❧

Insights that can help heal

- ✦ We can be a conduit for the flow of spiritual energy during an elder's final days.

- ✦ We are not the healer, only the instrument.

- ✦ When we turn away from illness and imbue ourselves with exalted thoughts or prayer, we become connected to wellness within.

- ✦ When suffering is accepted instead of denied, we may be able to transcend pain.

Helping yourself heal

1. Realize that to be effective with scriptures, you have to experience the sacred words and not simply read them. If you are unable to do this, trust that you will find the right path to illumine you and your elder.

2. If you want to try sharing scriptures with your elder, develop the habit of finding verses or phrases and let them speak or sing to you. Allow insights to flow.

3. Give up *trying* to be the sole helper with your elder and allow the energy of Love to take over. Your tension and anxiety may lessen.

Helping your elder heal

1. Have you ever experienced, or are you willing to experience, a Presence within the scriptures? Your response to this question will help you determine whether you are comfortable sharing scriptures with your elder.

2. For elders who do not have religious backgrounds, choose poetic verses. If you are not comfortable with prayer, seek images of beauty that uplift the soul.

For your inspiration

I am like a green olive tree whose branches spread to infinity.
Part of the earth, sea, and sky; part of the Infinite Invisible who
created all that is, I have a holy inheritance: love, wisdom, and
radiance. Such riches never die. Each day I die to my old self, to the
blemishes of rage, fear, and sorrow. Each day I am re-created anew.
In this, my elder and I are one.

EPILOGUE

A New Vision of Eldercare

SOME PEOPLE SLEEP until the morning; some people know they have to bring in the morning. This Talmudic teaching, as taught by Rabbi Shlomo Carlebach, can guide us to walk bravely into a new era of eldercare unprecedented in the history of our society. U.S. Census Bureau figures show that in 2004 one in every seven Americans was sixty-five or older. By 2050, it is predicted that this figure will increase to one in every five.

How will we greet this tremendous growth in the elder population? Will we wait until their population explosion is upon us and become overwhelmed with serving their needs? Or will we begin now to plan for their well-being? Are we creative enough to envision a new way of serving the needs of the oldest members of our society—a way that includes pathways to wholeness, so that elders will be cared for not only financially and physically but emotionally and spiritually as well?

The essence of eldercare needs to change: inner wellness and attention to the spiritual self need to become the core from which eldercare programs are developed. Spiritual dialogues, prayer therapy, the sharing of stories and dreams, the exploration of life's mysteries and miracles, and the enhancement of self-esteem and joy through music, dance, movement, poetry, and art—these all need to be integrated into ongoing programs for elders. And each of these experiences can be facilitated by

Healing Companions, whose role is to celebrate and honor the whole person, to fill the emotional and spiritual gap in eldercare.

Healing Companions not only attend to the emotional and spiritual needs of elders, they also prepare *themselves* for growing old. Most people have moments of anger, selfishness, fear, greed, and rigidity. Healing Companions face such feelings in themselves and hope to develop a yielding, open spirit of joy, equality, and oneness. Such open-heartedness naturally inspires more tolerance, compassion, and inspiration. This kind of transformation is healing for both elders and Healing Companions. The result is less stress and more joy.

Love can guide us to a new level beyond the values we have most prized: youth, glamour, physical prowess, and earning capacity. These values often lead us to abandon those who are old, ailing, and no longer productive. But as we reach out to honor elders, to seek the shining jewel within an old, decaying body, we encounter a human being who emanates a wondrous creation: himself, herself.

Unless individuals change, society can't. We need courage to overcome our resistance to change within ourselves, and within the very structure of society, which must accommodate, integrate, and care for the coming massive increase in the elder population. Each one of us can make a difference within the impersonal milieu in which many elders live and die.

To do this, we need a common vision. A place to begin is with the realization that we *are* a common vision. Each of us has the same longing to love and be loved, to live in peace, to experience joy. Underlying our ethnic, religious, and socioeconomic differences, we are one. If we act as a circle of friends helping one another to fulfill the dream of a peaceful and joyful existence—even at the end of life's journey—our time on earth will have been fruitful. We can be a light of warmth in a cold world; we can become people who bring in the morning with joy, bring in the light for a new dawn. And we can each look forward to joy in the evening of our lives.

About the Author

JOAN ENGLANDER is founder of Healing Companions® services, a holistic pioneering vision for eldercare. For twenty-seven years she has taught elders and nursing staffs, serving as a consultant and in-service trainer for geriatric care facilities in the California Central Coast region. She is also a holistic eldercare coach for families and friends. Her work is deeply inspired by Jungian psychology and by her own spiritual experiences.

Ms Englander sings by the bedside and offers poetry, storytelling, movement, inner reflection, Qigong, and chair dance in private sessions and for groups of elders. In addition, she offers retreat workshops for eldercare providers and for those interested in becoming Healing Companions. She gives musical presentations at healing, retirement and retreat centers; Hospice, nursing, geriatric, home health care and ministerial associations; churches and synagogues.

Her background includes extensive experience as a journalist and musician. For two years she traveled in Egypt, India, and Israel, where she studied spiritual healing traditions.

In 1983 Ms Englander attended an ecumenical gathering in Rome, where she had a private, life-transforming meeting with Mother Teresa. A series of cataclysmic experiences, including the death of a close friend and a serious injury, brought Ms Englander face to face with her own suffering. The healing she received for her own losses profoundly influenced her groundbreaking work as a Healing Companion.

Currently, Ms Englander is an oblate at the New Camaldoli Hermitage in Big Sur, and resides in Ojai, California.
Website: www.joanenglander.com
Email: healing@joanenglander.com

Notes

Introduction

Epigraph. Rabindranath Tagore, *Gitanjali* (New York: Scribner Poetry, 1997), 85.

Chapter 1

Epigraph. Judy Wechsler, "Lessons from a Service Conference," *Sathya Sai Newsletter* 9, no. 2 (Winter 1984-85); Sathya Sai Baba Book Center of America, Norwalk, Calif.

1. Joan Englander, "Shlomo Returns to Sing, Tell Tales," *Ojai Valley News*, March 16, 1983.

2. Anzia Yezierska, "We Go Forth All to Seek America," in *The Golden Land*, Azriel Eisenberg, ed. (New York: Yoseloff, 1964), 286. Reprinted in Samuel H. Dresner, *The Sabbath* (New York: Burning Bush Press, 1970), 67.

3. Englander, "Singing Rabbi Revisits Ojai Valley," *Ojai Valley News*, May 23, 1982.

4. Rabbi Shlomo, concert held in Santa Monica, Calif., June 10, 1981.

5. Englander, "For the Moment—All Will Be Well," *Ojai Valley News*, January 28, 1981.

6. Thich Nhat Hanh, *Plum Village Chanting and Recitation Book* (Berkeley: Parallax Press, 2000).

7. Englander, "For the Moment—All Will Be Well."

8. Tagore, *Gitanjali*, 18.

Chapter 2

Epigraphs. Jean-Paul Sartre, http://www.chatna.com/author/sartre.htm.2006; Joan Englander.

Chapter 3

Epigraph. Acts 2:17, from Witness Lee et al., trans., *The New Testament: Recovery Version* (Anaheim, Calif.: Living Stream Ministry, 1985).

1. Thomas Moore, *Care of the Soul: A Guide for Cultivating Depth and Sacredness in Everyday Life* (New York: HarperCollins, 1992).

2. Lee, trans., *New Testament* 2 Corinthians 4:6.

3. Edward F. Edinger, *Ego and Archetype: Individuation and the Religious Function of the Psyche* (New York: G. P. Putnam's Sons, 1972), 212-17.

Chapter 4

Epigraph. William Wordsworth, "I Wandered Lonely as a Cloud," from *Familiar Quotations*, John Bartlett, 16th ed. (Boston: Little, Brown, 1992), 375.

1. Kahlil Gibran, *Sand and Foam: Book of Aphorisms* (New York: Alfred A. Knopf, 1970), 72.

2. Thomas Moore, *Care of the Soul*, 289.

Chapter 5

Epigraphs. James Roose-Evans, *Passages of the Soul: Ritual Today* (Rockport, Mass.:

Element, 1994), 46; Proverbs 5:1 as quoted in Luke Dysinger, OSB, trans., *The Rule of Saint Benedict: Latin and English* (Trabuco Canyon, Calif.: Source Books, 1997), 3.

Chapter 6

Epigraph. Bernie S. Siegel, *Love, Medicine, and Miracles* (New York: Harper and Row, 1986), 66.

1. Tim Hansel, *You Gotta' Keep Dancin'* (Colorado Springs, Colo.: Cook Communications Ministries, 1985), 83.

2. Maxine Kumin, "History Lesson," in *Our Ground Time Here Will Be Brief* (New York: Viking, 1982), 92.

3. Louis Simpson, *Collected Poems* (New York: Paragon House, 1988), 356.

4. Eknath Easwaran, *Gandhi the Man* (Tomales, Calif.: Nilgiri Press, 1983), 12-20.

5. Ibid., 21-22.

6. Ibid., 28, 117, 140.

7. Susan Jeffers, *Feel the Fear and Do It Anyway* (New York: Ballantine Books, 1988), 75, 79-80, 127, 166.

8. For further information on Marilyn Grosboll's self-esteem seminars, contact Self-Esteem Enterprises, 1096 Casitas Pass Road, Suite 212, Carpinteria, Calif., 93013.

9. Lee, *The New Testament*, abridged from Luke 17:21.

10. Ibid., Ephesians 3:17.

11. Ibid., 2 Corinthians 3:5.

12. Ibid., 2 Corinthians 3:18.

Chapter 7

1. Norman Cousins, *Anatomy of an Illness: Reflections on Healing and Regeneration* (New York: W. W. Norton, 1979), 40.

2. Ed Wheat, MD, with Gloria Okes Perkins, *Love Life for Every Married Couple* (Grand Rapids, Mich.: Zondervan, 1980), 162. Proverbs 5:18-19 (NASB)

3. *The Holy Scriptures*, Harold Fisch, ed. (Jerusalem: Koren Publishers, 1969), Proverbs 5:18-19.

4. As interpreted by Rabbi Arthur Gross-Schaefer.

5. Wheat, *Love Life*, 73.

6. Ossie Davis, as quoted by Phillip L. Berman and Connie Goldman, eds., *The Ageless Spirit* (New York: Ballantine Books, 1992), 61-63.

Chapter 8

Epigraphs. Joan Englander.

1. Robert Muller, *Most of All They Taught Me Happiness* (New York: Doubleday, 1978), 106.

Chapter 9

Epigraphs. Joan Englander.

Chapter 10

Epigraphs. Carole Marie Kelly, *A Handful of Fire: Praying Contemplatively with Scripture* (Mystic, Conn.: Twenty-Third Publications, 2001), 97; Lee, *New Testament*, 2 Corinthians 6:10.

1. Grosboll, Self-Esteem Enterprises.

2. Lee, *New Testament*, Ephesians 4:22-24.

3. Ibid., 2 Corinthians 5:17.

4. *Bhagavad Gita*, 2:62-64, as quoted by Easwaran, *Gandhi the Man*, 121-22.

5. *The Holy Bible*, Authorized King James Version (Grand Rapids, Mich.: Zondervan, 1983), Genesis 22:1-19.

6. William Bridges, *Transitions: Making Sense of Life's Changes* (Cambridge, Mass.: Da Capo Press, 2004), 130, 154.

Chapter 11

Epigraph. Lewis Smedes, *How Can It Be All Right When Everything Is Wrong*, rev. ed. (Colorado Springs, Colo.: Waterbrook Press, 1999), 27, 32.

1. Tagore, *Gitanjali*, 88.

2. Center for Attitudinal Healing, 33 Buchanan Drive, Sausalito, Calif., 94965; 415-331-6161.

3. Shoshana Kalisch with Barbara Meister, *Yes We Sang! Songs of the Ghettos and Concentration Camps* (New York: Harper and Row, 1985), 3, 8-9.

4. Etty Hillesum, *An Interrupted Life: The Diaries of Etty Hillesum*, 1941-1943 (New York: Random House, 1981), 238.

5. Ibid., 247.

Chapter 12

Epigraph. Lee, *New Testament.*

1. Siegel, *Love, Medicine, and Miracles*, 71.

2. You can learn more about the work of Valerie Stevens in her book *12 Keys to Freedom in Christ* (Rancho Mirage, Calif.: Les Strang Group, 1998).

3. Hansel, *You Gotta Keep Dancin,'* 39.

4. Ibid., 54-55.

5. Ibid., 39.

6. Ibid., 42.

Chapter 13

Epigraphs. John Milton, *Paradise Lost, Paradise Regained* (Garden City, N.Y.: Doubleday, 1969), 19; trans. Soiku Shigematsu, *A Zen Harvest: Japanese Folk Zen Sayings, Haiku, Dodoitsu, and Waku* (San Francisco: North Point Press, 1988), 51.

1. Adolf Guggenbühl-Craig, *Power in the Helping Professions* (Dallas, Texas: Spring Publications, 1992), 94, 124, 153.

2. Joan Chittister, *There Is a Season* (New York: Orbis Books, 1995), 1, 68.

3. Morton T. Kelsey, *The Other Side of Silence: A Guide to Christian Meditation* (New York: Paulist Press, 1976), 52, 83.

4. Allan B. Chinen, "The Magic Towel," *In the Ever After: Fairy Tales and the Second Half of Life* (New York: Chiron Publications, 1990), 25-28; as summarized from "The Priest's Towel," *Folk Legends of Japan*, by R. Dorson (Tokyo: Tuttle, 1962).

5. Henry J. M. Nouwen, *The Wounded Healer: Ministry in Contemporary Society* (New York: Doubleday, 1979), 72.

6. Chittister, *There Is a Season*, 109.

Chapter 14

Epigraph. Elisabeth Leseur, *My Spirit Rejoices: The Diary of a Christian Soul in an Age of Disbelief* (Manchester, N. H.: Sophia Institute Press, 1996), 27.

1. Thomas Merton, *Seeds of Contemplation* (New York: New Directions, 1949), 2.

2. Zalman Schachter-Shalomi and Ronald S. Miller, *From Age-ing to Sage-ing: A Profound New Vision of Growing Older* (New York: Warner Books, 1995), 39.

3. Ibid., 40.

4. Sogyal Rinpoche, trans., *The Tibetan Book of Living and Dying*, Patrick Gaffney and Andrew Harvey, ed. (San Francisco: HarperCollins, 1992), 12.

5. Canticles 6:3, as quoted in S. Y. Agnon, *Days of Awe* (New York: Schocken Books, 1965), 18.

6. *New Testament & Psalms*, Revised Standard Version (New York: American Bible Society, 1971), Psalms 51:17.

7. Malachi 3:7, from Agnon, *Days of Awe*, 139.

8. Ibid., 20.

Chapter 15

Epigraph. St. Teresa of Avila, in Daniel Ladinsky, trans., *Love Poems from God: Twelve Sacred Voices from the East and the West* (New York: Penguin Compass, 2002), 291.

1. Schachter-Shalomi, *From Age-ing to Sage-ing*.

2. Jon Kabat-Zinn, *Wherever You Go, There You Are: Mindfulness Meditation in Everyday Life* (New York: Hyperion, 1994), 96-97.

3. The conversation took place with Father John Powell at the New Camaldoli Hermitage, Big Sur, Calif.

4. Rabbi Samuel Seicol, American Society on Aging Convention, March 1996, Anaheim, Calif.

5. Joe Portale, "Attacked by Killer Bees!" *Guidepost* magazine (July 1995), 24-27.

6. Virginia Harris, conference on "Spirituality and Healing in Medicine," sponsored by Harvard Medical School Department of Continuing Education and the Mind Body Institute of Beth Israel Deaconess Medical Center, March 16, 1997, Los Angeles.

7. *New Testament & Psalms*, Psalms 16:8-9.

8. Lee, *The New Testament*, abridged from Luke 11:5-9.

9. Larry Dossey, MD, *Healing Words: The Power of Prayer and the Practice of Medicine* (San Francisco: Harper, 1993), 116-17.

10. Margie Willers, *Awaiting the Healer* (Eastborne, Great Britain: Kingsway Publications, 1991).

11. Dossey, *Healing Words*, 64-65.

12. Ibid., 36.

Chapter 16

Epigraph. Roose-Evans, *Passages of the Soul*, 95.

1. Harvey Arden and Steve Wall, *Wisdom Keepers: Meetings with Native American Spiritual Elders* (Hillsboro, Ore.: Beyond Words Publishing, 1990), 86-91.

2. Michael Ozair, ed., *Let There Be Light: A Compilation of Torahs on the Essence of Hanukkah*, an unpublished collection distributed at Rabbi Shlomo Carlebach's memorial in Los Angeles.

Chapter 17

Epigraph. Joan Englander.

1. Isaiah 61:3, *The Holy Scriptures*, Fisch.

2. Thomas Moore, *Care of the Soul*, 173.

Chapter 18

Epigraph. Rabindranath Tagore, *Collected Poems and Plays of Rabindranath Tagore* (New York: Macmillan, 1944), 277.

1. Geoffrey Hodson, *First Steps on the Path* (Madras, India: Theosophical Publishing House, 1928), 131.

2. Jack and Marcia Kelly, "Sanctuaries: The Complete United States," *AARP Magazine* (November/December 2005).

3. Ezekiel 36:26-27, as found in Norvene Vest, *Bible Reading for Spiritual Growth* (San Francisco: Harper, 1993), 61.

4. Guigo II, *The Ladder of Monks*, trans. Edmund Colledge, OSA, and James Walsh, SJ (Kalamazoo, Mich.: Cistercian Publishers, 1981), 73.

5. Colm Luibheid, trans., *John Cassian Conferences* (New York: Paulist Press, 1985), 42-43.

6. Easwaran, *Gandhi the Man*, 117, 140.

Chapter 19

Epigraph. Michael Shapiro, as quoted by Joan Englander in "An Evening of Joy," *Voice* (Ojai, Calif.), December 29, 1995.

1. Aryeh Kaplan, *Jewish Meditation: A Practical Guide* (New York: Schocken Books, 1985), 68-69.

2. Thomas Keating, *Open Mind, Open Heart* (Rockport, Mass.: Element, 1991), 14, 61, 83, 87, 136-37.

3. Sogyal Rinpoche, trans., *Tibetan Book of Living and Dying*, 215-16.

4. Miroslava Linda Sabbath, "Dual Citizenship," from *Detour to Paradise* (Ottawa, Canada: Sasquach Publications, 2003).

Chapter 20

Epigraph. "Bless Your Heart," *Heartland Samplers*, Series 2, February 27 (Minneapolis, Minn.: Heartland Samplers, 1990).

1. David M. Mazie, "Music's Surprising Power to Heal," *Reader's Digest* (August 1992), 174-75.

2. Mary Kay Blakely, *Wake Me When It's Over* (New York: Times Books, 1989), 144, 167.

3. Rinpoche, *The Tibetan Book of Living and Dying*, 183-184.

4. Alan Loy McGinnis, *The Friendship Factor*, (Minn: Augsburg Publishing House, 1979), 51.

5. Leonard Bernstein, as quoted by Don G. Campbell, *Master Teacher* (Colo: Passacaglia Press, 2004), 12-13.

Chapter 21

1. Therese Schroeder-Sheker, "Music for the Dying: A Personal Account of the New Field of Music Thanatology—History, Theories, and Clinical Narratives," *Advances: The Journal of Mind-Body Health 9*, no. 1 (Winter 1993), 41.

Chapter 22

The Biblical verses in this chapter were spoken or sung extemporaneously. Some are direct quotations, others are paraphrases. The following citations refer to the originals from which they were derived.

1. Isaiah 43:2
2. Psalm 61:2
3. 2 Corinthians 5:2.
4. Isaiah 40:31.
5. 2 Peter 1:4.
6. Hebrews 12:1.
7. 2 Corinthians 12:9.
8. Ibid.
9. 2 Corinthians 12:10.
10. 2 Corinthians 5:17.
11. John 1:51.
12. Acts 17:25.
13. Hebrews 2:18.
14. *The Co-Worker Newsletter*, No. 37 (1992). Newsletter of the Missionaries of Charity, Mother Teresa's order.
15. Ephesians 3:17.
16. Psalms 16:11.
17. Mechtild of Magdeburg, as quoted by Kathleen Norris, *The Cloister Walk* (New York: Riverhead Books, 1996), 163.
18. Isaiah 55:12.

Resource Guide

Caregiving and aging

Caring Connections, a program of National Hospice and NHPCO
www.caringinfo.org

National Family Caregivers Association
www.nfcacares.org

National Organization for Empowering Caregivers
www.care-givers.com

Visiting Nurses Associations of America
www.vnaa.org

American Geriatrics Society, www.americangeriatrics.org
For other information, Google: Geriatric associations.

National Association of Area Agencies on Aging
www.n4a.org

American Society on Aging
www.asaging.org

Alzheimer's Association: www.alz.org
Dementia Information: www.ninds.nih.gov
The American Stroke Foundation: www.americanstroke.org
Cancer Society: www.cancersociety.com
National Parkinson Foundation: www.parkinson.org

Alternative healing and care

American Holistic Health: www.ahha.org

Association for Integrative Medicine: www.integrativemedicine.org

North American Society of Homeopaths: www.homeopathy.org

California Homeopathic Medical Society: www.homeopathywest.org

Circle of Care alternative: www.circleofcare.com. This site gives alternatives to institutional care, use of the arts for patients and professionals, and alternatives to medical intervention.

Holistic health. Google: Reiki healing; cranialsacral therapy, pranic healing, healing touch.

Rachel Remen: www.rachelremen.com. For health care professionals: reclaiming the heart and soul of medicine; the healing power of story.

Commonweal ISHI: www.commonweal.org/ishi. Curriculum for medical students: The Healer's Art. Storytelling workshops.

Eden Alternative; & thou shalt Honor: www.edenalt.com and www.pbs.org/thoushalthonor/eden. Alternative nursing home care. Dr. Bill Thomas, Geriatrician, envisions inspired alternatives.

Psychology & Therapy

American Psychological Association, www.apa.org

Institute of Transpersonal Psychology: www.itp.edu

Psychosynthesis: www.synthesiscenter.org

The CG Jung Institute: www.junginla.org

Pacifica Institute: www.pacifica.edu. Depth psychology studies and interns.

ACEP: www.energypsych.org. Research of current energy work and therapists.

Retreat and personal growth centers

Lani Luciano, Six Spiritual Getaways: Where the Spirit Moves You, retreat centers. AARP Magazine, November/December 2005, www.aarpmagazine.org

Jack Kelly, *Sanctuaries* (New York: Bell Tower, 1996).

Council training. Deep listening and communication. The Ojai Foundation, Ojai, CA, www.ojaifoundation.org

Esalen Institute, Big Sur, CA: www.esalen.org

Omega Institute, Rhinebeck, NY: www.eomega.org

The Crossings, Austin, TX: www.thecrossingsaustin.com

Elat Chayyim, Accord, NY: www.elatchayyim.org

Healing and spirituality

Spirituality, healing, and forgiveness. For each category, Google: Jewish, Buddhist, Native American, Islamic, Hindu, Christian Science, Sufi, Catholic, Episcopal, and the other Christian faiths (for Presbyterian: www.sbpres.org).

Interfaith prayers, meditations, and beliefs: beliefnet.com

Catholic Health Association www.chausa.org

Forgiveness, Azim Khamisa: www.azimkhamisa.com. The inspirational story of Azim's forgiveness of his son's murderer, and how he uses his grief to help others. Forgiveness workshops, tapes, and literature.

Gratefulness. Gratitude applied to all aspects of life with the focus on peacemaking. Brother David Stendl-Rast. www.gratefulness.org

Institute of Noetic Sciences: www.noetic.org. Building bridges between science and spirit. Founded by astronaut Edgar Mitchell.

Magazines and Journals

Spirituality & Health magazine
www.SpiritualityHealth.com

Healing Environments, Journal of Hope. Use of the arts for hospice, hospital, and nursing home rooms. www.healingenvironments.org
415-292-4040

Parabola Magazine: www.parabola.org

Shift at the Frontiers of Consciousness (Linked to Institute of Noetic Sciences)
www.shiftinaction.com

Eastern spirituality

Christian eastern orthodox: Google

His Holiness the Dalai Lama: www.dalailama.com

Thich Nhat Hanh: www.plumvillage.org

Ammachi. Hindu spiritual teacher who embraces everyone with love, speaks at the United Nations, and inspires thousands to work for the poor. www.amma.org

Sri Sathya Sai Baba. Hindu spiritual teacher who encourages human values, inspires unity by teaching that the only religion is love, and offers free health care and services for the poor through his followers. www.sathyasai.org

Music and meditation tapes for healing

CD: *Graceful Passages, A Companion for Living and Dying & ChantWave* at Grace Cathedral
www.innerharmony.com Michael Stillwater

CD: *The Blessings of Music*, James Schaller CMP
www.soundcovenant.org

CDs and videos: Therese Shroeder-Sheker
www.chaliceofrepose.org

Books for your elder

A journey of art and lyrical words to soothe the dying. The words can be sung. Warren Hanson, *The Next Place* (Golden Valley, Minn.: Waldman House Press, waldmanhouse.com, 1997).

An inspiring autobiography to read to your elder. A blind man finds inner sight and becomes a leader in the French Resistance. Jacques Lusseyran, *And There Was Light* (Sandpoint, Idaho: Morning Light Press, 2000).

Books for storytelling: Healing Story Alliance
www.storynet.org 1-800-525-4514

Two books of spiritual and transformational stories: Elisa Davy Pearmain, ed., *Doorways to the Soul* (Cleveland, Ohio: The Pilgrim Press,1998), and: Heather Forest, *Wisdom Tales From Around the World* (Little Rock, Arkansas: August House, 1996).

Some tales may appeal to Alzheimer's residents. Howard Schwartz, *Elijah's Violin & Other Jewish Fairy Tales* (New York: Oxford University Press, 1983).

Poetry for yourself and your elder. Roger Housden, *Ten Poems to Change Your Life* (New York: Harmony Books, 2001), and *Ten Poems to Open Your Heart* (2002).

Peace Pilgrim's walk across America and her spiritual teachings for yourself and your elder. Compiled by Friends of Peace Pilgrim, *Peace Pilgrim* (Santa Fe, New Mexico: Ocean Tree Book, 1983).

A guide for dealing with anger. The author was nominated for the Nobel Peace Prize by Martin Luther King. Thich Nhat Hanh, *Anger* (New York: Riverhead Books, 2001).

Some stories that appeal to elders. Rachel Naomi Remen, M.D., *Kitchen Table Wisdom* (New York: Riverhead Books, 1997).

Books for yourself

Families learn to listen with compassion and communicate with sensitivity to a loved one who has a serious illness. Stories that move you to tears. Jeff Kane, M.D., *How to Heal: A Guide to Caregivers* (New York: Allworth Press Books, 2003). Amazon.com

Compassionate communication. Marshall Rosenberg. www.cnvc.org

A lyrical exploration of Qigong philosophy and exercises. Roger Jahnke, *The Healing Promise of Qi* (New York: McGraw Hill, 2002).

A holistic personal journey when fighting cancer. Cheryl Canfield, *Profound Healing* (Rochester, Vt.: Healing Arts Press, 2003).

Poetry to touch your heart. Thich Nhat Hanh, *Call Me By My True Names* (Berkeley Calif.: Parallax Press, 1999).

Stories, commentaries, and meditation exercises on aging, death, and spirituality. Drew Leder, M.D., Ph.D., *Spiritual Passages* (New York: Jeremy P. Tarcher/Putnam, 1997).

Books for those drawn to mysticism

Mystical poetry and lyrical prayers open the doors of the heart to beauty, purity, mystery, and spiritual longing. They help grow the soul. A few lines prayed or contemplated on, for yourself or shared with an elder, may awaken a connection to soul life, and deepen your life of prayer or reflection.

A devotional, contemplative Christian journey with the mystics. A series of books that create 30 days with a Great Spiritual Teacher. One such book: Richard Chilson, *All Will Be Well, Based on the Classic Spirituality of Julian of Norwich* (Notre Dame, Indiana: Ave Maria Press, 2003).

Devotional poetry. Daniel James Ladinsky, trans., Hafiz, *The Subject Tonight is Love, Sixty Wild and Sweet Poems of Hafiz* (North Myrtle Beach, South Carolina: Pumpkin House Press,1997).

Mystical love poems by the 13th century Flemish Beguine, Hadewijch. Trans., Mother Columba Hart, OSB, *Hadewijch—The Complete Works* (Mahwah, N.J.Paulist Press, 1980).

Poetry integrating Chinese and Christian spirituality. Blessed by Jovan, Serbian Orthodox Bishop. Hieromonk Damascene, *Christ the Eternal Tao* (Platina, Calif., PO Box 70: Valaam Books, 2002).

The Hasidic masters on prayers, parables, aphorisms, and the Jewish inner life. Arthur Green, *Your Word is Fire* (Woodstock, Vt.: Jewish Lights Publication, 1993). Amazon.com

The poetry of Sufi mystic, Jalal-ud-Din Rumi with ecstatic commentaries to awaken the heart. The author relates Rumi's verses to the gospels, the Koran, Hindu scriptures and the teachings of spiritual masters. Andrew Harvey, *The Way of Passion, A Celebration of Rumi* (New York: Jeremy P. Tarcher/Putnam, 2001).

Order Form

TELEPHONE ORDERS: Call (805) 646-7700

EMAIL ORDERS: healing@joanenglander.com

POSTAL ORDERS: Make check or money order payable to:
Joan Englander
P.O. Box 385 Ojai, CA 93024

NAME: _____

ADDRESS _____

CITY / STATE / ZIP _____

TELEPHONE: _____

EMAIL ADDRESS: _____

NUMBER OF COPIES: _____

PRICE $19.95 EA.   _____

SALES TAX (7.25% for CA residents only) $ 1.88 EA.   _____

SHIPPING & HANDLING $ 6.00   _____

TOTAL   _____

IN ADDITION, PLEASE SEND ME INFORMATION FOR:

_____ Speaking Engagements

_____ Workshops/Retreats

_____ Consultations

Thank you for your order